"This volume adds to the existing Pink Therapy series by expanding the resources available for practitioners working with GSRD people across often challenging and, for some, controversial topics. The volume encompasses scenarios presenting in contemporary practice that are readily accessible for clinicians seeking knowledge from experienced practitioners. A clear message is that despite initially daunting and complex presentations, the volume provides authoritative practical pathways from top-notch experts to assist in identifying solutions within a competence informed therapeutic process."

Kevan Wylie, *MD FRCP FESCM. Past President, World Association For Sexual Health*

"It takes a while to acknowledge our biases and prejudices if we ever reach that point. Yet unchecked, we might think of providing the best service to our clients. 'Erotically Queer' questioned me: am I genuinely open to diversity? Through which lenses am I seeing my clients? When you come across such a book, you will know how much you commit to inclusivity and are brave to challenge your mindset constantly. It remains on my nightstand, as one reading is not enough."

Francesca Tripodi, *Director, International Online Sexology Supervisors (IOSS)*

"*Erotically Queer*, is a new volume of the Pink Therapy series, which brings together contributions from experts in the GSRD therapy field. Each chapter benefits from having the unfiltered and unique voice of the author as they take the reader on a rich and vibrant journey. This is an outstanding volume that is essential reading for all therapist at every level of experience whether in general or psychosexual practice."

Jo Coker, *AccCOSRT(Sen) AccCOSRT (Sup) MBPsS FCOSRT. HCPC Counselling Psychologist. Professional Standards Manager COSRT*

T0383619

Erotically Queer

Erotically Queer is a practice guide for clinicians, bringing together experts in their field with pioneering topics within GSRD (gender, sex and relationship diversity).

Chapters cover an array of topics rarely dicussed in either clinical or popular literature, including lesbian sex, queer menopause, bisexuality, working with shame, the sex lives of asexuals, sexuality and transgender people, treating anodyspareunia, compulsive sexual behaviours and chemsex. It also helps practitioners reflect on their biases regarding BDSM/kink and understand more regarding non-pathologising practices with intersex people.

The book aims to help all clinicians work more effectively with the Queer population, with the most contemporary sexological knowledge.

Silva Neves is a COSRT-accredited and UKCP-registered psychotherapist specialising in sexology and intimate relationships. He is a Pink Therapy clinical associate. He is a course director for the Contemporary Institute of Clinical Sexology (CICS), an international speaker, broadcaster and author.

Dominic Davies is the Founder of Pink Therapy, a clinical supervisor and sexologist and course director of two training programmes in gender, sex and relationship diversity therapy. He has been internationally recognised as one of 50 gender and sexual health revolutionaries.

Erotically Queer

A Pink Therapy Guide for Practitioners

Edited by Silva Neves and
Dominic Davies

Routledge
Taylor & Francis Group
LONDON AND NEW YORK

Designed cover image: Thomas Dyson

First published 2023
by Routledge
4 Park Square, Milton Park, Abingdon, Oxon OX14 4RN

and by Routledge
605 Third Avenue, New York, NY 10158

Routledge is an imprint of the Taylor & Francis Group, an informa business

British Library Cataloguing-in-Publication Data
A catalogue record for this book is available from the British Library

ISBN: 978-1-032-19732-6 (hbk)
ISBN: 978-1-032-19731-9 (pbk)
ISBN: 978-1-003-26060-8 (ebk)

DOI: 10.4324/9781003260608

The Open Access version of chapter 6 was funded by Y. Gávriel Ansara.

Contents

Acknowledgements

Silva and Dominic would like to thank:

Professor Esben Esther Pirelli Benestad for the most moving and poetic foreword. It brought us both to tears.

All our authors who contributed chapters to this book. We are grateful for their hard work, their time and their expert knowledge.

Our most eminent and internationally respected sexologists, Kevan Wylie, Francesca Tripodi and Jo Coker, for their thoughtful words of endorsement.

Our clients, who teach us more than textbooks.

Our students and supervisees, whose enquiring minds motivate us to find answers to support them.

Our peers and supporters in the Pink Therapy Facebook group.

Thomas Dyson for the fab book cover.

One final acknowledgement is to honour the passing of our dear friend and colleague David Stuart, who coined the term "chemsex" and worked tirelessly worldwide to help advise and support the development of services to support gay men whose chemsex use became out of control. Our world is poor for his passing. His kindness, compassion and generosity live on in his writings and the hearts of all who knew him.

Silva would like to thank:

Dominic Davies for his support in my work and for being a fabulous co-editor on this book. His knowledge and vast experience continues to feed me regularly. I'm also grateful for our shared sense of humour, which was much needed when we were both stuck in a hotel with COVID!

My colleagues whom I'm very lucky to call friends: Julie Sale, Rima Hawkins, Lorraine McGinlay, Dr Francesca Tripoli, Dr Meg-John Barker, Babette Rothschild, Kate Moyle, Dr Roberta Babb, Lohani Noor, Aoife Drury, Remziye Kunelaki, Juliette Clancy, Lisa Etherson, Diana Moffat, Andrew Mirrlees, Julie Gaudion, David Piner and Clare Staunton. I'm so grateful to have them in my life, sharing professional wisdom, personal stories, and laughs.

My followers on my professional social media platforms who identify as Queer and Queer allies. It feels good to see them out there, including the sex-positive trailblazers: Lucy Rowett, Gigi Engle, Alix Fox, Paisley Gilmour, Topher Taylor, Ruby Rare and Zachary Zane, to name just a few.

The College of Sexual and Relationship Therapists (COSRT). I'm proud to be an accredited member.

My husband Dr James Rafferty for his consistent love and support. He brings much Queer joy to my life.

Dominic:

I've spent over 40 years passionately engaged in the mental and sexual health of what we now call our GSRD communities. In the early days, I felt like a lone voice, but as the years have gone by, I've found a network of others in the UK and worldwide who are as passionate and engaged as I am. I am pleased to know them as friends and colleagues; they all sustain me in passion for my work as a therapist, supervisor and trainer.

Thank you, Charles Neal, Gail Simon and Keemar, for being amongst the very first of my UK professional support network. Looking across the oceans, I send thanks to Jack Drescher, Doug Braun-Harvey, Anna Randall, Richard Sprott, Cyndi Darnell, Margie Nichols, Markie Twist and Eli Coleman: you've influenced me more than you will ever know.

Kink has been an essential part of my identity, and it seems fitting in a book that celebrates the erotic to thank all those who have contributed to my erotic life over the years. I won't name you, but if your cheeks flush reading this, you know who you are! My life would have been much poorer without you in it. Thanks for the memories!

Contributors

Dr Y. Gávriel Ansara (he/him) lives on unceded Boonwurrung Country. He is a polycultural psychotherapist, educator and supervisor specialising in Anti-Oppressive/Liberating Practice approaches. He has received awards for his research, teaching and international human rights and social justice contributions. His positioning statement on his lived experiences of oppression and privilege is available at https://liberatingcentre.care/gavi/

Dr Annalisa Anzani is a postdoctoral researcher and psychologist working in Milan, Italy. She received her PhD at the University of Milano-Bicocca in 2020 with a thesis titled "Transgender Health. A Minority Stress Perspective on the Clinical Work with Transgender Clients". Her research interests are primarily trans health and sexuality.

Prof Esben Esther Pirelli Benestad is a physician, specialising in clinical sexology, NACS, professor in sexology at the University of Agder, Norway and a transgifted, proud father of two, grandparent of five.

Dr Lori Beth Bisbey is an HCPC registered practitioner psychologist, accredited advanced GSRD therapist, sex and intimacy coach, educator and author who has spent the last 30+ years working with people in private practice. Her specialities: treatment of PTSD, sex and relationships. Dr Bisbey identifies as a queer polyamorous leather woman.

Tania Glyde (MA, MNCS) (they/she) is a psychotherapist in private practice in London UK (londoncentralcounselling.com/; londonsexrelationshiptherapy.com/). They are a Pink Therapy advanced accredited GSRD therapist. In 2022 they started the Queer Menopause Collective. You can find resources for LGBTQ+ people experiencing menopause at queermenopause.com.

Dr Bartosz Grabski, MD, PhD, FECSM, WPATH-CM is a specialist in psychiatry and sexology, also trained in CBT. He works as an assistant professor at the Department of Psychiatry of the Jagiellonian University Medical College, where he is a head of the Sexology Lab. He practises and publishes in LGBT health.

Dr Benedict Hoff, PhD, is an integrative therapist, clinical sexologist and mindfulness teacher with an academic background in film, gender and queer theory. He has contributed to various publications in the fields of cultural studies, mindfulness and psychotherapy, and is based in London as an associate therapist at the Thought House Partnership.

Simon Alexander Lyne is an integrative cognitive behavioural and psychosexual psychotherapist with accreditation from BABCP. He is also trained in EMDR. He works full-time in the NHS and facilitates a group for GSRD doctors and dentists, and runs a busy private practice. He is particularly passionate about supporting GSRD clients.

Jenna McCaffrey (BSc Psychology Hons Queens University Belfast) has been working with LGBTQ+ couples and individuals since 2008. She holds a postgraduate diploma in relational therapy (Relate Institute/University of Hull), a diploma in sex and relationship therapy (Relationships Scotland) and a CICS diploma in compulsive sexual behaviour.

Ellis Morgan is a gender identity therapist in private practice in London. His writing includes collaborations with Strathclyde University and Scottish Transgender Alliance, "Dangerous Education: The Occupational Hazards of Teaching Transgender" (2018) and "Transforming Research Practice" (2016). He was previously a director within the LGBTQ+ mental health sector.

Serge Nicholson is a psychosexual and relationship therapist with a passion for working alongside GSRD clients. Serge has a private practice (London & Hastings), delivering individual and partner therapy, plus group work. In addition, Serge is a GSRD lecturer, and co-founder of hotpencilpress.co.uk. www.sergenicholson.org.uk

Dr Antonio Prunas, PhD, is a licensed psychologist and psychotherapist. He completed a training in sexology and is a graduate of the diploma in GSRD therapy at Pink Therapy. He currently works in private practice as a sex therapist. He is Associate Professor at the Department of Psychology of Milano-Bicocca University, Milan, Italy.

Jo Russell (she/they), is a senior accredited psychotherapist, supervisor and trainer in Glasgow. Jo has an MSc in counselling studies (advanced practice) from Edinburgh University, is a graduate of the Pink Therapy Post-Graduate Diploma and a clinical associate of Pink Therapy. Jo is a lifelong asexual. Publications: "Asexuals: a hidden one per cent" *Therapy Today* (March 2016).

Julie Sale is the Director of the Contemporary Institute of Clinical Sexology, a leading UK sex and relationship therapy training and education organisation. She is a UKCP registered and accredited general psychotherapist, COSRT senior accredited sex and relationship therapist and COSRT accredited clinical supervisor.

Foreword

Prof Esben Esther Pirelli Benestad

You cannot see the details, the pitfalls, the perils nor the splendours of any landscape from the perspective of some thousand feet above.

To really know the landscape or rather all the landscapes of human diversity, you must have been there, on the ground together with those who live in the territory. One time is not enough, nor two. In order to be reasonably familiar with the more unusual landscapes of human life, you must have walked there over and over again. Still, you must always realize that at any time a new aspect, a new perception of self, a new way to be erotically aroused may be disclosed to you. Disclosures of that which is unusual, especially when it concerns sex and gender, take a deeper and a more trustful alliance than anything we may encounter as fellow human beings and in context: as therapists.

Stories like these are clients' gifts to therapists who have proven worthy of deep confidence.

We are diverse, we perceive ourselves in many different ways as gender, as biologically sexed with genitals, as with brains telling other stories than the so-called sex organs, as with ways to express our love and as with ways to reach the realms of personal erotic heavens.

Hardly any major health education anywhere takes into account this vast and colourful human wealth. On the contrary, the cis- and heteronormative thinking has ruled the waves and left all too many with broken hearts, broken spirits, with shame and reinforced traumas of retention. Many have lived, and many still live in a constant state of shy alertness, fearing the different kinds of judgements thrown upon them with words like sick, disordered, sinful or non-existent. To retain talents of profound importance is harmful to any human being. It is a great and very timely challenge for all who claim to be therapists to have some hundred humility walks in the worlds of sex, gender and erotics. Those who have not done so should declare themselves not eligible to work with clients equipped with talents of the kind this book describes.

My first encounter with anyone, with any book, where I could feel that the authors had been in the landscape and not seen them from some thousand feet above. That book had the name Dominic Davies on the cover. It was a joyful relief! There was someone out there who did not see human diversities as rarities, who offered me not only knowledge but also compassion. This book "Pink therapy", the first one in the series, was, for me, the first book I read with insights from an outside that I myself belonged to.

It was a profound and healing process! Hence the names linked to that book have been in my treasure chest ever since, and here they are again!

Is it a minefield? Is sex and eroticism beside the scope of therapy, be it psychological, medical or in any other way aimed to assist the improvement of clients' lives?

In 2018 and 2021, I was invited to give Norwegian psychiatrists a "Day of sexology". All together, there were 72 of them. My first Question was: *Have any of you in your many years of education and training learned anything about sex and gender?* One had had a two-hour lecture, the rest: Nothing. My next question was: *Do any of you believe that sex and gender is of significance to mental health?* They all nodded, and I exclaimed: *Isn't it strange?*

This is I fear the state of therapeutic competence in this field in most corners of the globe. At places, it is much worse, condemning fellow human beings to death or oblivion. Only in some sacred spots, it is better.

Such a spot is in your hands right now.

It is my thorough belief that this book will improve the knowledge and, in consequence, the lives of many, including your own.

You must still step into the landscapes and have numerous equal and loving talks with all those people this book concerns.

Nevertheless, a detailed map like this will always come in handy!

Introduction

Silva Neves and Dominic Davies

The first three volumes of the Pink Therapy series (Davies & Neal, 1996, 2000; Neal & Davies, 2000) are regarded by the psychotherapy and psychology professions as pioneering books in offering specialist knowledge of working therapeutically with LGBTQ+ people. Since the last publication, there has been a growing interest in gender, sex and relationship diversities (GSRD), with many new books published on the subject (Moon, 2008, 2010; Nichols, 2020; Constantinides et al., 2019; Iasenza, 2020; Czyzselkska, 2022). Indeed, the field has grown exponentially.

Erotically Queer is one of the two new Pink Therapy volumes (alongside *Relationally Queer*), two decades since the last Pink Therapy publication. This book aims to guide practitioners on how to work with the GSRD populations who present with difficulties in their sex lives, sexual behaviours or erotic themes.

Sex is often a taboo topic that therapists find hard to approach, preferring to talk about anxiety, depression and other mental health concerns. But people with GSRD identities need a safe space to talk about their sex lives and explore their eroticism without fearing that their therapists will see them through cisgender-heteronormative lenses.

What is GSRD?

Pink Therapy as an organisation has always viewed our therapeutic and training services beyond the more traditional lesbian, gay, bisexual and transgender (LGBT) terms as we knew there were many other marginalised groups with an equal or greater need for good mental health support, in particular, heterosexual kinksters or intersex clients might not feel comfortable approaching LGBT counselling organisations. For many years, we have settled on the phrase gender, sex and relationship diversity (GSRD) to refer to these categories.

We didn't find adding more letters to the acronym helpful as this was also limiting and exclusionary, despite it getting as complicated as LGBTTQQIAAP (lesbian, gay, bisexual, transgender, transsexual, queer, questioning, intersex, asexual, ally, pansexual). Our descriptions that follow are our current understanding of marginalised identities, consensual relationships and practices, and are not meant to

DOI: 10.4324/9781003260608-1

be exclusive. They will probably continue to change as our understanding of the biopsychosocial approach to gender/sex and relationships develops.

G = Gender

Within Gender, we include people on the gender spectrum who identify as trans, agender, bi-gender, crossdressers, genderqueer, gender fluid, non-binary and gender non-conforming.

S = Sex

We are using two different understandings of the word Sex: sex as in sexuality, sexual orientation/identities: lesbian, gay, bi- and pansexual and those on the asexual spectrum, celibate and those engaged in BDSM/Kink and Fetish.

Sex is also used to mean biological sex, including intersex people, born with sex characteristics (including genitals, gonads and chromosome patterns) that do not fit typical binary notions of male or female bodies.

R = Relationship

In Relationship, we include people on the aromantic (aro) spectrum, those involved in BDSM/Kink power exchange relationships, sex work relationships, people in multi-partnered relationships (swingers, non-monogamous, polyamorous people, etc.), as well as those in 'monogamish' forms of partnership.

D = Diversity

Diversity encompasses the diversities and differences within each of the earlier categories. As you will see, we have a passion for embracing differences and diversities.

What is GSRD therapy?

We believe GSRD therapy is an emerging modality arising from the collective work of researchers and therapists over the past half a century. It has been pioneered in the UK by Dominic Davies, who has been working as a specialist GSRD psychotherapist for 40 years. He has pulled together the many research threads with colleagues and applied clinical wisdom and lived experience from various GSRD identities into this nascent theoretical approach. He co-edited (with Charles Neal) the first three UK textbooks on LGBT therapy in 1996 and 2000 and established the Pink Therapy organisation (www.pinktherapy.com) in 1999. Since then, GSRD therapy has developed our greater understanding of human diversities. As such, the skills necessary in working with GSRD people are becoming established in an emerging therapeutic modality rather than a mere set of techniques. This is partly because GSRD therapy has a specific philosophy of inclusivity, humility and specialist theories embedded in the practice (Davies & Neves, 2023).

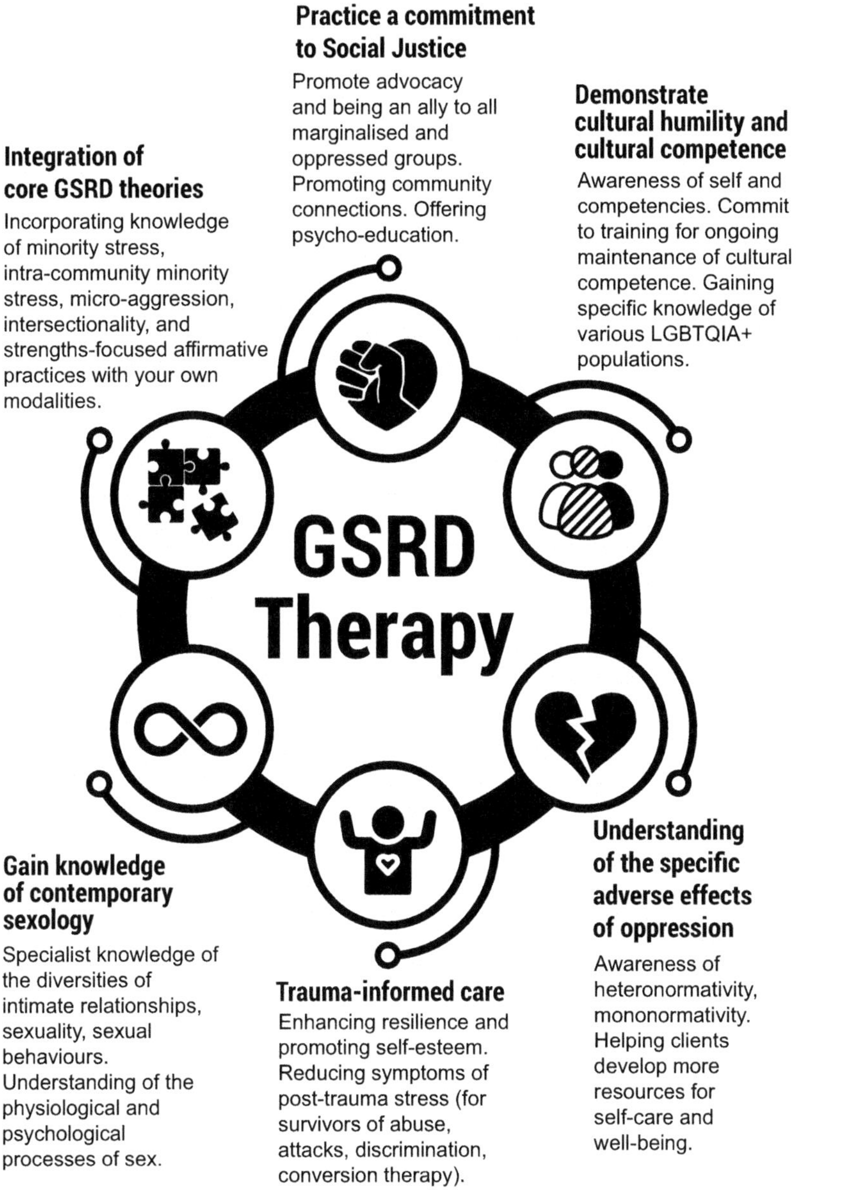

Practice a commitment to Social Justice

Promote advocacy and being an ally to all marginalised and oppressed groups. Promoting community connections. Offering psycho-education.

Demonstrate cultural humility and cultural competence

Awareness of self and competencies. Commit to training for ongoing maintenance of cultural competence. Gaining specific knowledge of various LGBTQIA+ populations.

Integration of core GSRD theories

Incorporating knowledge of minority stress, intra-community minority stress, micro-aggression, intersectionality, and strengths-focused affirmative practices with your own modalities.

GSRD Therapy

Gain knowledge of contemporary sexology

Specialist knowledge of the diversities of intimate relationships, sexuality, sexual behaviours. Understanding of the physiological and psychological processes of sex.

Trauma-informed care

Enhancing resilience and promoting self-esteem. Reducing symptoms of post-trauma stress (for survivors of abuse, attacks, discrimination, conversion therapy).

Understanding of the specific adverse effects of oppression

Awareness of heteronormativity, mononormativity. Helping clients develop more resources for self-care and well-being.

Figure 0.1 The six core principles of GSRD therapy

There are currently six core principles of GSRD therapy (Figure 0.1).

1   *Practice a commitment to social justice.* This emergent modality is rooted in social justice, arguing against our professions' unchecked heteronormative,

mononormative and cisgenderist biases. GSRD therapy has grown from other social justice approaches like feminist therapy and Cross-Cultural and Black psychologies; therefore, it is the first core component of practising GSRD therapy, which includes promoting advocacy and being an ally to all marginalised and oppressed groups, for example, by researching the impact of government policy on the well-being of GSRD people (Rucco et al., 2022). Psychotherapy and psychology are notorious fields for being largely middle-class, white heterosexual professions, training therapists to work with themselves as the 'typical' people, and the rest are 'alternative' people. It is now changing slowly. The philosophy of GSRD therapy is motivated by a passion for embracing differences and diversities and therefore takes a firm stance of being of service to all people, not leaving a section of our community out. For example, at the time of writing in the UK, we are actively fighting to ensure Trans and gender non-conforming communities are included in any legal ban on Conversion Practices (Jowett et al., 2021; MoU, 2022). Through our international training programmes and network, we commit ourselves to fight for queer rights overseas. From as far back as Maslow's (1943) Hierarchy of Needs, we know how important it is for us to be psychologically and physically safe to begin to thrive. The therapeutic space can be the starting point for that safe environment, but it is also part of social justice to promote community connections; we need to do what we can to help promote safe spaces for GSRD people to meet. For example, LGBTQIA+ spaces where people can meet and connect are necessary for developing resilience to minority stress and microaggressions (Meyer, 1995) The commitment to social justice also involves being able to engage in psychoeducation with clients depending on their needs. For example, it may be crucial for some clients to understand that their mental health difficulties occur not because they're 'broken' or 'diseased', but because of homophobia, biphobia, transphobia and cisgenderism; in other words, it is because of what happened to them not who they are. Our roles as therapists may also extend to advocacy and allyship.

2   *Demonstrate cultural humility and cultural competence.* Even the most experienced therapist in GSRD cannot know everything about all communities. Therefore, we must maintain self-awareness regarding our positionality, privileges, biases, assumptions, blind spots and cultural competencies. Therapists must cultivate cultural humility (Tervalon & Murray-Garcia, 1998) by reminding themselves that they do not know everything. A GSRD therapist will commit to regular training for their ongoing maintenance of cultural competence and gain specific knowledge of various LGBTQIA+ populations, as well as staying updated on what they used to know, which may no longer apply because the language of GSRD changes rapidly. For example, the language around gender has been evolving as we expand our understanding and learn from our trans colleagues, researchers and clients.

3 *Understanding of the specific adverse effects of oppression.* All the populations under GSRD are those who have been othered by our society, and pressure is unrelenting. It can be challenging for white, cisgender heterosexual therapists to understand or remind themselves of what it is like to be seen as 'other'. It is also necessary to realise that cisgenderism, heteronormativity and mononormativity, so ubiquitous in our daily lives, hurt and oppress GSRD people. Understanding the specific adverse effects of minority stress (Meyer, 2003) and realising that this oppression is pervasive and continuous means that therapists can guide their sessions by helping clients develop more resources for self-care and well-being in navigating an inhospitable world (Dunlop, 2022).

4 *Trauma-informed care.* Most of the trauma literature is concerned with treating post-trauma symptoms. Still, for the GSRD community, there is a blend of post-trauma events (e.g., childhood bullying, survivors of abuse, discrimination and conversion practices) and ongoing trauma (e.g., distal and proximal minority stress). Therefore, it is essential to have specific knowledge of trauma so that therapists can feel confident in reducing post-trauma symptoms and helping clients enhance their resilience and self-esteem–promoting strategies when faced with ongoing trauma. Not all clients will need focused trauma treatment, but most will benefit from trauma-informed therapists.

5 *Gain knowledge of contemporary sexology.* A GSRD therapist must have contemporary knowledge of and be comfortable talking about the diversity of intimate relationships, sexuality, sexual behaviours and sexual fantasies because many of these areas are where GSRD clients have been wounded by being insulted, pathologised or attacked because of whom they love and are in a relationship with, whom they have sex with and what turns them on. Normalising the diversities of sexual desires, arousals, behaviours and fantasies and the diversity of sexualities and relationships is often where profound healing occurs. The therapist needs to be confident in their understanding of the physiological and psychological processes of sex to help clients explore their intimate relational and erotic lives in a safe space. It's a travesty that so few sex and relationship therapists are trained well enough to understand and treat anodyspareunia (see Chapter 10), a common sexual problem not even documented in the heteronormative DSM-5 (2013) and WHO (2019, ICD-11).

6 *Integration of core GSRD theories.* It is essential when working with GSRD clients to have a robust grasp of core GSRD theories and their application in therapy, such as minority stress (Meyer, 2003), intra-community minority stress (Pachankis et al., 2020), micro-aggressions (Nadal, 2013), intersectionality (Freeman-Coppadge & Langroudi, 2021) and strengths-focused affirmative practices (see Dunlop, 2022, for some excellent examples), which can all be integrated within existing modalities, whether therapists are already trained in person-centred therapy, or psychodynamic, Gestalt, TA, CBT and so on. As such, GSRD therapy can be used as a modality within modalities.

Why this book?

We are not proposing a ghettoisation of therapy for GSRD folks as we believe all therapists need to be trained and competent to work with GSRD clients, who, after all, are over-represented in the therapy population. Also, we recognise that some therapists wish to specialise in GSRD therapy like there are other specialists such as sex and relationship therapists.

There is increasing visibility and acceptance of GSRD people in our Western societies. More people are becoming empowered to identify in ways closer to their authentic selves. Yet, minority stress theory is still relevant across the generations (Frost et al., 2022). This is why we have decided to publish our book. We have gathered an excellent team of experts to help clinicians understand the critical elements of GSRD therapy in the context of their erotic lives. You will see all the six principles of GSRD therapy weaved throughout this book, bringing the modality alive with case studies.

How to read this book

Chapters are individual. In the spirit of diversity, we have retained each author's voice in the writing of their chapters, so not all chapters follow the same structure. However, all chapters will present cutting-edge knowledge in the field of GSRD and sexology. Each chapter can be read separately or together. Please note that all case studies presented in this book are composite of various clients, with all identifying features removed to respect their confidentiality.

A note on the terminology

There isn't one terminology that fits everybody. This is the beauty of diversity. Some authors use certain words (gay men, e.g.), and others will use terms such as MSM (Men who have Sex with Men). We commit to keeping updated with the current inclusive language, which changes fast. Authors explain their rationale for using certain words over others. Readers may agree or disagree and take the opportunity as food for thought.

In any case, we are together, discussing words that feel right for individuals. The intention of inclusion starts with a broad language and not a certainty of 'right' or 'wrong'.

References

Constantinides, D.M., Sennott, S.L., & Chandler, D. (2019). *Sex Therapy with Erotically Marginalised Clients Nine Principles of Clinical Support*. Abingdon, UK: Routledge.

Czyzselska, J.C. (Ed.). (2022). *Queering Psychotherapy*. London, Karnac Books.

Davies, D., & Neal, C.E. (Eds.). (1996). *Pink Therapy: A Guide for Counsellors Working with Lesbian, Gay and Bisexual Clients*. Buckingham, UK: McGraw-Hill.

Davies, D., & Neal, C.E. (Eds.). (2000). *Therapeutic Perspectives on Working with Lesbian, Gay and Bisexual Clients*. Buckingham, UK: McGraw-Hill.

Davies, D., & Neves, S. (2023). Gender, sex and relationship diversity therapy. In T. Hanley & L. Winter (Eds.), *The SAGE Handbook of Counselling and Psychotherapy* (5th ed.). London: Sage.

DSM-5. (2013). American psychiatric association. In *Diagnostic and Statistical Manual of Mental Health Disorders* (5th ed.). Arlington, VA: American Psychiatric Publishing.

Dunlop, B. (2022). *The Queer Mental Health Handbook*. London: Jessica Kinglsey Publishers.

Freeman-Coppadge, D.J., & Langroudi, K.F. (2021). Beyond LGBTQ-affirmative therapy: Fostering growth and healing through intersectionality. In K.L. Nadal & M.R. Scharrón-del Río (Eds.), *Queer Psychology Intersectional Perspectives*. Cham, Switzerland: Springer Nature.

Frost, D.M., Fingerhut, A.W., & Meyer, I.H. (2022). Social change and relationship quality among sexual minority individuals: Does minority stress still matter? *Journal of Marriage and Family*, 84(3), 920–933. https://doi.org/10.1111/jomf.12827

Iasenza, S. (2020). *Transforming Sexual Narratives: A Relational Approach to Sex Therapy*. London: Routledge.

Jowett, A., Brady, G., Goodman, S., Pillinger, C., & Bradley, L. (2021). Conversion Therapy: An Evidence Assessment and Qualitative Study. *Government Equalities Office*. www.gov.uk/government/publications/conversion-therapy-an-evidence-assessment-and-qualitative-study/conversion-therapy-an-evidence-assessment-and-qualitative-study (Accessed: 6 September 2022).

Maslow, A.H. (1943). A theory of human motivation. *Psychological Review*, 50(4), 370–379.

Meyer, I.H. (1995). Minority stress and mental health in gay men. *Journal of Health and Social Behavior*, 36(1), 38. doi:10.2307/2137286

Meyer, I.H. (2003, September). Prejudice, social stress, and mental health in lesbian, gay, and bisexual populations: Conceptual issues and research evidence. *Psychological Bulletin*, 129(5), 674–697. doi:10.1037/0033-2909.129.5.674. PMID: 12956539; PMCID: PMC2072932.

Moon, L. (Ed.). (2008). *Feeling Queer or Queer Feelings? Radical Approaches to Counselling Sex, Sexualities and Genders*. London: Routledge.

Moon, L. (Ed.). (2010). *Counselling Ideologies: Queer Challenges to Heteronormativity*. Farnham: Ashgate.

MoU (2022). *Memorandum of Understanding on Conversion Therapy in the UK*. Updated November 2022. https://www.bacp.co.uk/events-and-resources/ethics-and-standards/mou/ (Accessed: 6 September 2022).

Nadal, K.L. (2013). *That's So Gay!: Microaggressions and the Lesbian, Gay, Bisexual, and Transgender Community*. Washington, DC: American Psychological Assoc.

Neal, C.E., & Davies, D. (Eds.). (2000). *Issues in Therapy with Lesbian, Gay, Bisexual and Transgender Clients*. Buckingham, UK: McGraw-Hill.

Nichols, M. (2020). *The Modern Clinician's Guide to Working with LGBTQ+ Clients*. London: Routledge.

Pachankis, J.E., Clark, K.A., Burton, C.L., Hughto, J.M.W., Bränström, R., & Keene, D.E. (2020). Sex, status, competition, and exclusion: Intraminority stress from within the gay community and gay and bisexual men's mental health. *Journal of Personality and Social Psychology*, 119(3), 713–740. https://doi.org/10.1037/pspp0000282

Rucco, D., Anzani, A., Scandurra, C., Pennasilico, A., & Prunas, A. (2022). Structural stigma and bisexual+ people: Effects of the rejection of the Zan Bill in Italy on minority stress and mental health. *Journal of Bisexuality*. doi:10.1080/15299716.2022.2119629

Tervalon, M., & Murray-Garcia, J. (1998). Cultural humility versus cultural competence: A critical distinction in defining physician training outcomes in multicultural education. *Journal of Health Care for the Poor and Underserved*, 9(2), 117–125. https://doi.org/10.1353/hpu.2010.0233

World Health Organization. (2019). ICD-11. In *International Statistical Classification of Diseases and Related Health Problems* (11th ed.). https://icd.who.int/

Chapter 1

Attachment narrative therapy as a tool for sex therapy with lesbian couples

Jenna McCaffrey

Research regarding the prevalence of sexual problems among lesbian couples remains scarce (Peixoto, 2017), with a paucity of writing on the subject in general (Armstrong & Reissing, 2013).

Traditional sex therapy has been criticised as being patriarchal and pathology-orientated (Tiefer, 2001). The medical model established by Masters and Johnson (1970) is based on a problematic conceptualisation of women's response cycles, assuming sequential stages of desire, arousal and orgasm, more suited to men (Meston & Bradford, 2007). A rethink is notably pertinent in dealing with 'desire disorder', which is hindered by the prevailing myth of 'lesbian bed death' (Hall, 1987), despite having been debunked (Iasenza, 2002, 2004; Nichols, 2004). There has been a concerted effort to create more inclusive ways of approaching lesbian sexuality.

A key aspect of working well with lesbian couples is to place them in the context of the society they operate within, taking a multi-contextual perspective (Iasenza, 2004). Acknowledging the impact of internalised heteronormativity (Moon, 2016) and sexism (Cobin & Angelo, 2015) on the sexual identity and self-concept of lesbian women is vital to forging a therapeutic relationship and to challenging the underlying causes of the presentation of low desire in the therapy room.

This chapter is an invitation for sex and relationship therapists to consider several questions in relation to lesbian couples presenting with such difficulties: What is sex? What is good sex? What is good sex therapy?

This is not a suggestion to ditch traditional sex therapy altogether – self and sensate focus (Weiner & Avery-Clark, 2017) can provide a useful framework for change. This chapter is, however, a proposal, illustrated by casework, of an integration of systemic approaches with sex therapy, using attachment narrative therapy (ANT; Dallos, 2006; Vetere & Dallos, 2008) as a vehicle to re-establish the sexual connection of the couple.

Thus, we can acknowledge the importance of the context of the relationship, normalise that experience, externalise the problem-saturated dialogue and unpack the factors that created the issue in the first place.

I am both mindful and respectful that women in same-sex relationships may not identify as lesbian, or that lesbian clients might not identify as women. I use

DOI: 10.4324/9781003260608-2

the words women and lesbian here for the purpose of brevity, with the caveat that language should be attended to carefully in client work (Riggs, 2015).

Lesbian bed death

It is an indictment of our culture that the idea of lesbian bed death (Hall, 1987) retains weight, even within the LGBTQ+ communities, with some couples self-diagnosing (Cobin & Angelo, 2015). This can be recognised as a symptom of internalised homophobia, which can bequeath a pessimistic evaluation of the potential quality and duration of same-sex intimate relationships (Lingiardi et al., 2012). Consideration should be given to how that may impact upon lesbian clients, or perhaps even hinder accessing sex therapy in the first place.

The most common presenting issue for lesbian couples is that of desire (Cobin & Angelo, 2015). However, lesbians demonstrate lower reporting of sexual difficulty compared with their heterosexual counterparts, along with higher levels of arousal and increased orgasmic function (Beaber & Werner, 2009), achieving orgasm more reliably (Nichols & Shernoff, 2007).

The primary difficulty is the mainstream definition of sex as including genital contact with the goal of reaching orgasm. Many lesbian couples have more frequent whole-body interactions that may simply not involve genital contact or orgasm (Nichols, 2004).

Systemic principles and sex and relationship therapy (SRT) with lesbian couples

Whilst sex and relationship therapy (SRT) and systemic therapy might not initially appear comfortable bedfellows, systemic therapy has much to offer in the resolution of sexual difficulty (Markovic, 2013). Green and Flemons assert that: "systemic framework offers a unique and generative framework from which to create positive sexual change for clients" (2004, p. xxiv). This is particularly relevant when dealing with sexual minorities, given the natural disposition of systemic ideology toward a de-pathologising, non-normative stance (Anderson & Goolishian, 1992). Systemic tenets of curiosity (Cecchin, 1987); the creation of safe uncertainty (Mason, 1993); taking a non-expert, not knowing approach (Anderson & Goolishian, 1992); collaborative therapy (Anderson & Gehart, 2007); utilising circular, reflexive questioning to deconstruct misconceptions about sex and explore how these affect sexual functioning (Markovic, 2013) as well as using reflexivity to check and maintain an open position (Burnham, 2005) are all fundamental to respecting the unique position of lesbian couples. Long-held accepted elements of SRT, such as the key role of education, structuring the sessions, etc. (Hawton, 1985) can occur within a systemic framework.

Multi-contextual models of SRT with lesbian couples, such as that proposed by Iasenza (2004), centre on the appreciation of the influences of family, culture and society alongside the perspective of the couple, or the individuals within it, acknowledging the power hierarchy they are operating within. Narrative therapy (Dallos, 1997) provides a useful framework for the exploration of these influences and the identification of problem-saturated descriptions becoming the dominant story. These ideas have been successfully married by Iasenza to create Narrative Relational Sex Therapy (2020).

Externalisation and reframing separate clients from the problematic narrative (White & Epston, 1990), portraying difficulties as external, transient states, rather than a fundamental part of, or quality in, the client or relationship (Dallos, 2006). The normalisation of the impact of growing up in a sexist, homophobic society (Iasenza, 2004) and the Ericksonian technique of utilisation, identifying competencies and resources (Zeig, 1994), are further tools of benefit.

Understanding attachment patterns is of prime importance in working with lesbian couples because of the unique impact on attachment bonds of internalised shame due to misattunement, or indeed rejection by important others, which differs from other minority experiences in that the children of other oppressed groups usually have a role model providing a counter-narrative from the mainstream which can affirm them in the shape of a similar parent (Rohleder, 2020).

Therefore ANT, the integration of systemic, narrative and attachment theories, has much to offer this client group in SRT. It provides a framework to explore the creation of relational constructs (Dallos, 2006), generating multiple perspectives about the connections between narratives of relationships and behaviours, or events, as well as a clear structure for addressing the implications of preferred narratives generated in therapeutic work (Vetere & Dallos, 2008). This allows the enhanced version of solution-oriented therapy described as 'Possibility Therapy' by O'Hanlon (2004).

What is sex?

SRT tools such as the Female Sexual Functioning Index (FSFI; Rosen et al., 2000) can be a hindrance in the conceptualisation of lesbian sex. These demonstrate the patriarchal and pathology orientated position of traditional sex therapy highlighted by Tiefer (2001), overlooking that it is often not lust driving sex for women, but rather a desire for intimacy (Nichols & Shernoff, 2007), with many women experiencing desire responsively (Basson, 2007).

Nichols (2004) poses the question as to why only genital contact toward the goal of an orgasm counts? Can sex not also include mutual, sensual physical contact, for example, masturbating with a partner while watching porn together? Komisaruk and Whipple (2011) point out the capabilities of bodies to orgasm without genital contact at all.

The focus of SRT originates in dysfunction. Therefore lesbian sexuality is often approached from the problem-focussed point of view, rather than the joyous celebration of female sexuality reflected in the work of Fahs and Plante (2017), which depicts a wide range of activities described by women under the umbrella of sexual encounters, some as simple as the skin on skin contact of lying peacefully naked together.

Cultural, individual and interpersonal factors influence how sex is/is not defined for individuals (Bowling et al., 2020). Types of enquiry and the language used are highly influential in responses to questions surrounding sexual activity, particularly in the case of activities which are socially or culturally censured (Mavhu et al., 2008).

ANT allows us, as therapists, to home in on how our clients perceive sex, to draw out the narratives, providing a vehicle for clients to understand not only their narratives around what sex is in terms of repertoire, but the meanings placed on those activities, or on sexual connections generally, along with where these ideas originated. In many ways, our own ideas as therapists, or the views of traditional sex therapy, are irrelevant. All that truly matters is that clients can define for themselves what sex means and to make choices to work toward establishing the sexual relationship they desire. There should be no assumptions of normality, no definition of what sex means or how it should happen (Cobin & Angelo, 2015).

What is good sex?

Tiefer highlights the notion of false equivalency between men and women in SRT, describing the definition of 'normal' sexual function as a "totally arbitrary exercise", resulting in performance standards mandating "regular and routine desire for sexual relations, genital arousal and orgasm" (2003, p. 15), without which, a label of deficiency can be applied, which is singularly unhelpful to an already marginalised group (Cobin & Angelo, 2015).

The heteronormative focus on an expected outcome from a sexual encounter (orgasm) is problematic as a tool for defining what constitutes sexual success; it is not relevant or pertinent for those who might find great joy and pleasure through sensuality, without experiencing orgasm (Anderson & Cyranowski, 1996). Heimann (2017) expounds that lack of orgasm does not necessarily equate to a problem.

More useful than a dysfunction-orientated perspective, perhaps, is measuring successes and competency in terms of the eight factors contributing directly to sexual functioning identified by Armstrong and Reissing (2013): age, income, religion, cultural recognition, relationship duration, sexual satisfaction, psychological well-being and relationship satisfaction, which can assist in the identification of areas beyond the bedroom that can be worked upon to underpin sexual satisfaction.

The primary purpose of SRT is not to follow a pre-determined set of objective sexual criteria, but instead to enable a mutually satisfactory sexual relationship (Leiblum, 2007). The very idea of good vs bad sex echoes the patriarchal vocabulary of winners and losers. If we are to challenge a binary worldview, attending to the narratives of the couple surrounding 'good' sex and linguistic nuances within that becomes imperative.

ANT provides a useful tool for the exploration of narratives around 'good' sex, whether narratives reflect personal beliefs or have been integrated from societal messages, and how attachment narratives intersect with sexual ones in the creation of sexual self-esteem. The erotic template (Morin, 1995) can be effectively utilised to narrow down broader narratives to individual preferences, tuning into peak erotic turn-ons and focusing on the subjective nature of the sexual interchange between two people.

Recognition of subjectivity is crucial while working with sexual minorities. Sex is not just about repertoire, encompassing feelings evoked. It can be a joyous experience, however, Nichols and Shernoff (2007) point out that it can also provoke shame or anxiety.

The 'Good Enough' sex model takes account of the multiple functions of sex, from stress reliever to spiritual experience, alongside pleasure (Metz & McCarthy, 2007), providing principles to guide sex therapists in the task of client satisfaction. This may well include various types of sex, with different measures of success, depending on the functionality of the experience.

What is good sex therapy?

> Constructing a therapeutic relationship is in itself an intervention and arguably one of the most powerful aspects of therapy.
>
> (Dallos, 2006, p. 125)

At the heart of any good therapy is the therapeutic relationship. A good relationship in SRT with lesbian clients is not possible without considering the unique position of lesbians in terms of living within a societal structure that is both sexist and heterosexist. Overtly locating couples within this context provides a reassurance to clients that the therapist holds an awareness of these systemic contributors, thus Iasenza (2004) advocates directly asking how sexism and homophobia impact sexual functioning.

Cobin and Angelo (2015) propound that when working with an already stigmatised group, it is inadequate to merely not be homophobic; therapists must actively avoid the heterosexist position, being mindful of using gender-neutral language. Women in same-sex partnerships may not identify as lesbian, but rather perhaps as queer, bisexual, etc., and lesbians presenting for sex therapy may not identify as women, but perhaps non-binary, etc. It is imperative to identify the preferred terms of clients and ensure their usage (Riggs, 2015). An awareness of the dynamical systems approach to sexuality (Diamond, 2009) is useful, stepping away from the overly rigid view that traditional models of SRT assume, which are too simplistic, towards an awareness of the sexual fluidity many women experience.

Whilst approaching the experience of a lesbian couple with openness, knowledge of issues which may impact upon lesbian couples is important (Biaggio et al., 2002). Green (2004) points out the lack of normative paradigms of lesbian partnerships, the increased possibility of reduced levels of family and societal support, and the potential for conformation to stereotypical gender roles for both partners. The significance of gender role socialisation and its implications cannot be overlooked

(Connolly, 2015), for example, the possibility of a reduced likelihood of requesting sex perhaps being socialised into women (Cobin & Angelo, 2015).

In order to cope with hostile external forces, a feature of lesbian couplehood may well be fusion, an understanding of which better prepares therapists to provide an affirmative experience to clients (Connolly, 2015). Biaggio et al. (2002) caution that misunderstanding, or the interpretation of the emotional intensity of fusion as problematic, assumes the normativity of heterosexual relationship bonds. Mutual engagement and empowerment and increased closeness (Green et al., 1996) can be considered beneficial.

In addition to acknowledging the dual minority status of lesbian couples in terms of heterosexism and sexism (Berry & Lezos, 2017) is the necessity for an awareness of further intersectionality, for which familiarity with the Social GGRRAAACCEEESSS (aspects of difference and diversity: gender, geography, race, religion, age, ability, appearance, class/caste, culture, ethnicity, education, economics/employment, sexuality, sexual orientation and spirituality; (Burnham, 2012) and the potential for them to remain invisible or unvoiced (Krause, 2012) is useful. Cobin and Angelo state that ignoring differences is: "equivalent to working from an ethnocentric, white, heterosexist view that not only is limited but also can be damaging" (2015, p. 105). Ideally, the goal of good therapy should be to surpass doing no harm, into practicing aspirational ethics (Riggs, 2015).

Given that sexuality is conventionally viewed from a heteronormative position the institutions of society are ingrained with heterosexuality, inevitably finding its way into clinical practice (Hertzmann & Newbigin, 2020). Although we have come a long way from lesbian sex being ignored, or viewed as an aberration, the need remains to acknowledge the "oppressive weight of professional ignorance" (Masters & Johnson, 1979, p. 3) that SRT has grown from. Lesbian couples may well be wary of engaging in SRT, or indeed therapy in general (Iasenza, 2004). This is understandable, as central to good sex therapy with lesbian clients is the issue of specific training (Riggs, 2015). Studies researching the frequency of LGBT affirmative training received by sex therapists reveal startlingly low results – Corturillo et al. (2016) found less than half, whilst Zeglin et al. (2021) just 25.5%, which they rightly point out creates a space for the marginalisation or exclusion of clients in the therapy room. Therapists without specific training are left to rely on their own ideologies around sexuality (Speciale, 2020). It is the duty of sex therapists seeking to work well with this client group to ensure an appropriate knowledge base.

A strengths-based approach, recognising LGBT+ communities as healthy, is of critical importance (Riggs, 2015), as is the acknowledgement that lesbians sustaining relationships despite societal stressors exhibit a high degree of resilience and strength (Connolly, 2015).

Consideration should be given to the appropriateness of diagnosis. It is the position of Green and Flemons (2004) that it is unnecessary to diagnose in order to resolve difficulties, whilst Iasenza (2004) robustly regards an anti-pathological, thus anti-diagnosis stance to be imperative.

Berry and Lezos (2017) position that sexual difficulties are natural and understandable responses to relational and psychological factors exhorting the explicit questioning of normative standards and the identification of expectations around sex. These are crucial elements of good sex therapy with non-normative client groups, along with accounting for the influence of internalised homophobia in initial goals for therapy. Furthermore, they point out the need for distinctive competencies, offering six clinical techniques which include the following: a non-judgemental stance, affirmation, an appreciation of fluidity, normalising (part of which is deconstructing abnormal), horizontalising (contextualising the concern in the client's lived experience) and a high level of knowledge and literacy about sexual diversity and intersections. Additionally, they highlight the particular importance of reflective practice.

It is my view that ANT provides a vehicle which can encompass all of the above, as well as providing tools to work with. If therapists consider what constitutes sex, deconstruct good sex, identify problematic sexual narratives, take consideration of attachment narratives, locate the couple in wider societal structures and consider intersectionality, and engage in reflexive and ethical practice attending to our own position in the system, in my opinion, we have established the parameters for successful sex therapy

History taking

Leiblum (2007) identifies assessment as a critical component of SRT for effective formulation. Markovic (2013) advocates for history taking to be viewed as a therapeutic tool, not just a diagnostic one. My view is that history taking allows me, as a therapist, into each client's circle of trust. It is an opportunity to draw out attachment narratives, uncovering tales of inclusion/exclusion, gain an understanding of a client's sense of their place in society and explore sexual narratives.

I draw on the influences of Iasenza (2004, 2020) and Weiner and Avery-Clark (2017), as well as training resources I have come across, to gather a wide range of information. Rather than having set questions, I use systemic techniques to draw out problematic narratives and explore potential intersectionality.

In terms of childhood stories, I seek to understand a variety of factors: the family relational dynamic, particularly relating to perceived loving behaviours; relationships with peers and connection to wider society; the effects of the Social GRRRAAACCEEESSS (Burnham, 2012); introduction to the concept of sex; familial/peer narratives of nudity/modesty/appropriate behaviours; early sexual experiences; body image; self-esteem and narratives of self. I seek out experience of (or lack of) positive exposure to LGBTQ+ relationships.

In addition to standard enquiries into medical history – health, psychological, sexual and relational history – and perceived sexual functioning, I seek to understand each client's narratives of sexual self and sexual relationships, their peak turn-ons and fantasies (Lehmiller, 2018), and their pillars of sexuality (Morin, 1995). I inquire about the health of the current relationship, level of attraction and narratives of couplehood, the connectedness of the couple to others, especially the LGBTQ+ communities, their experience of coming out and whether there are places they are not out.

This list is by no means exhaustive. I aim to build up an idea of the sexual self of each client within the couple.

Round table

Iasenza (2004) described the usefulness of partners sharing history highlights with one another. I employ this technique prior to adding my own input, to open up discussion and assist in the feeling of collaboration, which is further enhanced by offering choices when possible.

Dallos (2006) describes formulation with an attachment narrative perspective as centring on relational patterns of beliefs and actions driven by attachment processes. The round table stage is an opportunity to draw together all of the narratives feeding into the difficulty and gain clients' consent for the projected work.

Case study

This case study is an abridged version. Details have been changed to protect identities. Permissions are held on file.

Initial meetings

Tess presented alone, describing her sex drive as non-existent, threatening her marriage of three years. Tess (38) and Amy (35) had been together for five years and had enjoyed fulfilling sex up until the birth of their son 18 months prior. Tess couldn't understand the disconnect between them, given their happiness should be complete. She blamed herself, describing "not being very good" at relationships and a previous inability to let down her guard and connect.

From the dearth of sex, a divide was growing. Amy felt rejected and resentful. Tess "knew" the problem was hers, as Amy had tried to initiate but she couldn't engage, feeling no arousal. She was afraid, as Amy had stopped trying and had withdrawn.

They engaged in SRT together, and Tess had been diagnosed with Female Sexual Interest/Desire Disorder. She described their experience as "sex therapy for straight people" and felt that "the touching thing" only served to increase the gap between them as Amy felt Tess was "making herself" do it and Tess felt under pressure to feel arousal. When she couldn't, she questioned whether she was cut out for a long-term relationship. The therapy had ended when they were set the task of scissoring, which felt alien to both, leaving them feeling the therapist didn't understand how they had sex. Having decided that SRT as a couple was not the right fit for them, Tess came alone, feeling that she needed to "fix her sex drive" for the relationship to work.

The initial session was an exploration of what form the work might be, taking a "not knowing" approach (Anderson & Goolishian, 1992) and offering Tess choices. Given her feelings of disempowerment in her previous therapeutic encounter, I considered it imperative for her to feel a sense of collaboration (Anderson & Gehart, 2007). I might have training and SRT skills, but I wanted her to know that she held the expertise regarding her relationships, with Amy and with her own sexual self. I would not be fixing Tess, as I did not believe she was broken.

An investigation of the relationship revealed a story of strength. The initial stages of their relationship had been difficult. Amy's family found it hard to accept Tess. Amy's previous heterosexual marriage produced a seven-year-old son. Although they currently co-parented with a stable shared custody agreement, navigating that had been arduous.

Early in their relationship, Tess's diagnosis of breast cancer resulted in a double mastectomy. Amy carried their son, as Tess had been unable to. She was sometimes unsure of her role in their family unit, which was compounded by the views of members of her wider family expressing sympathy for their son because they felt it was "not right for a boy to have no daddy". Watching Amy breastfeed the baby made her feel less womanly.

The baby also impacted their time together. Their older son spent every other weekend and a midweek night with his father, so the couple had enjoyed time to connect, which often led to physical intimacy. The effect of the absence of that time was keenly felt.

Tess was overcome with emotion at the idea that something as personal as her desire levels might not be a failing of hers, or indicate an inability to sustain a relationship, but rather that the changing relationship dynamic and external pressures placed upon the couple might contribute to her lack of sexual engagement. Tess and Amy had managed to sustain a close bond, despite hostility to their relationship, a major health crisis and the changes to their dynamic. Our conversation opened the door to reframing problematic narratives, and Tess wished to continue.

The session ended with a consideration of the potential benefits of re-engaging with couple work. Subsequently, the couple booked a session for Amy, followed by a joint session.

Amy arrived intrigued by the idea that problematic narratives, rather than she or Tess personally, might be derailing their sex life and interested in an approach that didn't jump into "the touching thing". Amy described her upset at Tess's self-blame for the situation, worried that her own insistence on co-sleeping to facilitate breastfeeding pushed Tess away. She was concerned that giving birth changed the way Tess viewed her; perhaps she was no longer a sexual being in Tess's eyes. She struggled to lose weight following the pregnancy and felt unattractive. Her previous marriage had broken down following pregnancy, as her husband found her body unappealing. Amy feared that it was happening again. She needed their previous level of intimacy to be restored to feel desirable.

Amy related that the prompt for seeking therapy initially was a conversation in which Tess described her sense of being useless – she couldn't have the baby, or breastfeed, she looked at Amy with her ex and felt that they were more of a proper family than she and Amy could be. She questioned Amy's sexuality; perhaps Amy would be better off with a man. Amy had been horrified and felt that they needed to repair the sexual relationship so that Tess could see that she was secure in her identity.

Amy worried that she didn't know how to be a "proper lesbian" and a full-time parent at the same time, and whether that was a turn off to Tess. Previously, the couple had an active social life on the gay scene while their older son was away. Since having their baby, they socialised more often with heterosexual couples met through pregnancy and baby groups, or with family, rather than with their gay friends. Amy's family made comments about her children being exposed to "unsuitable people", which enraged Amy. However, whilst she found their views abhorrent, she found herself "living a pretty straight life, just with a woman".

An examination of what "proper lesbian" meant afforded Amy the opportunity to realise how much her unconscious scripts influenced how she interpreted her relationship. She was keen to explore these themes with Tess.

The first joint session delved into what it meant to Tess and Amy to be a lesbian couple, raising children in a heteronormative society, and how it impacted on their sense of self and sexual identity. Tess raised her fear of lesbian bed death. Amy explained that she struggled with her mother's words, that choosing to be gay was choosing a lifetime of unhappiness, despite her personal belief that her sexual orientation was not a choice and her view that their happiness was possible. She had tried her best to live as she was expected to by her family, but had never experienced relational joy until she met Tess.

Neither had thought about the narratives they held; however, by identifying external forces being exerted upon them, they began the normalisation of their experience, begging the question if any relationship could be expected to encounter no difficulty, given the strength of "The Force"? Their joint love of Star Wars sparked a connection with the idea of "The Force", which we utilised throughout the work.

The idea of history taking evoked memories of their previous experience; however, framed as an opportunity to explore their narratives and enhance the understanding of the wider picture for themselves as well as for me, Tess and Amy saw the merit of it. It came with a guarantee that it was not the pathway to "the touching thing" they didn't want. If we collectively felt that some aspect of sensate focus might be useful, it would not be a directive process, but rather a collaborative one. Attending to their story dispelled their fear.

Formulation

The history taking encompassed the elements previously outlined, the key threads of which are summarised.

Predisposing factors

Both came from conservative, religious families – Tess Catholic, Amy Presbyterian – in heterosexist communities. They had in common an entirely heteronormative sex education in religious schools, and both came from homes with clearly defined gender roles, lacking in physical and emotional intimacy.

Tess lived in the shadow of her older sister, who was smarter, thinner, more attractive, and heterosexual. Tess internalised the words her mother used: "stupid, fat, and useless". She struggled at her school due to dyslexia and ADHD (undiagnosed until she was 12 and 15, respectively), and she suffered homophobic bullying. She was rejected by her parents at 16 upon coming out. Tess developed an avoidant attachment style. Tess had a plethora of sexual experiences, only ever with women, but had only experienced short-term relationships, mostly ended by her, or following her withdrawal.

Amy was the only child of a controlling mother. Her father left when she was three, and they had no relationship. She found it difficult to resist her mother's influence, even pursuing the career of her mother's choosing. Amy had married her first boyfriend at 21, following an eight-year relationship. She had three sexual partners prior to Tess, who was her first same-sex relationship. Amy exhibited an anxious attachment style.

Precipitating factors

Tess's breast cancer treatment reinforced her poor body image. Simultaneously to becoming a mother herself, she felt obliged to reconnect with her own parents due to her mother's failing health. The change in dynamic following the birth of her son shook Tess's security in the relationship and led to her concerns about Amy's sexuality.

Pregnancy and childbirth led to the resurfacing of Amy's body image issues and created anxiety around her desirability. Furthermore, it engendered an increase in criticism from her mother about her marriage to Tess.

Maintaining factors

Communicating around intimacy was difficult given the couple's differing attachment styles. Criticism of their family dynamic and internalised homophobia created a cognitive dissonance around parenthood and their relationship.

The work

I offered no diagnosis, opening the round table session with history highlights from the couple, then focussed solely on the attachment and problematic narratives drawn out through the history taking stage. I offered Tess and Amy the opportunity to consider the contributing factors and to decide which conversations they wished to prioritise. There was no physical element to the treatment programme in the initial stage.

We began with an exploration of sex, how it differed from other intimacy, what constituted good sex and the functionality of sex in their relationship. Sex was being used as a measuring tool for relational health. This realisation helped the couple to examine what other measures of relational health they might use to focus on relational strengths.

It also provided the basis for the exploration of problematic narratives. This work unearthed the penetration narrative Tess held. Amy loved to be penetrated with a strap-on. When Tess placed this alongside her fears around their family, it fuelled her concern about Amy's sexuality. However, far from fantasising about being with a man, the joy of penetration for Amy was feeling the soft hairlessness of Tess's skin, their breasts pressing together, and the variability of size and texture that she was able to control in terms of choosing the attachments to Tess's strap-on. The penetrative sex they had was not a poor substitute for a penis, but rather, perceived by Amy as better than sex with any man.

Recognition of attachment styles (Bowlby, 1988) facilitated the reframing of Tess's closing off as a fear response – a reaction to insecurity and how that fitted with Amy responding to feelings of insecurity with neediness. This enabled behaviours to be reframed and perceived as less threatening. The couple was able to see dealing with feelings of insecurity as a management issue, rather than a catastrophe, and strategise towards resolutions.

Educational aspects (Hawton, 1985) included acknowledging the role of internalised homophobia in Amy's heterosexual marriage (Fioravanti et al., 2021), along with the preponderance of gay people towards a pessimistic evaluation of the potential quality and duration of same-sex intimate relationships (Lingiardi et al., 2012). This, alongside the exploration of Tess's fear of lesbian bed death, contextualised her fatalistic attitude towards relationships. Joint resistance to homophobia increased closeness and renewed hope.

During a session exploring intersectionality, Tess said, "All this internalised stuff is just rubbish isn't it? It makes you want just to wreck something". So, we explored what to do with it. We wrote down all of the things identified from the formulation, added things from the discussions, creating a pile of pages which we ripped to pieces. They scrunched it all into a big ball, named Bob. We reflected about the impact Bob had exerted over them when they hadn't realised he was there and how their knowledge now gave them wider choices. When I asked what they wanted to do with Bob, they decided to take him home and put him in their fire.

The couple merged their thinking of "The Force", with the Bob exercise, creating "Bob Force". This became a platform to discuss when they were feeling a greater impact from external forces and created a shared language: for example, "Bob is trying my patience today". Furthermore, it widened to incorporate "Bob people" – Tess's mother (Bob force factor 10/10), Amy's mother (Bob force factor 6/10), and some friends. This opened discussions about how to navigate relationships with "Bob people", whether they should cut them out or minimise the amount of time spent with them. Additionally, it highlighted the dearth of interaction with "Non-Bob" people, leading to reconnecting with their gay network and joining groups for lesbian parents.

Some of the exercises the couple worked on related to self-esteem. They each completed individual work, but given their heightened awareness of this shared difficulty, they very quickly merged working on positive self-talk into a joint enterprise, affirming one another daily and solidifying their connection.

The first piece of practical work for the couple was engaging in self-focus, to get each of them in touch with their sexual selves. This was accompanied by a conversation about receptive desire (Basson, 2007). Simmering (Barbach, 2001), building sexual arousal and strengthening the erotic bond through brief intimacies was encouraged. Individual mirror work (Griffen et al., 2018) followed, as both had anxieties about their bodies. Shortly after, they did mirror work together, discussing what they liked about their bodies and listening to what they each liked about the other. They did not contain the exercise to looking at one another. Touching came naturally, they became aroused and had sex. In fact, they had sex the following morning, too.

Although our work carried on for a few more sessions, it was apparent that they had moved on emotionally and sexually. They had exposed their vulnerabilities conversationally, felt held, and once the barrier had been overcome physically, there was no need for any guided programme.

Conclusion

My usage of ANT was borne from necessity, as the couple described did not wish to pursue traditional SRT. Coming from a systemic background and practising ANT in couple work, it seemed like the obvious choice to bring about change in this situation. However, it worked so effectively that I felt empowered to challenge what I had considered to be the only way of working as a newly qualified SRT therapist and move beyond it. I do use sensate focus, sometimes to great effect, but find that ANT is present in all of my SRT work.

I believe there needs to be more research around the skills to work with LGBTQ+ client populations. There are particular gaps in our knowledge when it comes to lesbian couples. Empirical research into how such couples define sex would be most beneficial.

It is imperative for SRT therapists to take into consideration societal heterosexism and sexism prior to pathologising lesbian couples with diagnoses and embarking on treatment plans. It is quite possible that many women are enjoying the sexual relationships that suit them, but problematic narratives are the cause of their discomfort. It is of course important to put in place interventions to facilitate change when change is needed, but only after collaborative discussion with clients to establish if it is in fact necessary. In this way, we truly respect the uniqueness of the couples who present for SRT.

References

Anderson, B.L., & Cyranowski, J.M. (1996). Women's sexuality: Behaviours, responses and individual responses. *Journal of Consulting and Clinical Psychology*, 63(6), 891–906.
Anderson, H. (2007). The heart and spirit of collaborative therapy. In H. Anderson & D. Gehart, (eds). *Collaborative Therapy: Relationships and Conversations That Make a Difference*. London: Routledge.

Anderson, H., & Goolishian, H. (1992). The client is the expert: A not-knowing approach to therapy. In S. McNamee & K.J. Gergen (Eds.), *Therapy as a Social Construction* (pp. 25–39). London: Sage Publications.

Armstrong, H.L., & Reissing, E.D. (2013). Women who have sex with women: A comprehensive review of the literature and conceptual model of sexual function. *Sex and Relationship Therapy*, 28(4), 364–399.

Barbach, L. (2001). *For Each Other: Strong Sexual Intimacy*. New York: Signet Books.

Basson, R. (2007). Sexual desire/arousal disorders in women. In S.R. Leiblum (Ed.), *Principals and Practice of Sex Therapy* (pp. 25–53). New York: Guilford Press.

Beaber, T., & Werner, P. (2009). The relationship between anxiety and sexual functioning in lesbians and heterosexual women. *Journal of Homosexuality*, 56(5), 639–654.

Berry, M.D., & Lezos, A.N. (2017). Inclusive sex therapy practices: A qualitative study of the techniques sex therapists use when working with diverse sexual populations. *Sexual and Relationship Therapy*, 32(1), 2–21.

Biaggio, M., Coan, S., & Adams, W. (2002). Couples therapy for lesbians: Understanding merger and impact of homophobia. *Journal of Lesbian Studies*, 6(1), 129–138.

Bowlby, J. (1988). *A Secure Base: Clinical Applications of Attachment Theory*. London: Routledge.

Bowling, J., et al. (2020). Definitions of sex and intimacy among gender and sexual minoritised groups in urban India. *Culture, Health and Sexuality*, 22(5), 520–534.

Burnham, J.B. (2005). Relational reflexivity: A tool for socially constructing therapeutic relationships. In C. Flaskas, B. Masson, & Perlesz (Eds.), *The Space Between* (pp. 45–67). London: Karnac.

Burnham, J.B. (2012). Developments in social GRRRAAACCEEESSS: Visible-invisible and voiced-unvoiced. In I.B. Krause (Ed.), *Culture and Reflexivity in Systemic Psychotherapy: Mutual Perspectives*. London: Routledge.

Cecchin, G. (1987). Hypothesising, circularity and neutrality revisited: An invitation to curiosity. *Family Processes*, 26, 405–413.

Cobin, M., & Angelo, M. (2015). Sex therapy with lesbian couples. In J.J. Bigner & J.L. Wetchler (Eds.), *Handbook of LGBT-Affirmative Couple and Family Therapy* (pp. 99–112). London: Routledge.

Connolly, C.M. (2015). Lesbian couple therapy. In J.J. Bigner & J.L. Wetchler (Eds.), *Handbook of LGBT-Affirmative Couple and Family Therapy* (pp. 43–56). London: Routledge.

Corturillo, E.M., McGeorge, C.R., & Stone Carlson, T. (2016). How prepared are they? Exploring couple and family therapy members' training experiences in lesbian, gay and bisexual affirmative therapy. *Journal of Feminist Family Therapy*, 28(2–3), 55–75.

Dallos, R. (1997). *Interacting Stories: Narratives, Family Beliefs and Therapy*. London: Routledge.

Dallos, R. (2006). *Attachment Narrative Therapy: Integrating Systemic, Narrative and Attachment Approaches*. London: Open University Press.

Diamond, L.M. (2009). *Sexual Fluidity: Understanding Women's Love and Desire*. Cambridge: Harvard University Press.

Fahs, B., & Plante, R. (2017). On 'good sex' and other dangerous ideas: Woman narrate their joyous and happy sexual encounters. *Journal of Gender Studies*, 26(1), 33–34.

Fioravanti, G., Banchi, V., & Giunti, D. (2021). Sexual functioning of group of a group of gay and lesbian parents who have children from heterosexual relationships: An exploratory study. *Sex and Relationship Therapy*, 36(2–3), 256–257.

Green, R.J. (2004). Foreword. In J.J. Bigner & J.L. Wetchler (Eds.), *Relationship Therapy with Same-Sex Couples* (pp. xii–xvii). New York: Haworth Press.

Green, R.J., Bettinger, M., & Zacks, E. (1996). Are lesbian couples fused and gay male couples disengaged? In J. Laird & R.J. Green (Eds.), *Lesbians and Gays in Couples and Families: A Handbook for Therapists* (pp. 185–230). San Francisco: Jossey Bass.

Green, S.R., & Flemons, D. (Eds.). (2004). *Quickies: The Handbook of Brief Sex Therapy*. London: W.W. Norton and Co.

Griffen, T.C., Naumann, E., & Hildebrandt, T. (2018). Mirror exposure therapy for body image disturbances and eating disorders: A review. *Clinical Psychology Review*, 65, 163–174.

Hall, M. (1987). Sex therapy with lesbian couples: A four-stage approach. *Journal of Homosexuality*, 14(1–2), 137–156.

Hawton, K. (1985). *Sex Therapy: A Practical Guide*. New York: Oxford University Press.

Heimann, J. (2017). Orgasmic disorders in women. In S.R. Leiblum (Ed.) (2007), *Principles and Practice of Sex Therapy*. New York: Guilford Press.

Hertzmann, L., & Newbigin, J. (Eds.). (2020). *Sexuality and Gender Now: Moving Beyond Heteronormativity*. Abingdon: Routledge.

Iasenza, S. (2002). Beyond 'lesbian bed death': The passion and play in lesbian relationships. *Journal of Lesbian Studies*, 6(1), 111–120.

Iasenza, S. (2004). Multicontextual sex therapy with lesbian couples. In S.R. Green & D. Flemons (Eds.), *Quickies: The Handbook of Brief Sex Therapy* (pp. 15–25). London: W.W. Norton and Co.

Iasenza, S. (2020). *Transforming Sexual Narratives: A Relational Approach to Sex Therapy*. London: Routledge.

Komisaruk, B.R., & Whipple, B. (2011). Non-genital orgasms. *Sexual and Relationship Therapy*, 26(4), 356–372.

Krause, I.B. (Ed.). (2012). *Culture and Reflexivity in Systemic Psychotherapy: Mutual Perspectives*. London: Routledge.

Lehmiller, J. (2018). *Tell Me What You Want*. London: Robinson.

Leiblum, S.R. (Ed.). (2007). *Principles and Practice of Sex Therapy*. New York: Guilford Press.

Lingiardi, V., Baiocco, R., & Nardelli, N. (2012). Measures of internal sexual stigma for lesbians and gay men: A new scale. *Journal of Homosexuality*, 59(8), 1191–1210.

Markovic, D. (2013). Multidimensional psychosexual therapy: A model of integration between sexology and systemic therapy. *Sexual and Relationship Therapy*, 28(4), 311–323.

Mason, B. (1993). Towards positions of safe uncertainty. *Human Systems: The Journal of Systemic Consultation & Management*, 4, 189–200.

Masters, W.H., & Johnson, V.E. (1970). *Human Sexual Inadequacy*. Boston: Little Brown and Company.

Masters, W.H., & Johnson, V.E. (1979). *Homosexuality in Perspective*. Philadelphia: Lippincott Williams and Wilkens.

Mavhu, W., Langhaug, L., Manyonga, B., Power, P., & Cowan, F. (2008). What is sex exactly? Using cognitive interviewing to improve the validity of sexual behaviour reporting among young people in rural Zimbabwe. *Culture, Health and Sexuality*, 10(6), 563–572.

Meston, C.M., & Bradford, A. (2007). Sexual dysfunctions in women. *Annual Review of Clinical Psychology*, 3, 233–256.

Metz, M.E., & McCarthy, B.W. (2007). The 'good-enough sex' model for couple satisfaction. *Sex and Relationship Therapy*, 22(3), 351–262.

Moon, L. (2016). Counselling Ideologies: Queer Challenges to Heteronormativity. London: Routledge.

Morin, J. (1995). *The Erotic Mind*. London: HarperCollins.

Nichols, M. (2004). Lesbian sexuality/female sexuality: Rethinking 'lesbian bed death'. *Sexual and Relationship Therapy*, 19(4), 363–371.

Nichols, M., & Shernoff, M. (2007). Therapy with sexual minorities: Queering practice. In S.R. Lieblum (Ed.), *Principles and Practice of Sex Therapy* (pp. 379–415). New York: Guilford Press.

O'Hanlon, B. (2004). Come again? From possibility therapy to sex therapy. In S. Green & D. Flemons (Eds.), *Quickies: The Handbook of Brief Sex Therapy* (pp. 1–14). London: W.W. Norton and Co.

Peixoto, M.M. (2017). Sex and sexual orientation. In W. IsHak (Ed.), *The Textbook of Clinical Sexual Medicine* (pp. 433–445). Cham, Switzerland: Springer International Publishing AG.

Riggs, D.W. (2015). Ethical issues in LGBT couple and family therapy. In J.J. Bigner & J.L. Wetchler (Eds.), *Handbook of LGBT-Affirmative Couple and Family Therapy* (pp. 421–432). London: Routledge.

Rohleder, P. (2020). Homophobia, heteronormativity and shame. In L. Hertzmann & J. Newbigin (Eds.), *Sexuality and Gender Now: Moving Beyond Heteronormativity* (pp. 40–56). Abingdon: Routledge.

Rosen, R., et al. (2000). The Female Sexual Function index (FSFI): A multidimensional self-report instrument for the assessment of female sexual function. *Journal of Sex and Marital Therapy*, 26(2), 191–208.

Speciale, M. (2020). Negotiating sexual values in counsellor education: A qualitative case exploration. *Journal of Counselling Sexology and Sexual Wellness: Research Practice and Education*, 2(1), 10–21.

Tiefer, L. (2001). A new view of women's sexual problems: Why new? Why now? *The Journal of Sexual Research*, 38(2), 89–96.

Tiefer, L. (2003). Taking back women's sexuality. *In the Family*, 4, 14–16.

Vetere, A., & Dallos, R. (2008). Systemic therapy and attachment narratives. *The Journal of Family Therapy*, 30, 374–385.

Weiner, L., & Avery-Clark, C. (2017). *Sensate Focus in Sex Therapy: The Illustrated Manual*. London: Routledge.

White, M., & Epston, D. (1990). *Narrative Means to Therapeutic Ends*. New York: Norton.

Zeglin, R.J., Goldberg, S., Stalnaker-Shofner, D.M., Walker, B.M., & Schubert, A.M. (2021). Sex therapy credentials: A descriptive analysis of the training of clinicians who do sex therapy. *Sex and Relationship Therapy*. doi:10:1080/14681994.2021.1937598

Zeig, J.K. (Ed.). (1994). *Ericksonian Methods: The Essence of the Story*. New York: Brunner-Mazel.

Chapter 2

Queer menopause
Working with the LGBTQIA+ menopausal client

Tania Glyde

Part one: what is menopause? (overview)

Introduction

Depending on who you are, you may have been tempted to skip this chapter. *'Menopause? What even is that?'* You might have heard of it, perhaps from a parent or caregiver, or via some mother-in-law jokes off the telly. Actually, you've done yourself a favour by taking an interest, because menopause is a very significant societal and health-related issue that affects a large number of people. We all, therapists in particular, need to be talking about it, no matter who we are or how we work.

The menopause I am mainly (though not entirely) focusing on in this chapter is what happens in bodies with ovarian systems, when the ovaries slow down and then stop producing oestrogen, causing menstruation to stop, resulting in infertility. However, as you will see later in this chapter, the biopsychosocial nature of menopause means there are other ways a person might experience menopause-like symptoms, and clinicians need to take this into account.

A major factor, perhaps *the* major factor, is the length of time a person may be experiencing menopause-related side effects and body/mood changes. Enter perimenopause, a term that is only just beginning to be understood. If you know a little bit about menopause, you will likely associate it with a person's menstruation stopping at 50. This, unfortunately, barely touches on what really happens. In reality, the side effects of oestrogen fluctuation can start in a person's late 30s or earlier. And the effects may last beyond the 60s and into the 70s.

The menopause focus in the mainstream media is very much on the experience of cisgender heterosexual women (and, while we're here, mostly white and middle class). And while it's true that the majority of people who experience menopause do belong to that group, it's important to say that even this large number of people has historically (Corinna, 2021), and unfortunately is currently still, getting a raw deal over education, information, healthcare, and medical support.

DOI: 10.4324/9781003260608-3

But what about all the people in menopause who are not heterosexual, and/or are not cisgender? There is almost nothing written on the menopause experience of people who are LGBTQIA+. And yet, as a therapist, GSRD-focused or not, you are going to see perimenopause and menopause in your therapy room, whether you realise it or not. (And whether your client realises or not either, such is the inadequacy of education at the time of writing.) You are particularly going to have younger clients who may be desperately struggling with perimenopause without knowing what is actually going on for them.

Thanks to activism, children are now going to be taught about menopause at school. But there is a long way to go. If neither you nor your client know anything about perimenopause or menopause, your client will miss out, and this may affect their health because perimenopause can exacerbate existing health and mental health issues.

So, in this chapter, I am first going to give a general introduction, explain the essentials of perimenopause and menopause, who experiences it and how, and take a look at the social context and how it's portrayed in the media and mainstream resources. We will look at the different ways a person may become menopausal, and how menopause may intersect with various identities.

In Part two, I will summarise my research as well as signpost other resources, and in Part Three, I will offer a list of guidelines for therapists.

What is menopause?

Menopause is a form of hormonal transition. People may refer to the 'natural' menopause, when the ovaries have stopped working in midlife, although there are other ways to experience it, as I will outline in this chapter.

Menopause is also an umbrella term for a multi-stage process which can be summarised as follows: somewhere, approximately in middle age, but absolutely can be younger, the ovaries' oestrogen production starts to fluctuate and eventually diminish, and the ovaries gradually cease egg production. This period of time, which can be years long, is *perimenopause*. During this time, menstruation may become irregular; I say 'may' because sometimes periods can remain regular when the body has begun having other side effects. Eventually, menstruation stops altogether. When menstruation has stopped for a year or more, the person is finally said to be 'in menopause'. And then, in an odd quirk of medical timekeeping, the next day they are henceforth known as *post-menopausal*.

When does it happen?

While the age of 50 is frequently declared to be the age when menstruation finally stops (one of the reasons it doesn't come up on many younger people's radar), this process can absolutely happen earlier or later. Significantly, perimenopause can last up to 10 years or more. So, to reiterate, menopause information is relevant to people long before they are 50. This is what everyone needs to be shouting about, whether they are queer or not.

Systemic and intersectional factors

When doing this work, it's important to remember the potentially compounding factors in a person's life that will impact their experience of menopause. Think about the impact on a person when they are having difficult health experiences but don't know why. Add to this the impact of any existing trauma, health issues, and life difficulties they have (Gibson et al., 2019). And add on top of this the impact of any marginalised identities that person holds.

Other ways menopause can occur

It's important to know that menopause can occur in ways other than the age-related slowing down of the ovaries, for example:

- If the ovaries have been removed, at any age for any reason, including as a teenager. It's important to remember the needs of younger people who experience premature menopause, for whatever reason. For them, the popular 'ageing is terrible' narrative may feel alienating and irrelevant.
- Premature Ovarian Insufficiency (POI), when the ovaries cease to function properly.
- After chemotherapy, in some instances.
- If the person starts taking exogenous hormones or hormone blockers, this can also bring on menopause-like experiences. As with all menopausal people, these changes in the body may affect quality of life, including in relationships and the workplace (Reese, 2020).
- For a transmasculine person, lowering the oestrogen in the body will bring on menopause-like side effects; subsequently, taking testosterone may erase these effects, or it may not (Casimiro & Cohen, 2019).
- For a transfeminine person, having to come off supplemental oestrogen, for example, in order to have gender confirmation (or other) surgery, can also bring on similar side effects, as can testosterone blockers (Mason, 2021; Tangpricha & den Heijer, 2017).

What are the side-effects of menopause?

Following is a range of side effects that can begin in perimenopause and continue post-cessation of menstruation. There is a wide variety of experiences, depending on genetics, overall health, class, race, trauma, and current life situation. Some people experience very little and only know what's happening because their periods have stopped; many will have some of these, and some will find their lives drastically affected.

1   **Mental health**

    Insomnia (which may exacerbate poor mental health overall), anxiety, depression, mood swings, irritability or rage (further reading: Corinna, 2021, pp. 129–153).

2 **Physical health**

Hot flushes (or vasomotor symptoms), sweating and night sweats, overheating, tingling hands and feet, chronic pain, eczema, itching and skin dryness, hair loss, unusual hair growth, weight gain.

3 **Cognitive capacity**

Brain fog, trouble with word-finding, forgetfulness, memory loss.

4 **Gynaecological and sexual health**

- Increasingly irregular and/or very heavy periods (confined-to-the-home levels of heavy).
- Genitourinary Symptoms of Menopause (GSM), previously known as *vaginal atrophy*. This is the thinning and drying of the vaginal, urethral, and other surrounding tissue, making any penetration very painful (this includes medical examinations). The likelihood of bladder infections and stress incontinence increases. Also increased odour as the vagina becomes more alkaline, leading sometimes to BV (Bacterial Vaginosis).
- Lowered libido. In perimenopause, libido can also be raised, which brings its own potential challenges.

Overview of impact

All these side effects may have a compound effect on mental health and sexual self-confidence, along with shame, internalised ageism, and internalised ableism. They can also exacerbate some existing health conditions, particularly in terms of mental health, and Premenstrual Dysphoric Disorder (PMDD).

In the longer term, as a result of low oestrogen, someone may experience osteoporosis (or brittle bones), stroke, heart disease, and dementia.

In terms of mental wellbeing, menopause may dovetail with existing life challenges, and also existing trauma. If you are already on the edge mentally and physically, and your health is bad and you cannot sleep, everything will seem worse, and sometimes *become* worse, doubly if you are impacted by racism, misogyny, homophobia, biphobia, transphobia, and ableism.

And of course, it dovetails with poverty. Another mainstream menopause narrative trope you may have noticed is the 'wealthy middle-aged white woman going on spa weekends'. This is true for some, and untrue for many.

Menopause also intersects with neurodivergence, as well as potentially instigating neurodivergence of its own (Moseley et al., 2020).

Once you have properly reached post-menopause, you are infertile. Many people of all identities experience grief at the end of menstruation and at the same time a lot of relief. However, some cis women may feel they have lost their femininity or even their sense of being a woman at all; this may be negative for some, and positive for others (Glyde, 2021c, 05:46–08:59).

Menopause in the media and public life

In terms of research and reported experiences, the majority focus is still on – as well as cisgender and heterosexual – the white, European, Western, Anglo, middle-class, well resourced, and medicalised experience of menopause.

Responses to menopause in public life generally relate to how cisgender heterosexual women are supposedly feeling about it, and often focus on physical appearance, capacity to have PIV (penis-in-vagina) sex, and general ability to please men and keep their interest visually and sexually.

Conversely, there is also a narrative of repulsion, with imagery of things being rotten, faded, or comical (Glyde, 2020, 04:36–09:25). As menopause is overwhelmingly associated publicly with women, misogyny and ageism go hand in hand here. Ageism in mainstream media also means older women are seen as redundant.

So the mainstream narrative is along the lines of the destruction of femininity and terrifying slide into old age, and consequent loss of both status and worth. Of course, you don't have to be queer or trans to feel alienated by the angles taken in the media and popular culture, whether what you see is heteronormative, cisnormative, repulsively humorous, or financially out of reach.

Of course, it's important to say that many people also rejoice in this phase of life. Menopause can bring a sense of freedom, and many people report an improved experience of life, despite health difficulties. However, as the playing field is not remotely level, and information and access are so patchy, it is important not to assume all clients will experience this, particularly not if they are at the start of their menopause transition.

As you can see, there are many factors to menopause, which can be seen as both a stage of life and a potential health condition. Practitioners need to be aware of all the potential intersections here, and also of the many opportunities to be tripped up by their own unconscious prejudices.

Menopause healthcare and treatment

A person with an ovarian system may take replacement hormones, which will initially be oestrogen and likely progesterone (the latter definitely if the person still has their uterus). This medication has generally been known as HRT (Hormone Replacement Therapy), although the acronym MHT (Menopausal Hormone Therapy) is increasingly preferred, in order to be more specific and not to be confused with other forms of hormone treatment.

Some people are advised not to take HRT for existing health reasons, including high blood pressure, a stroke or blood clotting disorder history, or a history of oestrogen positive cancer, and other cancers. It can be taken in pill form, gel, and patches. If the person is still menstruating, the oestrogen and progesterone are taken separately. There are many combinations. Patches, and anything applied to the skin rather than ingested, are seen to be safer because they lower the risk of blood clots and digestive issues.

It is clear from the thousands of desperate people posting in menopause groups on social media that there is a great disparity in how GPs view menopause, and whether they take it seriously at all. A survey by the campaigning group Menopause Matters found that nearly half of all UK universities with medical schools do not have mandatory menopause education on the curriculum (Menopause Matters, 2021). It is not certain that a patient will easily obtain a prescription for replacement hormones. Some have antidepressants thrust on them whether this is suitable or not, and others are denied treatment, being told that menopause is 'natural'. Which is, of course, one step away from 'women's lot'.

None of this has been helped by previous research, in particular, the very large HRT study, the Women's Health Initiative in 2002, the outcome of which (and whose poor interpretations) was to cause a generation of people to be too scared to take HRT. 'The damage done was huge, basically leaving many symptomatic women without an effective treatment, even if the epidemiological data were not strong enough to document a clear harm to women's health' (Cagnacci & Venier, 2019, p. 6). Although there have been studies subsequently, work is still being done to unpick the damage (Robinson, 2020).

Ovarian-based bodies also produce testosterone, and low levels can also impact wellbeing and health. At the time of writing, there is still no licensed testosterone preparation for women in the UK. However, there are increasingly loud calls for this to be changed (International Menopause Society, 2019). Currently in the UK, prescribing is at the discretion of GPs, who may refer to specialist NHS menopause clinics. Otherwise, patients go private if they can afford it.

There are various alternative remedies, such as black cohosh, sage, and red clover, which have many supporters, but which have not been well studied (Corinna, 2021, pp. 279–283).

There has been extensive political discussion around supplemental oestrogen. In the past, it has been seen as a saviour of cisgender heterosexual women from a terrible fate. Corinna (2021, p. 32) quotes the notorious *Feminine Forever* by Robert A Wilson, where he describes the menopausal woman as 'a dull-minded but sharp-tongued caricature of her former self'. A feminist/queer backlash was inevitable, where taking HRT was seen as bending to the patriarchy through compliance with patriarchal values (Kelly, 2008).

A note on hormones and gender

It's important to talk about hormones and their (supposedly) gendered nature. People attach great cultural and personal meaning to the idea that oestrogen is the GIRL hormone and testosterone is the BOY hormone. While this is not the place for a detailed explainer, I can assure you that it is far more complicated than that, and a lot less binary. While different bodies may have different proportions of them, all bodies make oestrogen, progesterone, and testosterone and need them to function. Testosterone levels, like all hormones, also fluctuate in all bodies and have been shown to go up and down depending on status (Fine, 2017).

Also, it's important to remember that, in an Assigned Female At Birth (AFAB) body, it is actually the ovaries that produce a good proportion of testosterone (Abdel-Rahman & Hurd, 2020; Burger, 2002), and in Assigned Male At Birth (AMAB) bodies, the testes produce some oestrogen along with testosterone (Hussain & Gilloteaux, 2020; Hess, 2003). To gender hormones in the specific and exclusive binary way that we do is therefore incredibly unhelpful, and creates unnecessary issues for many.

One of the worst outcomes of this enforced binary is doctors operating on Intersex (InterAct, undated) babies and young people, born with variations in their sexual or reproductive anatomy, without their consent. This is also sometimes done through subterfuge and deceit, simply in order to normalise and binarise the child's gender. 'Many intersex women never experience periods, yet as part of the powerful medical institution, doctors wrongly tell intersex people that they are in post surgical menopause' (Davis & Khan, 2021).

And this is where we need to look in more detail at how menopause intersects with LGBTQIA+ identities. Very little academic work exists on the LGBTQIA+ experience of menopause.

Part two: supporting research

The current situation

There is much research concerned with (and entire journals dedicated to) ageing and health (e.g. the *Journal of Ageing and Health*), LGBTQIA+ health (e.g. Lefevor et al., 2019), older LGBTQIA+ health (e.g. Hoy-Ellis, 2016), and about menopause itself (e.g. Monteleone et al., 2018). But almost nothing that combines them all. And it is not edifying that we had to wait until 2021 before an actually inclusive book on menopause was published: *What Fresh Hell Is This? Perimenopause, Menopause, Other Indignities, and You* by Heather Corinna (2021). (Disclosure: I am quoted in it and wrote the foreword to the UK edition. If there were other books like this, I would be glad to reference them.)

Up until now, queer approaches to menopause have barely been written about, and – some blogs and art projects aside – resources are almost non-existent (Glyde, 2021b, pp. 5–6). However, the increasing existence of a trans/queer menstruation movement (e.g. www.bleedingthunder.com/; Rydstrom, 2020) means that, somewhere down the line, a trans/queer menopause movement is sure to follow. And it's wise to future-proof your practice on this because of the increasing number of younger people who are taking gender expansiveness to new levels.

Connected subjects

Before coming to menopause, it's worth looking briefly from a wider angle at some of the outside factors that affect this client group. Disparities between the experiences of LGBTQ+ people and the mainstream population are not hard to find.

'Older LGBTQ+ adults experience specific issues, including social stigma, isolation, financial issues and concerns about disclosure, as well as major health disparities when compared with heterosexuals (Fredriksen-Goldsen et al., 2011, cited in McGlotten & Moore, 2013)' (Glyde, 2021b, p. 4).

Looking at the entire population, 50 is generally the age when chronic health conditions start to occur (Hoy-Ellis, 2016). However, while the general population may in fact start to experience a reduction in psychological distress around this time, LGB adults aged 50+ remain significantly more vulnerable in this regard (Hoy-Ellis, 2016).

Rowan et al. (2021) noted that 'Older lesbian and bisexual women had high rates of tobacco use, alcohol use, and substance abuse and reported more inpatient stays and emergency department visits related to substance use disorders' (p. 1).

Unfortunately, LGBTQ+ identified clients could not be guaranteed a good experience in therapy either, and it was possible they would not return, even if they needed it, after a bad experience. This negative experience might involve being pathologised or erased (Glyde, 2021b, p. 4).

Research shows that trans and non-binary people are vulnerable to mental health issues and are more likely to carry out suicide attempts. Many trans clients have very low expectations of how they will be treated by therapists (Glyde, 2021b, p. 4). I will go into this further in the third section. 'I note the disturbing number of counsellors who claim in online discussion that they can work with anyone, simply by asserting that they don't judge' (Glyde, 2021b, p. 15). This is not enough to claim cultural competency.

How can therapists and healthcare practitioners best support and validate their queer menopausal clients?

For my research, I interviewed 12 LGBTQIA+ identified and menopausal people about their experiences (Glyde, 2021b). I did this research after a number of conversations about menopause with queer and non-binary AFAB friends. I initially focused on counselling and psychotherapy, but then I decided to open my questions to experiences of the wider healthcare system. In the case of LGBTQIA+ menopause, many of the issues are similar.

Imagine going to see a practitioner (therapeutic or medical) whom you are likely unsure of due to your past experiences with similar ones, perpetually braced for a potentially difficult encounter, having to explain your gender or sexuality and even debate them about it, then talk about something you don't really understand, and which you don't realise your practitioner neither knows nor cares much about. Overall, there is potential for a wasted journey or an uncomfortable experience at best, and a disaster at worst.

Summary of my findings

I pulled five main conclusions out of the data (Glyde, 2021b, pp. 9–15):

1 **Therapists need to acknowledge their Queer Menopausal Clients' experiences rather than make assumptions about them.**

   Many participants spoke about the assumptions that therapists and practitioners made about their lives and bodies. Along with this came the minimisation of clients' experiences and needs. There are still heterosexist and cissexist assumptions made about what the client does with their body and whom they may do it with, for example, the gender of a partner, or an assumption that PIV sex will be happening.

2 **Queer Menopausal Clients are likely to have had previous negative experiences in the healthcare system, in therapy and in life in general.**

   Many participants had had negative experiences already and were braced for more. They ranged from irritating and disempowering to actively traumatic.

3 **Available information about menopause is inadequate, and therapists need to realise that both they and their clients may hold inaccurate knowledge about it.**

   There was confusion, mixed up with memories from family and cliches from the media. Some participants reported having to educate their therapists and doctors.

4 **Therapists should not assume the Queer Menopausal experience is exclusively negative.**

   Despite some health challenges, some participants welcomed a shift in values, and menstruation ending, and there was some reflection about the benefits of queerness as protective against cisgender heterosexual and patriarchal norms.

5 **Therapists need more training in gender, sex and relationship diversity, menopause, and hormones.**

   This is my overall conclusion and, of course, the purpose of this book.

My research revealed a huge disjunct between client experiences and the attitudes of practitioners, and showed that there is a great need for training and knowledge.

A further word on hormones

You may feel you are entering a potential minefield. After all, 'It's your hormones, dear' has been used as a form of mockery (ageist and otherwise) – towards women in particular – since time immemorial. It's easy to see why a therapist might hesitate before mentioning this to a client.

However, hormones have many meanings and resonances, depending on who is taking them. One of the participants in my study referred to the 'hormone hacks' that their friends undertook, buying them online, in order to bring their bodies more into line with their true selves. Non-binary people may, for example, talk of 'microdosing' hormones. Hormones, both endogenous and exogenous, may affect someone's experience of menopause.

For example, an adult transmasculine person who starts taking testosterone and oestrogen blockers will be going into a second puberty at the same time as having a menopause, at any age. If someone has been taking testosterone for a long time before hitting 'natural' menopausal age, they may avoid a lot of the effects of 'natural' menopause, but not all. At any point, the consequent reduction in oestrogen may lead to vaginal dryness and other symptoms of GSM. This can be remedied by topical oestrogen cream. But for some, the idea of taking supplemental oestrogen may bring fears of being feminised by it and cause dysphoria, not least due to having to insert it into the vagina.

So it's best to be open to whatever your client is bringing on this and respect their choices to medicate or not. And there may be some grieving for what might have been if they cannot take hormones for health reasons.

Trans men and non-binary clients in menopause

Trans men and AFAB non-binary people may have a particularly challenging experience when seeking support. There are a number of potential reasons for this.

- Trying to concentrate on heavily gendered information resources. A sense of being excluded and potential for loss of interest.
- The pressure to either stay quiet or spend ages explaining themselves to incredulous or potentially hostile staff.
- The anticipatory stress of having to do either of these.
- Being repeatedly misgendered by healthcare staff. The medical/healthcare world is particularly bad for this, as well as the hospitality industry (Glyde, 2021a).
- Experiencing dysphoria due to body parts being touched or named as feminine. Not everyone experiences this, but many do.
- Even if done kindly, the 'woman to woman' support in breast/gynae clinics, etc., does not help.
- Feminine-styled information portals, leaflets, etc., may also discourage someone from seeking help.

- The need for knowledge about hormones and their significance. As noted previously, someone might not realise that adding in a small dose of oestrogen may be helpful with GSM, and not feminise them. Remember that dysphoria is powerful.
- For someone non-binary, the challenge of discussing hormones with a GP simultaneously regarding menopause, and microdosing for gender affirmation reasons, and the fear of having to perform for multiple gatekeepers (Glyde, 2021b, p. 12).

Queerness as a potentially protective factor

Being LGBTQ+ may be a protective factor in terms of some of the biopsychosocial aspects of menopause.

- Some people are less attached to the idea of fertility and giving birth.
- The absence of needing to please cis men through youthful appearance, slimness, and conventional sexual availability.
- More immunity to conventional beauty standards.
- Fewer escalator relationships, and more expansive notions of what relationships are and could be.
- Having more expansive forms and definitions of sex – for example, no focus on PIV – means that bodily changes can be worked around.
- There seems to be a higher incidence of and awareness of disability and physical and mental health issues among the LGBTQ+ population, both when younger and older. Awareness of this may be protective when menopause symptoms come around. Some queer people have thus had time to work on internalised ableism and ageism.
- A sense of community and therefore support.

(Glyde, 2021c, 14:23–15:44)

Sexual and gender evolution in midlife

It is very possible that menopause has its own queering properties. Of course, once again we are in biopsychosocial territory. Don't discount that your client, whom you may, for example, have been reading as a cisgender heterosexual woman, could be identifying in some other way, or moving towards this.

Menopause impacts people and brings out all sorts of things that may have been dormant. Someone may experience a shift in perception of their own sexuality and attractions, and of their gender. There is a relatively common narrative of cis women, who were previously living as heterosexual, starting to date other women in middle age. Some report menopause promoting a return to a pre-puberty self. We need more research on the idea of re-gendering in midlife.

Part three: how can therapists improve their practice and better serve LGBTQIA+ clients in menopause?

Initial Work

Check your own assumptions

Examine any binary assumptions in your mind (we all have them, as most of us grew up with them), and learn how much the gender binary is linked to racism and colonialism (Iantaffi, 2020; Barker & Iantaffi, 2019). It's essential to look at this, as binary language may feel unhelpful and even traumatising to your client.

Examine your own biases

It is painfully apparent that a therapist may attend all the high-quality trainings in the world, and have a huge pile of qualifications, but until you have truly processed your feelings about sexuality, gender, race, disability, age, sex worker status, lifestyle, including examining your own traumas around them, you may still inadvertently harm your client and be unable to truly affirm them. It may help to organise awareness training for you and a group of colleagues. For example, Gendered Intelligence (https://genderedintelligence.co.uk/) and GIRES (www.gires.org.uk/) offer trans awareness training. *Me and White Supremacy* by Leila F Saad has a guided learning process attached to it (www.meandwhitesupremacybook.com/). Guilaine Kinouani offers Race Reflections courses (https://racereflections.co.uk/).

Get trained

Get trained in and informed about GSRD/LGBTQIA+ identities. This could be via longer trainings or individual CPD. Pink Therapy offers a diploma and a number of courses (https://pinktherapy.org/). Also, try TASHRA (www.tashra.org/) for kink-related training.

Join a menopause group, or start your own

If you are struggling with the idea of your own menopause (if that applies to you), reflect on this. Why not think about creating or joining a discussion group? Menopause Cafes are a thing (www.menopausecafe.net/) – perhaps you could start a queer, kink, or polyamory friendly one? Or you could meet with colleagues.

Remember: your clients may be bringing negative past healthcare experiences

Remember that your GSRD identified clients (and your menopausal clients) have very likely already experienced prejudice in therapy and almost certainly in healthcare. Your clients may be hypervigilant, traumatised, or just plain tired of having to explain themselves over and over again.

Attend to your own somatic needs as a practitioner

Experiential workshops (or self-practice in the pandemic), involving movement and consensual touch, can also help you inhabit your body and go deeper into somatic awareness. This in turn will open you up to general awareness and greater ability to feel where difficult feelings are stored in your body.

Menopause

Educate yourself

You need to know about menopause, whether it is likely to happen to you personally or not. When neither therapist nor client understands menopause, this will neither benefit the client nor the work. Queermenopause.com has a growing resources page (www.queermenopause.com/resources-1).

Take care when accessing mainstream menopause information

Mainstream menopause information is often aimed at older cis women who are well resourced financially. Don't assume that this is the case for everyone.

Seek out those who may share your specific menopause experience

If you yourself are experiencing menopause (or going to) and you have a marginalised or minoritised identity, there are an increasing number of activists and groups doing public engagement who may share your identity. For example:

> The Queer Menopause Collective: www.queermenopausecollective.com
> The Menopause Inclusion Collective: www.menopausecollective.org/
> Karen Arthur: www.reddskin.co.uk/menopausewhilstblack
> Nina Kuypers: www.lattelounge.co.uk/my-menopause-nina-kuypers/
> Sophia Forum: https://sophiaforum.net/ (for women with HIV)

Take care around using gendered language

Your queer menopausal client may have been avoiding resources that invoke dysphoria and may not know what is going on with them. Some transmasculine and nonbinary people may struggle to even think about the idea of menopause. While the current post-menopausal generation is only starting to be aware, more and younger people will be coming up and needing gender-neutral resources. So please take care around the language you use, including pronouns.

Take care when accessing menopause resources on social media

Both you (depending on your identity) and your client may need to take care when looking online for support. There are a number of menopause groups, but they are generally, with notable exceptions, very focused on the needs of cisgender hetero-sexual women and can sometimes be transphobic.

Be proactive in raising the idea of menopause

There may be room for some psychoeducation here, and your client may thank you for it. Also, menopause has some heritability to it. If your client knows their biological mother, and if it is safe for them to do so, it might be worth them asking them about it.

Find an appropriately knowledgeable supervisor

Make sure you have a supervisor who understands GSRD and also understands menopause.

Queer menopause in sex and relationships

Again, take care around language

Get used to saying that menopause happens to *people* rather than women. As more and more people evolve to, and/or come out as, non-binary, genderqueer, agender, genderfluid, and gender expansive, there will be a greater and greater need for gender-inclusive language.

Take special care around the language your client uses for their genitals

See if someone has a particular language for their genitals. Using a traditional medical name may be fine for some clients, and not for others. Be guided by your client (Thom, no date).

Your client's desires may be evolving

Remember that people's sexual relationships with themselves evolve as they age. If menopause is affecting them, it may well be changing their levels of desire, and their perception of themselves. This may in turn bring grief or relief.

Your client's sense of their gender and sexuality may also be evolving

Your client may have experienced a shift in sexuality, expression, or gender around menopausal age and need support with it. They may want to transition and need support navigating this. Recognise also that there will be a variety of positions among your clients about being 'born this way'. Some may stick to that, and consider anyone who comes out later in life as not the same. Others accept the mutability of many human attributes.

Your client may need to grieve something

Menopause is experienced differently by every person. And it is certainly not all negative. But a client may well need to adapt to it and do some work around acceptance. If they have never had children, they may have a grieving process to go through, even if they did not particularly want them.

Do some psychoeducation around hormones

Hormones, as I described previously, have been gendered and this can create problems. It may be helpful to remind your client that all bodies need them to function.

Take care making assumptions around your asexual client

Don't assume your asexual client has not met the right person, or that they have a sexual self waiting to come out, or that they want to mourn sex they never had.

Also, some asexual people are not comfortable with someone claiming an asexual identity after menopause. Similarly, don't assume that allosexual (non-asexual) people will mourn a lost libido after menopause. It may be a relief.

Remember: every client will experience a different kind of response to menopause

If your AFAB client is experiencing depression or anxiety, reflect on what may be causing this in terms of perimenopause. Find out if they have seen their GP and what was said. Many GPs are not up to speed on menopause and the needs of patients. Doubly so if they are gender variant or gender non-conforming. Is your client neurodivergent as well as GSRD identified? What impact may menopause be having on them?

Conclusion

LGBTQIA+ awareness is growing, and so is awareness of menopause. As this life stage can last up to several decades, and represent many different things to different people, the attentive therapist will seek a good understanding of menopause before working with GSRD clients where this may come up as an issue.

References

Abdel-Rahman and Hurd. (2020). Androgen excess: Practice essentials. *Medscape*. [online] https://emedicine.medscape.com/article/273153-overview (Accessed: 22 August 2021).

Barker, M., & Iantaffi, A. (2019). *Life Isn't Binary*. London: Jessica Kingsley.

Burger, H.G. (2002). Androgen production in women. *Fertility and Sterility*, *77*(Suppl 4), S3–S5. https://doi.org/10.1016/s0015-0282(02)02985-0

Cagnacci, A., & Venier, M. (2019, September). The controversial history of hormone replacement therapy. *Medicina (Kaunas)*, 55(9), 602. Published online 2019 Sep 18. https://doi.org/10.3390/medicina55090602

Casimiro, I., & Cohen, R.N. (2019, April 1). Severe vasomotor symptoms post-oophorectomy despite testosterone therapy in a transgender man: A unique case study. *Journal of the Endocrine Society*, 3(4), 734–736. www.ncbi.nlm.nih.gov/pmc/articles/PMC6436763/ Published online 2019 Feb 13. https://doi.org/10.1210/js.2018-00367

Corinna, H. (2021). *What Fresh Hell Is This? Perimenopause, Menopause, Other Indignities, and You*. London: Hachette.

Davis, G., & Khan, K. (2021). Patches not pads: An intersex experience with postsurgical (pseudo) menopause. In H. Dillaway & L. Wershle (Eds.), *Musings on Perimenopause and Menopause: Identity, Experience, Transition, Chapter 9*. Bradford, Ontario: Demeter Press.

Fine, C. (2017). *Testosterone Rex: Unmaking the Myths of Our Gendered Minds*. London: Icon Books.

Fredriksen-Goldsen, K.I., Hyun-Jun, K., Emlet, C., Muraco, A., Erosheva, E. A., Hoy-Ellis, C.P., Goldsen, J., & Petry, H. (2011). *The Aging and Health Report: Disparities and Resilience among Lesbian, Gay, Bisexual, and Transgender Older Adults*. Seattle, WA: Institute for Multigenerational Health.

Gibson, C.J., Huang, A.J., McCaw, B., Subak, L.S., Thom, D.H., & Van Den Eeden, S.K. (2019). Associations of intimate partner violence, sexual assault, and posttraumatic stress disorder with menopause symptoms among midlife and older women. *Journal of the American Medical Association Internal Medicine*, 179(1), 80–87. https://doi.org/10.1001/jamainternmed.2018.5233. https://jamanetwork.com/journals/jamainternalmedicine/fullarticle/2715160

Glyde, T.L. (2020, March 28). *Queer Menopause: Where Gender, Sexuality and Age Collide*. [online] Video from Pink Therapy Queer Desire Conference. www.youtube.com/watch?v=7g8eb2ojBZ4 (Accessed: 21 August 2021).

Glyde, T.L. (2021a, May 5). Dear menopause community. *Queer Menopause*. [online] www.queermenopause.com/blog/2021/4/19/dear-menopause-community (Accessed: 21 August 2021).

Glyde, T.L. (2021b). How can therapists and other healthcare practitioners best support and validate their queer menopausal clients? *Sexual and Relationship Therapy*. https://doi.org/10.1080/14681994.2021.1881770

Glyde, T.L. (2021c, May 14). *Menopause: Agent of Queerness?* Video from AltSex NYC Conference. [online] www.youtube.com/watch?v=Sv8zrIo_tn8 (Accessed: 21 August 2021).

Hess, R.A. (2003). Oestrogen in the adult male reproductive tract: A review. *Reproductive Biology and Endocrinology: RB&E*, 1, 52. https://doi.org/10.1186/1477-7827-1-52

Hoy-Ellis, C.P. (2016). Concealing concealment: The mediating role of internalized heterosexism in psychological distress among lesbian, gay, and bisexual older adults. *Journal of Homosexuality*, 63(4), 487–506. https://doi.org/10.1080/00918369.2015.1088317

Hussain, A., & Gilloteaux, J. (2020). The human testes: Oestrogen and ageing outlooks. *Translational Research in Anatomy*, 20. https://doi.org/10.1016/j.tria.2020.100073

Iantaffi, A. (2020). *Gender Trauma*. London: Jessica Kingsley.

InterACT. (undated). FAQ: What is intersex? *InterACT Advocates.* [online] https://interactadvocates.org/faq/ (Accessed: 22 August 2021).

International Menopause Society. (2019). *Special Edition: International Menopause Society Consensus Statement on Testosterone Treatment for Women: Key Messages.* [online] www.imsociety.org/2019/09/04/special-edition-international-menopause-society-consensus-statement-on-testosterone-treatment-for-women-key-messages/ (Accessed: 13 November 2021).

Kelly, J. (2008). A lesbian feminist analysis of the demise of hormone replacement therapy. *Women's Studies International Forum,* 31(4), 300–307. https://doi.org/10.1016/j.wsif.2008.05.002

Lefevor, G.T., Boyd-Rogers, C.C., Sprague, B.M., & Janis, R. (2019). Health disparities between genderqueer, transgender, and cisgender individuals: An extension of minority stress theory. *Journal of Counseling Psychology,* 66(4), 385–395. https://doi.org/10.1037/cou0000339

Mason, J. (2021). Menopause for the rest of us (AKA people born with testicular systems). In H. Corinna (Ed.), *What Fresh Hell Is This? Perimenopause, Menopause, Other Indignities, and You* (pp. 285–292). London: Hachette.

McGlotten, S., & Moore, L.J. (2013). The geriatric clinic: Dry and limp: Aging queers, zombies, and sexual reanimation. *The Journal of Medical Humanities,* 34(2), 261–268. https://doi.org/ 10.1007/s10912-013-9226-8

Menopause Matters. (2021). *Menopause Support Survey Reveals Shocking Disparity in Menopause Training in Medical Schools.* [online] https://menopausesupport.co.uk/?p=14434 (Accessed: 13 November 2021).

Monteleone, P., Mascagni, G., Giannini, A., Genazzani, A.R., & Simoncini, T. (2018). Symptoms of menopause: Global prevalence, physiology and implications. *Nature Reviews Endocrinology,* 14(4), 199–215. https://doi.org/10.1038/nrendo.2017.180

Moseley, R.L., Druce, T., & Turner-Cobb, J.M. (2020). 'When my autism broke': A qualitative study spotlighting autistic voices on menopause. *Autism: The International Journal of Research and Practice,* 24(6), 1423–1437. https://doi.org/10.1177/1362361319901184

Reese, R. (2020). How Do Hormonal Changes Affect the Trans and Non-Binary Community? *Menopause In the Workplace.* [online] https://menopauseintheworkplace.co.uk/articles/how-do-hormonal-changes-affect-the-trans-and-non-binary-community/ (Accessed: 21 August 2021).

Robinson, L. (2020). *HRT: The History.* Women's Health Concern. [online] www.womens-health-concern.org/help-and-advice/factsheets/hrt-the-history/ (Accessed: 21 August 2021).

Rowan, G.A., Frimpong, E.Y., Li, M., Chaudhry, S., & Radigan, M. (2021). Health disparities between older lesbian, gay, and bisexual adults and heterosexual adults in the public mental health system. *Psychiatric Services (Washington, D.C.).* Advance online publication. https://doi.org/10.1176/appi.ps.202000940

Rydstrom, K. (2020). Degendering menstruation: Making trans menstruators matter. In C. Bobel, I.T. Winkler, B. Fahs, et al. (Eds.), *The Palgrave Handbook of Critical Menstruation Studies [internet]* (Vol. 68). Singapore: Palgrave MacMillan. https://doi.org/10.1007/978-981-15-0614-7_68. www.ncbi.nlm.nih.gov/books/NBK565621/ (Accessed: 22 August 2021).

Tangpricha, V., & den Heijer, M. (2017). Oestrogen and anti-androgen therapy for transgender women. *Lancet Diabetes & Endocrinology.* Author Manuscript. Published online 2016 Dec 2. https://doi.org/10.1016/S2213-8587(16)30319-9. Published in final edited form as: *Lancet Diabetes & Endocrinology*, 5(4), 291–300. www.ncbi.nlm.nih.gov/pmc/articles/PMC5366074/ (Accessed: 21 August 2021).

Thom, B. (no date). Words for junk (for sex educators!) What do you call yours? *Body Curious*. [online] www.body-curious.co.uk/genitals/ (Accessed: 21 August 2021).

Chapter 3

Working with sexual shame

Simon Alexander Lyne

Shame is a human emotion that has probably been experienced since the dawn of consciousness (or since 'Eve' was tricked by a naughty little snake, depending on beliefs). Many scholars have developed theories about how it operates. Sexual shame, however, does not seem to be so openly or widely discussed. In this chapter, I share some thoughts on how to identify and work with sexual shame. I will use a current general shame theory to explain how it manifests within the sexual arena.

In ancient times, sex may have been viewed as healthy and natural; but by 600 AD, Western Christianity had come to see sexual desire as inherently sinful and, thus, shameful (Stone, 2017). For all recorded time, the prevailing attitude towards sex has largely favoured wealthy, heterosexual, cis-gendered, and able-bodied men. This group has generally been admitted into positions of power and created legislation. I am aware as the author of this chapter that I identify with at least two of those categories. I want to caveat that, although I endeavour to encompass the entire rainbow family in my writing, undoubtedly, my perspective will have flaws and biases – of which I hope the reader can be forgiving.

Defining shame

Shame is a potent emotion, to which all humans are vulnerable. John Bowlby (1980) believed shame to be a by-product of negative attachment relationships stemming back to early childhood. Not many of us get through life without experiencing some form of relational trauma, so shame is an emotion that we experience throughout our lifespan. Despite its universal nature, shame feels like a solitary pain. Tomkins (1963) calls shame "an inner torment, a sickness of the soul" (1963, p. 351). It is an effect of alienation and indignity, related to self-loathing, a sort of disgust aimed at the self. The more self-hatred we have, the worse our mental health (Allen & Oleson, 1999).

Most of us will be aware how harsh our 'inner critics' can be, and the danger in believing them, but the core experience of shame is non-verbal; we feel it deep within. Patricia DeYoung (2015) believes that despite shame feeling like an individual problem, all shame is, in fact, relational: "Shame is an experience of one's

DOI: 10.4324/9781003260608-4

felt sense of self disintegrating in relation to a dysregulating other" (2015, p. 18). So, shame may be understood as the symptom of relational trauma, and the physiological response akin to what we experience in trauma; hyperarousal (fight or flight) and hypoarousal (freeze or dissociation) (Van der Kolk, 2015).

The excruciating physical state is usually followed by behavioural attempts to hide, for example, shrinking, averting our eyes, covering our face. We cannot bear to look at others or for others to see us. We might want the 'ground to swallow us up', a common metaphor for the experience of shame. Gershen Kaufman (1974) asserts that shame stems from the shattering of meaningful interpersonal connection; one person's emotional and relational need is unmet by another's response, or those needs are rejected or dismissed, and the connection is lost.

Impact of shame

Various forms of psychopathology have been linked with shame, including depression, anxiety, low self-esteem, eating disorders, sub-clinical sociopathy, suicidality, self-injury, substance abuse, and compulsive behaviours (Tangney & Dearing, 2003). At its most extreme, shame has led some people to kill (Adshead & Horne, 2021).

There is a lack of research related to the effects of shame on sex. Still, it appears that symptoms of sexual shame include low sexual energy, low self-acceptance, avoidance of intimacy, sexual compulsivity, and sexual avoidance (Kyle, 2013).

Repressed shame clearly can cause damage, but in order not to pathologise all shame experiences, it can be helpful to think of shame as existing on a spectrum – from functional to maladaptive. We need to explore an individual's experiences within cultural contexts to assess whether shame has had a positive outcome or a corrosive, dehumanising effect. Clients may describe mild shame and embarrassment through to humiliation and degradation. Different people will perceive and express things uniquely, so it is inappropriate to impose blanket interpretations on all shame experiences (DeYoung, 2015).

Origins of shame

According to Schore (2003), shame first appears as a primary social emotion when aged 14–16 months. Most interactions at 10 months will be focused on play, affection, and caregiving. As the baby becomes a toddler, the parent starts to inhibit free exploratory or unwanted behaviours, thereby socialising the child. Face-to-face encounters that previously only generated interest and joy can now cause intense distress. The dismay communicated by the parent's face triggers shocking evaporation of positive affect. This sudden misattunement represents a regulatory failure intended to influence the child's behaviour. The child learns quickly, but if this perceived failure to meet expectations is frequent and prolonged, it may have a detrimental effect on emotional development, often leading to 'guilt-ridden' or 'shame-driven' character types (Piers & Singer, 1954).

Developmental psychologist Erik Erikson (1995) believed shame to be essential on the journey into autonomy, the second of eight stages of psychosocial development. Other theorists contend that self-conscious emotions such as guilt and shame serve as warnings that social norms, or rules have been violated, alerting the individual and motivating avoidance of wrongdoing in the future (Barrett, 1995). Where there are standards, there is often judgement. We are social animals, and it has long benefited us to belong to a social group; otherwise, our ancestors would not have survived in isolation. The terror that comes with being shamed is an evolutionary survival mechanism. Therefore, shame can be reframed as a measure of how much we care and want to belong, rather than how awful we are (Neves, 2021).

Ian Kerner (2021) describes the different childhood environments that give rise to our internal models for sex: Ideal, Evasive, Permissive, Negative, and Abusive. Kerner discusses how the majority of us do not grow up in ideal, sex-positive environments in which we can talk openly and receive developmentally appropriate information. Emotion regulation requires adequate attention and mirroring of affect from our primary caregivers. If sex is ignored or our sexuality is discussed in derogatory ways, our sexual feelings can become dysregulated.

In his late thirties, a client told me about exclusion from his extended family in Eastern Europe throughout his childhood. His extended family made their disgust of his perceived femininity clear, and, unfortunately, his parents allowed their bullying. His father told him that if he were to find out any of his children are gay, he would shoot them and not think twice about it. At thirteen, he had little understanding of what 'gay' was, but he understood it to be extremely bad. Another client remembered asking their mother what a "faggot" was, having heard the word at school. The mother recoiled and told them to stop being disgusting. The same client's father would pretend to vomit when seeing an image of same-sex love on the television. Another client remembered being called "wicked" and having a bar of soap forced into her mouth by her mother for having kissed her female classmate. It is common among the LGBTQ+ populations to report such violent memories from childhood.

Parents and their adolescent children often differ in their values, with discrepancies emerging in high contrast during the teenage years. During this time, shame and shaming experiences can create emotional wounds that leave lasting scars. The rollercoaster of adolescence and its potential for shame cannot be underestimated (Shadbolt, 2009). Young people are curious, and more tech-savvy on this side of the millennium, thus capable of searching out novel sexual content and hiding their internet search history. Still, I have had many clients mortified by their parents' discovery of porn under the bed or on their computer. If said porn does not align with the heteronormative model, this can cause further problems. For many, these incidents 'outed' them, exacerbating their sexual shame. As the young person moves into adulthood, experiences of shame from development can profoundly negatively affect interpersonal relationships, particularly sexual and romantic ones (Kyle, 2013).

Internalising shame

We rely on our primary caregivers' attunement to our feelings and needs when we are children. We learn to self-regulate through having someone consistently care for us, be alert to our emotions, and help us tolerate and understand them. If this does not happen, the misattunement can be very distressing. The feelings become overwhelming, and the child starts to internalise that there must be something wrong with them. This internalisation can happen without any intention to cause shame. There is no perfect parenting, and caregivers may have their own struggles with emotional dysregulation or shame (Perry, 2019). It is hard to model self-acceptance and self-compassion when we do not embrace them for ourselves.

Rather than gaining the knowledge we can do something 'bad' and still be lovable, our core emotional self gets entangled with a sense of inherent badness, and shame can feel overwhelming. We may attempt the 'perfect' performance to regain the affection of our caregivers. As we grow through adolescence, we attach shame to parts of our experience that are most challenging: our emotions, bodies, gender, sexuality, and competence. For survival, we become experts at avoiding or masking our shame. These strategies often alienate us and prevent authentic connection with ourselves and others.

Through the repeated shaming of expression of affect, needs and desires, shame becomes linked with these expressions so that just experiencing them starts to become shameful (Kaufman & Raphael, 1996). Consider a child told repeatedly with disgust not to play with their genitals. The child soon learns that genitals are shameful, even thinking about them, let alone touching or enjoying them. As the child grows, they are likely to associate feeling sexual desire with shame. The heteronormative world will compound the original sexual shame instilled by the parents' prohibitions, increase it, and consolidate it. It is not uncommon for parents to be horrified and bewildered if they find their child masturbating, and we do not often grow up with a positive view of sexual self-pleasure. One middle-aged client still reported finding it hard to look at her genitals. Her vulva was scrubbed sore as a young child by her mother, who called her 'dirty' after finding her exploring her own body in the bath. Though shame is conceptualised as an interpersonal process involving shamer and shamed, shame is also self-perpetuated via internal processes; links between past and present experiences (Kyle, 2013). Furthermore, shaming experiences are not always extreme; consistent disappointment and disapproval (rather than validation and celebration) can also cause long-term internalised shame.

Gender and sexuality are central to our social identity. Messages regarding expected gender roles and early shaming around sexuality begin long before our developing brains have the conscious critical faculty for analysis and comparison against other data. We cannot yet filter information critically, so the sense of being 'wrong' is automatically internalised as 'truth'. We do not realise that *we* are not the problem; the messages we unconsciously internalise need deconstruction.

The trauma of growing up in shame often goes unacknowledged and reverberates through entire lifetimes. How many of us were told directly or indirectly by family, religion, peers, school, society or the law that our gender identity, sexuality, sexual orientation, or sexual practices are "bad", 'wrong", "immoral", "weird", or "(insert mortifying adjective here)"? Once implanted, the seed takes root as a core belief which gets watered (unconsciously reinforced), eventually becoming our felt 'truth', the most prolific weed in our garden. It is socially-sanctioned brainwashing. When we live in chronic shame, it permeates everything; the way we see ourselves, the way we relate to others, and how we move through the world. When shame runs the show, we are its prisoners.

Psychological wellness requires a coherent sense of self, but chronic shame has such a deleterious effect that it fragments our sense of who we are and prevents us from being who we want to be. As Schore (2003) noted, when the two sides of the brain are not structurally integrated (as happens in attunement), the self a person aspires to can be quite different from the self they present with their language, emotions, and behaviours. Psychoanalytic theory suggests this disparity between our self-image and the idealised one we want to portray is where shame thrives (Wurmser, 1981).

Shame creates rigid, global beliefs centred on the self as essentially flawed; we feel unable to connect, despite really wanting to. Patricia DeYoung (2015) writes that chronically shamed people are often incredibly lonely and experience particular difficulty with love or accepting that anyone can love them. Regardless, chronically shamed individuals keep trying to love and be loved, believing that finding a partner is the answer to their discomfort. This is a fragile position, as others then have the power to not only rescue, but to trigger their sense of psychological annihilation.

Shame vs guilt

Brené Brown, who developed Shame Resilience Theory (Brown, 2006), has spoken about shame as a focus on the self (e.g., 'I am bad') as opposed to guilt, which is a focus on behaviour (e.g., 'I did a bad thing'; Brown, 2012). Guilt does not usually affect our core identity because there are ways to assuage it, for example, showing remorse or making reparations. However, when we experience ourselves as shameful, we absorb increasing amounts of negative ideas about who we are, like a sort of inverse narcissism. We feel exposed and fundamentally worthless.

GSRD shame

People in the GSRD community experience daily microaggressions, homophobia, biphobia, transphobia, ignorance, heterocentrism, bullying, and time spent 'in the closet'. This shame can be profoundly disturbing.

When we grow up in an environment that does not celebrate us, disconnection abounds. Relational ruptures threaten our well-being, and our ability to live and love authentically. Despite considerable progress in some small pockets of the world, society remains largely heteronormative, and we continue to experience ongoing trauma.

Walt Odets (2020) has written poignantly on how the AIDS epidemic created a legacy burden that endures today. Even after we learn to accept ourselves, we may retain some deep-seated beliefs that a part of us is 'bad'. The only upside is the potential erotic charge in being a 'sexual outlaw', according to Jack Morin's conceptualisation of the cornerstones of eroticism, one being "violating prohibition", which, for some, may be a powerful erotic space for enjoying their sex lives (Morin, 1995).

In the past, the fields of psychiatry, psychology and psychotherapy have contributed to cultural indoctrination of sexual shame by 'treating' gay patients with electro-shock therapy, medication, and chemical castration, and, even today, 'conversion' practices are still being offered and implemented. Homosexuality was considered a pathology by the medical and psychiatric professions until as recently as 1990 (Cochran et al., 2014). We are still witnessing the impact of this pathologizing, harmful approach. We live in a cis-het mononormative world; a world based on traditional relationships, roles, and assumptions. Even therapists who believe themselves to be GSRD-affirmative may try to encourage asexual clients to be sexual, non-monogamous clients monogamous, kinky clients 'vanilla', or bisexual or non-binary clients to choose one or the other (Barker, 2019).

George came to therapy with a great deal of shame around his identity. He grew up in a patriarchal South American family culture with strong messaging around what it means to 'be a man'. Yet what excited him was playing with gender expression and being penetrated by dominant women. George had been to therapists previously who led him to believe what he found erotic was the consequence of unidentified trauma, and if he were to overcome this, he would find 'normal' sex more exciting. What helped him eventually was greater sexual self-acceptance and finding his 'tribe'.

Though many of us have sex for relational and recreational purposes (Kerner, 2021), sex education today remains focused on the reproductive model, which marginalises anyone not planning on procreation. We are taught about sexually transmitted infections, but pleasure is not on the curriculum, nor are other kinds of relationships. We do not have the same bodies, and differences are not celebrated enough, even when our population is diverse and complex.

As Chris Donaghue (2015) writes, moving away from the confines of the medical model (and the binaries of order vs disorder) allows for new visions of healthy, non-normative sexual-relational styles. Undoubtedly one of the great things about being part of the GSRD community is that we get to challenge convention and create our own rules for living and loving. After all, there's not only one way to have sex, be in a relationship, or live a meaningful life.

Sexual shame

Clearly, shame related to sexual orientation, desire, arousal, and behaviour can have a disastrous impact on an individual's psychological well-being. The endless messaging regarding what is 'normal' shapes all of us. Therefore, it is helpful to conceptualise sexual shame as a phenomenon experienced the same way as general shame but specifically related to our thoughts, feelings and behaviours regarding sex, sexuality, and intimate relationships.

Sexual shame stems from morality, ideas about good and bad, right, and wrong. We learn these concepts from many sources, often without consideration for what makes sense to us personally. Bradshaw (1988) and Hastings (1998) note that no other facet of human activity or emotion is so dysfunctionally shamed as that of our sexuality.

Donald Nathanson (1992) wrote that shame "hovers everywhere in the bed of lust" (1992, p. 300). Brené Brown (2012) asserts that vulnerability is at the core of shame and the birthplace of joy, belonging, and love. What could be more vulnerable than being naked in front of another (or others) or the experience of dyscontrol during orgasm?

Sexual shame starts with the presiding culture's dominant narrative, which the people within that system internalise and then use to police each other (Moon, 2020). It is experienced when individuals measure themselves against the cultural standard, find themselves below the bar, and explain this failure via negative global self-evaluation (Lewis, 2003). Sexual shame prevents us from acknowledging and healing our trauma and stops many abuse survivors from reporting the crimes committed against them. At its most extreme, shame causes people to join hate groups and enact offences against those who trigger their own self-loathing (Moon, 2020).

Sexual shame is multi-layered, particularly for many in the GSRD community. Whether sex is a source of pride or shame depends on a complex interplay between biological factors and socially constructed messages about sex and sexuality (Sanderson, 2015). Sexuality and gender have been discussed as 'biopsychosocial' (Barker & Hancock, 2017), and shame can be viewed in a similarly intricate and multidimensional way (Gilbert, 2006).

Gay, bi, or trans people are perceived by many cultures as a perversion or deviancy that is criminal, punishable even by death, creating a great deal of fear, secrecy, and internalised shame about sexual and/or gender identity. Even in the UK, where the social environment is more progressive, being part of the GSRD community puts us at risk of discrimination, ostracisation, and violence.

Many experiences can spark sexual shame, including sexual abuse, sexual assault, exposure to pornography, religious shaming, excessive modesty or promiscuity (Hastings, 1998). We might feel shame about our body (size, shape, weight, musculature, genitals, sexual characteristics, bodily fluids, smells, sounds of pleasure), sexual arousal, desire, fantasies/fetishes/kinks, performance, sexual behaviours, sexual experience (or inexperience), sexual difficulties, sexual orientation, when/how we want to have sex and with whom, what we want to use in sex, relationships, sexual compulsions, sexual health, cultural and religious sanctions, the list goes on.

Karen Gurney (2020) specifies three conditions for good sex: psychological arousal, physical touch, and being present-moment-focused. Attention in sex is an important factor, and focusing on problematic areas (for example, performance rather than sensation) can sometimes result in dysfunction or difficulty (Lewis, 1995).

Receptive anal intercourse still holds stigma and shame. Gay men who identify as 'bottom' may be perceived to be effeminate, and people who are 'top' to be masculine, which colludes with the heteronormative and sexist societal narrative.

The HIV status is another significant source of shaming, particularly in the gay male populations. Potential sexual partners ask, "are you clean?" as if being HIV+ is dirty.

People of ethnic or racial minorities often experience more shame and shaming than their white peers (Odets, 2020). Black and ethnic minority clients usually report overt racism through online platforms and apps, with users advertising slogans such as "looking for BBC", "No fats, femmes or Asians", or responding to messages with "sorry, I don't eat curry" before blocking the other person. Of course, all these examples may well be symptoms of users' own internalised shame.

Connection is integral to relationships and sex. Fear of disconnection is a primal panic that can truly destabilise us (Johnson, 2011). Repairing a rupture involves reconnection. We need to remember the danger in detachment not only from others but also from ourselves. For this, we need to embrace our shamed parts and restore leadership to our core compassionate self.

Behavioural responses to shame

Karen Horney (1993) describes three ways to manage shame anxiety: moving toward, moving against, and moving away from people. There are pros and cons to each. With the first strategy, we focus on pleasing other people to retain their affection. We then come to depend on others for our self-worth. Moving against people feels powerful, but we must conquer everyone and everything to remain invincible, and nobody is bulletproof. Moving away from people means we have nobody to shame us, but the result is a life of isolation.

Donald Nathanson (1992) developed the Compass of Shame, similar to Horney's theory. Nathanson divided reactions to shame into four categories: (1) Withdrawal (isolating, hiding, running away), (2) Attack Self (judging, criticising, demeaning ourselves), (3) Avoidance (denial, using substances, or distracting through another means), and (4) Attack Others (blaming, lashing out in anger). An example of an 'attack other' response is seen in male machismo, where fear is viewed as weakness and converted into excitement and anger.

Connection and mutuality can be difficult because of shame, particularly for gay and bisexual men. Pachankis et al. (2020) assert that gay and bi men face status-based competitive pressures within their communities, which could very well be a response to shame, both judging themselves and rejecting others. In my experience, I frequently see this in the gay male community where there is a heavy reliance on the objectification of 'perfect' bodies and body parts.

Schema therapy, developed by Jeffrey Young (1990), suggests three maladaptive coping modes for habitual self-defeating themes (also called "lifetraps"): overcompensation, avoidance, and surrender. A typical example of overcompensation is perfectionism. Perfectionism is an attempt to ward off further criticism and defend against a feeling of inferiority (Gilbert, 1998). Unfortunately, perfectionism only reinforces deep-seated feelings of shame. Perfection is limitless, the goalposts constantly moving, and we live in fear of not achieving the conditions we think we need to feel worthwhile. Olivier, a gay man in his thirties, strived to project the illusion of perfection. His role as a doctor reinforced this trait, as mistakes in medicine can occasionally be fatal and must be avoided. His identity merged with his profession, and he felt his job 'made up for' his parents' disappointment in his sexuality, at least in part. This is a precarious position, as self-esteem is unreliable whenever perfection is not attained (it never is). When Olivier did make even a minor mistake, he was flooded with shame and experienced an influx of negative thoughts about himself.

Avoidance is a common strategy with all uncomfortable emotions. With sexual shame, alcohol may be used for its numbing effects, and drugs like crystal methamphetamine almost completely bypass shame (until the high runs out). Roberto, a young man in his twenties, had become involved in the chemsex scene as he found out that his awkwardness in the bedroom and his "unreliable" erections were instantly overcome with the use of "party" drugs. This resulted in a perceived inability to have sex sober and an increasing reliance on drugs to the extent he lost his job as a lawyer and experienced a psychotic episode.

Surrendering to shame means we succumb to whatever shame-based beliefs we hold, then think and act accordingly. We may pendulate between avoidance and over-compensatory strategies, but when these do not work, we are liable to experience the full weight of shame. Toby, a young student, found it hard to accept his same-sex attraction and would try to masturbate to heterosexual porn in a bid to 'turn himself straight', a sort of auto-conversion practice. In his teens, Toby had been out with girls and attempted sex but found he could not get aroused. Latterly, Toby tried dating men via apps. Messages from social media and the gay scene suggested everyone else was confident of their sexuality and that finding a partner was easy. He had not established a relationship and had come to view himself as "unattractive and unlovable". Sex was "terrifying". He felt shame about his body, his penis size, his use of porn, and his perceived lack of experience compared to his peers. He also felt shame about feeling shame (meta-shame). In the therapy room, Toby could barely look at me. His face reddened, and his eyes welled up every session for the first few months.

Rather than submitting to shamefulness, another recognized coping strategy is shamelessness (Roberts, 2020). Shamelessness differs from sex-positivity as it involves a total discarding of sexual values to avoid shame.

Silva Neves (2021) gives a solid account of how clients may engage in compulsive sexual behaviours to defend against the pain of shame and end up feeling yet more shame. This soon develops into a Moebius loop, a self-perpetuating cycle so strong that people describe shame as if it were encoded in their genes (also, see Chapter 11).

Cognitive responses to shame

Self-attack and self-blame are ways of regaining a sense of control and avoiding future humiliation or abandonment. They are common 'self-corrective' strategies when we have become hypersensitised to external insults (Gilbert, 2010). Now both the outer and the internal worlds are experienced as hostile. Shame feels like rejection, but here we are rejecting ourselves.

Human brains have the capacity for limitless imagination, fantasy, and psychological arousal, but this means we are also vulnerable to negative, threat-based (or shame-based) loops in the mind. We experience this as worry and rumination. Without any actual threat, our brain and bodies respond as if the danger is real, yet it is impossible to flee from an imagined menace. We may withdraw and isolate, resulting in loneliness and increased negative thoughts (Irons & Beaumont, 2017). Some of the common cognitive responses to shame are self-loathing and/ or self-defectiveness: "I'm ugly", "I'm stupid", "I'm worthless". Some are rejecting others: "all men are pigs", "gay men only want sex – they're not interested in love", "camp guys are always bottoms". Some cognition may ruminate on distorted stories, for example: "my girlfriend didn't respond to my text. I must have done something wrong, and she hates me now. Why do my girlfriends always hate me?" Robert had trouble being physically intimate for years with his husband because his first sexual partner told him he was "terrible in bed". Robert continued to have (and believe) the same negative thought about himself until it became an unquestioned part of his narrative. His shame prevented him from analysing his past lover's comment and realizing it was only one (harsh) opinion and not an absolute truth.

Working with shame

Black lesbian poet and activist Audre Lorde once said, "Your silence will not protect you" (Lorde, 2017, p. 2). This is especially true regarding shame, which needs secrecy, silence, and judgement to survive (Brown, 2010). Defusing shame involves bringing it into the light and air (DeYoung, 2015).

There is evident stigma about having psychological or emotional problems and seeking therapy. As psychotherapy is by nature a focus on the self (particularly the most problematic aspects of the self), working with shame in therapy is fraught with complications. Shame wants to be concealed, so speaking of shame involves courage and vulnerability. Even admitting to shame feels shameful. Furthermore, the client may view the therapist as an exemplar of mental wellness. Therapists are not immune to shame, and we need to keep in touch with our own shame in transference and countertransference processes in order to untangle it (Tangney & Dearing, 2003).

Babette Rothschild (2000) explains a particular difficulty with shame: it is not expressed or released the way other emotions are, and the way to begin decontaminating it is through accepting and non-judgemental contact with another. Facing shame can be incredibly daunting. Connection binds us together and certainly underpins effective therapy. It is a generally accepted truth that a crucial part of any therapy is the relationship with the therapist, and most therapies espouse the importance of authentic human connection.

Meg-John Barker (2013) proposes in *Rewriting the Rules* that we are plural rather than singular. We have many parts. We show certain aspects of ourselves to particular people in different contexts. This concept is integral to Internal Family Systems therapy, developed by Richard Schwartz (Schwartz & Sweezy, 2019). Schwartz highlights the need to work with, rather than against, the inner critic before accessing the vulnerable, shamed parts that the critic may be working hard to protect. Even the critic deserves compassion. The internal system needs upgrading, so we no longer utilise outdated ways to deal with new situations. Less judgement, more ways to be confidently vulnerable.

If chronic shame is one of the most poisonous experiences, compassion is the antidote. True self-compassion (from the heart rather than the head) is a powerhouse. It is sometimes viewed as weak or self-pitying, but in actuality, compassion gives us strength and courage to face painful challenges. We may know this intrinsically, but the truth gets occluded by the defences we employ to avoid feeling vulnerable. These defences separate us, and we struggle to harness our true nature even when innately capable of it. For the many clients who baulk at the idea of compassion, 'supreme friendliness' might be a more palatable alternative. Whatever the nomenclature, there is not a facet of life that cannot be improved with the compassionate approach.

Generating feelings of love, warmth, safety, and connection is tough for people who experience high levels of shame and self-criticism (Petrocchi et al., 2016). Like learning a new language, moving into a new way of being is not an event but a process; it takes time, consistent practice, and has a cumulative effect.

Compassion-focused therapy (CFT) and compassionate mind training evolved from clinical observations with clients who displayed deep core shame. CFT proposes that self-criticism and self-compassion are both self-evaluative systems.

Interpersonal cues from the therapist associated with social safety and acceptance create the secure container for the client to tolerate whatever is discussed and begin to internalise the regulation of emotions (Gilbert, 1998). Specific therapeutic strategies involve (but are not limited to) refocusing attention, controlled breathing, imagery work, writing, and engaging in conversation with our various parts. The self-compassion component involves three core elements: self-kindness, mindfulness, and common humanity.

Acceptance and Commitment Therapy (ACT), created by Steven Hayes (see, e.g., Hayes et al., 2016), has also been found effective at treating shame (Luoma & Platt, 2015) and with clients from sexual and gender minorities (Skinta & D'Alton, 2016).

ACT promotes psychological flexibility via the use of six core processes:

1   Acceptance (e.g., of uncomfortable emotions, thoughts, experiences)
2   Defusion (from thoughts and the idea that they are automatically accurate, relevant, or significant)
3   Present-moment awareness (a focus on the now, with a non-judgemental stance)
4   Self-as-context (connecting with the conscious 'observer self' rather than identifying too closely with or getting swept away by internal experiences)
5   Values (identifying what we find truly meaningful to guide our behaviour)
6   Committed action (living in line with our core values and being willing to do so in the knowledge that it may be uncomfortable at times)

Discovering what ingredients come together to make our unique erotic template and exploring our erotic mind (Morin, 1995) helps us understand what turns us on, as well as what may slam the brake on our arousal. Chloe, a young trans woman attracted to masculine men (believing them to be sturdy and able to protect her against shame), found herself turned off and sometimes even disgusted when they showed any sign of vulnerability. Chloe came to see everyone as a vast and complex mix of strengths and weaknesses, assets, and liabilities. Accepting her own and her boyfriend's vulnerabilities while celebrating their respective sexual power helped transform their relationship.

It may not be possible to be completely free of our internalised shame. Instead, we can find ways to understand and reduce shame to thrive. As with grief, we need to stop wishing for a different past and learn methods to live alongside it. Old stories and deep-rooted beliefs fight for survival, but shame can have much less hold over us than it once did.

Unconditional positive regard is a core foundational process of therapy. Professionals' genuine acceptance of non-normative identities, sexualities, and lifestyles can be profoundly transformative, helping clients overcome years of marginalisation and shame (Shahbaz & Chirinos, 2017). The therapist's presence in non-verbal, affective, and unconscious ways has the potential to heal. Whilst self-disclosure needs to be handled with caution, being a therapist from the GSRD community and being unashamed and open about our own identity holds its own capacity for healing. A relational, reciprocal style nurtures engagement and intimacy, whereas a hierarchical therapist may engender disconnection and disengagement (Cadwell, 2009).

Careful and well-timed use of good-natured humour can also have a powerful effect on disrupting the cycle of shame (Scheff, 1990). Active listening and awareness of changes in facial movement, body language, and tone of voice are essential. Curiosity, empathy, and the willingness to get up close while maintaining the delicate balance of professional detachment and discernment are invaluable tools.

Conclusion

Ultimately, we find ways to walk alongside our clients, assisting them to change what they can and accepting what they cannot. We help them let go of unrealistic ideals, seeing that they were born good enough, neither perfect nor flawed beyond repair. We affirm diversity and each client's unique identity. We witness shame and with its dissipation, come to a space of openness, willingness to be seen, less fear of rejection and abandonment. New intimacy is experienced in an expanded world. With radical, compassionate self-acceptance, we can reconnect with our true nature.

It is not our fault that we feel shame, but it *is* our responsibility to repair the damage. I think we owe it to ourselves, and to each other.

References

Adshead, G., & Horne, E. (2021). *The Devil You Know: Stories of Human Cruelty and Compassion*. New York, NY: Simon and Schuster.

Allen, D.J., & Oleson, T. (1999). Shame and internalized homophobia in gay men. *Journal of Homosexuality*, 37(3), 33–43.

Barker, M.J. (2013). *Rewriting the Rules*. New York, NY: Routledge.

Barker, M.J. (2019). *Good Practice across the Counselling Professions 001: Gender, Sexual, and Relationship Diversity (GSRD)*. Leicestershire, UK: British Association for Counselling and Psychotherapy.

Barker, M.J., & Hancock, J. (2017). *Enjoy Sex (How, When and If You Want To): A Practical and Inclusive Guide*. London, UK: Icon.

Barrett, K.C. (1995). A functionalist approach to shame and guilt. In J.P. Tangney & K.W. Fischer (Eds.), *Self-Conscious Emotions: The Psychology of Shame, Guilt, Embarrassment, and Pride* (pp. 25–63). New York, NY: The Guilford Press.

Bowlby, J. (1980). *Attachment and Loss: Loss, Sadness, and Depression* (Vol. 2). New York, NY: Basic Books.

Bradshaw, J. (1988). *Healing the Shame That Binds You*. Deerfield Beach, FL: Health Communications.

Brown, B. (2006). Shame resilience theory: A grounded theory study on women and shame. *Families in Society*, 87(1), 43–52.

Brown, B. (2010). *The Gifts of Imperfection: Let Go of Who You Think You're Supposed to Be and Embrace Who You Are*. Minneapolis, MN: Hazelden Publishing.

Brown, B. (2012). *The Power of Vulnerability: Teachings on Authenticity, Connection and Courage*. www.audible.co.uk/pd/The-Power-of-Vulnerability-Audiobook/

B00CYKEBVI?source_code=M2M30DFT1BkSH101514006R&ipRedirectOverride=t
rue&gclid=EAIaIQobChMIwYOu4pW49AIVVJnVCh2Fxg5UEAAYASAAEgKcfvD_
BwE&gclsrc=aw.ds (Accessed: 13 June 2017).

Cadwell, S. (2009). Shame, gender, and sexuality in gay men's group therapy. *Group*, 33(3), 197–212.

Cochran, S.D., Drescher, J., Kismödi, E., Giami, A., García-Moreno, C., Atalla, E., Marais, A., Vieira, E.M., & Reed, G.M. (2014, September 1). Proposed declassification of disease categories related to sexual orientation in the International Statistical Classification of Diseases and Related Health Problems (ICD-11). *Bulletin World Health Organization*, 92(9), 672–679. doi:10.2471/BLT.14.135541. Epub 2014 Jun 17. PMID: 25378758; PMCID: PMC4208576.

DeYoung, P.A. (2015). *Understanding and Treating Chronic Shame: A Relational/Neurobiological Approach*. New York, NY: Routledge.

Donaghue, C. (2015). *Sex Outside the Lines: Authentic Sexuality in a Sexually Dysfunctional Culture*. Dallas, TX: BenBella Books.

Erikson, E.H. (1995). *Childhood and Society*. London, UK: Vintage Books.

Gilbert, P. (1998). What is shame? Some core issues and controversies. In P. Gilbert & B. Andrews (Eds.), *Shame: Interpersonal Behavior, Psychopathology, and Culture* (pp. 3–38). Oxford, UK: Oxford University Press.

Gilbert, P. (2006). A biopsychosocial and evolutionary approach to formulation with a special focus on shame. In N. Tarrier (Ed.), *Case Formulation in Cognitive Behaviour Therapy: The Treatment of Challenging and Complex Cases* (pp. 81–112). New York, NY: Routledge.

Gilbert, P. (2010). *Compassion Focused Therapy: Distinctive Features*. Hove, UK: Routledge.

Gurney, K. (2020). *Mind the Gap: The Truth about Desire and How to Futureproof Your Sex Life*. London, UK: Headline Publishing Group.

Hastings, A.S. (1998). *Treating Sexual Shame: A New Map for Overcoming Dysfunction, Abuse, and Addiction*. Northvale, NJ: Jason Aronson Inc.

Hayes, S.C., Strosahl, K.D., & Wilson, K.G. (2016). *Acceptance and Commitment Therapy: The Process and Practice of Mindful Change*. New York, NY: The Guilford Press.

Horney, K. (1993). *Our Inner Conflicts: A Constructive Theory of Neurosis*. New York, NY: W. W. Norton & Co.

Irons, C., & Beaumont, E. (2017). *The Compassionate Mind Workbook: A Step-by-Step Guide to Developing Your Compassionate Self*. London, UK: Robinson.

Johnson, S. (2011). *Hold Me Tight: Your Guide to the Most Successful Approach to Building Loving Relationships*. London, UK: Piatkus.

Kaufman, G. (1974). The meaning of shame: Toward a self-affirming identity. *Journal of Counseling Psychology*, 21(6), 568.

Kaufman, G., & Raphael, L. (1996). *Coming Out of Shame: Transforming Gay and Lesbian Lives*. London, UK: Doubleday Books.

Kerner, I. (2021). *So Tell Me about the Last Time You Had Sex: Laying Bare and Learning to Repair Our Love Lives*. London, UK: Scribe Publications.

Kyle, S.E. (2013). *Identification and Treatment of Sexual Shame: Development of a Measurement Tool and Group Therapy Protocol* [Unpublished doctoral dissertation]. American Academy of Clinical Sexologists, Austin, TX.

Lewis, M. (1995). *Shame: The Exposed Self*. New York, NY: The Free Press.

Lewis, M. (2003). The role of the self in shame. *Social Research*, 70(4), 1181–1204.

Lorde, A. (2017). *Your Silence Will Not Protect You*. London, UK: Silver Press.

Luoma, J.B., & Platt, M.G. (2015). Shame, self-criticism, self-stigma, and compassion in acceptance and commitment therapy. *Current Opinion in Psychology*, 2, 97–101.

Moon, A. (2020). *Getting It: A Guide to Hot, Healthy Hookups and Shame-Free Sex*. New York, NY: Ten Speed Press.

Morin, J. (1995). *The Erotic Mind: Unlocking the Inner Sources of Sexual Passion and Fulfillment*. New York, NY: HarperCollins.

Nathanson, D.L. (1992). *Shame and Pride: Affect, Sex, and the Birth of the Self*. New York, NY: W.W. Norton & Company.

Neves, S. (2021). *Compulsive Sexual Behaviours: A Psycho-Sexual Treatment Guide for Clinicians*. Oxon, UK: Routledge.

Odets, W. (2020). *Out of the Shadows: Reimagining Gay Men's Lives*. London, UK: Penguin Books.

Pachankis, J.E., Clark, K.A., Burton, C.L., Hughto, J.M.W., Bränström, R., & Keene, D.E. (2020). Sex, status, competition, and exclusion: Intraminority stress from within the gay community and gay and bisexual men's mental health. *Journal of Personality and Social Psychology*, 119(3), 713.

Perry, P. (2019). *The Book You Wish Your Parents Had Read (and Your Children Will Be Glad That You Did)*. London, UK: Penguin Life.

Petrocchi, N., Matos, M., Carvalho, S., & Baiocco, R. (2016). Compassion-focused therapy in the treatment of shame-based difficulties in gender and sexual minorities. In M. Skinta & A. Curtin (Eds.), *Mindfulness and Acceptance for Gender and Sexual Minorities: A Clinician's Guide to Fostering Compassion, Connection, and Equality Using Contextual Strategies* (pp. 69–86). Oakland, CA: Context Press.

Piers, G., & Singer, M.B. (1954). Shame and guilt: A psychoanalytic and a cultural study. *Philosophy and Phenomenological Research*, 15(2), 279–80.

Roberts, M. (2020). *Beyond Shame: Creating a Healthy Sex Life on Your Own Terms*. Minneapolis, MN: Fortress Press.

Rothschild, B. (2000). *The Body Remembers: The Psychophysiology of Trauma & Trauma Treatment*. New York, NY: W.W. Norton & Company.

Sanderson, C. (2015). *Counselling Skills for Working with Shame*. London, UK: Jessica Kingsley Publishers.

Scheff, T.J. (1990). *Microsociology: Discourse, Emotion, and Social Structure*. Chicago, IL: The University of Chicago Press.

Schore, A.N. (2003). *Affect Dysregulation and Disorders of the Self (Norton Series on Interpersonal Neurobiology)*. New York, NY: W.W. Norton & Company.

Schwartz, R.C., & Sweezy, M. (2019). *Internal Family Systems Therapy* (2nd ed.). New York, NY: The Guilford Press.

Shadbolt, C. (2009). Sexuality and shame. *Transactional Analysis Journal*, 39(2), 163–172.

Shahbaz, C., & Chirinos, P. (2017). *Becoming a Kink Aware Therapist*. Oxon, UK: Routledge.

Skinta, M., & D'Alton, P. (2016). Mindfulness and acceptance for malignant shame. In M. Skinta & A. Curtin (Eds.), *Mindfulness and Acceptance for Gender and Sexual Minorities: A Clinician's Guide to Fostering Compassion, Connection, and Equality Using Contextual Strategies* (pp. 87–104). Oakland, CA: Context Press.

Stone, G.R. (2017). *Sex and the Constitution: Sex, Religion, and Law from America's Origins to the Twenty-First Century*. New York, NY: Liveright Publishing.

Tangney, J.P., & Dearing, R.L. (2003). *Shame and Guilt*. New York, NY: The Guilford Press.

Tomkins, S.S. (1963). *Affect, Imagery, Consciousness: Vol. 2: The Negative Affects*. New York, NY: Springer.

Van der Kolk, B. (2015). *The Body Keeps the Score: Mind, Brain and Body in the Transformation of Trauma*. London, UK: Penguin Books.

Wurmser, L. (1981). *The Mask of Shame*. London, UK: Johns Hopkins University Press.

Young, J.E. (1990). *Cognitive Therapy for Personality Disorders: A Schema-Focused Approach*. Sarasota, FL: Professional Resource Exchange, Inc.

Chapter 4

The sex lives of asexuals

Jo Russell

Asexuality – an introduction

"You mean there are people like that, and they're not lying?" "Yeah, I know!", the tutor responded, and the class sniggered. The course on sexuality and gender was part of a counselling advanced practice degree, and in the 40 taught hours, asexuality was acknowledged for less than three minutes, and dismissed in even less time. I felt angry, ashamed and odd in some unacceptable way. The response in the class demonstrates that most therapists are both unaware of and under-educated around asexuality.

Writing this chapter has been informed by a very personal journey. Now in my 60th year, I identify as asexual, having first heard the term aged 46. I had met with a counsellor for several years, during most of which any conversation about sexual thoughts, feelings, behaviours, or even sexuality in general, was unbearable to me. Eventually, I read a little about asexuality and tried to bring the idea into a session; my counsellor was more inclined to 'wait and see' how things might develop as I processed other parts of my story. We 'waited and saw' for three years before I moved on to a counsellor familiar with asexuality.

This chapter aims to offer an introduction to working therapeutically in a positive way with those experiencing low, or no, sexual attraction. There is space here for little more than mapping out some of the terrain you might explore with your asexual clients as you walk with them on their particular journeys, which may leave you with more questions or wonderings than answers.

Asexuality is a sexual orientation like any other. However, it is signified by a lack of something rather than a presence. The most widely used definition is offered by AVEN (the Asexuality Visibility and Education Network), which states:

> An asexual person does not experience sexual attraction – they are not drawn to people sexually and do not desire to act upon attraction to others in a sexual way. Unlike celibacy, which is a choice to abstain from sexual activity, asexuality is an intrinsic part of who we are, just like other sexual orientations.
>
> (www.asexuality.org)

DOI: 10.4324/9781003260608-5

Sexual attraction, sexual desire and sexual behaviour are different processes. Sexual behaviour indicates a choice, or intention, and is generally under one's control. Sexual attraction, on the other hand, is not a choice. It is sometimes difficult for asexuals to grasp what sexual attraction feels like. Angela Chen (2020) gives us a useful indication:

> Sexual attraction can be instantaneous and involuntary: a heightened awareness, physical alertness combined with a mental wanting.
>
> (p. 20)

As with the general population, asexual people may experience physiological responses to sexual arousal, and may even find it pleasurable, but the arousal is unlikely to lead to a desire to engage in partnered sexual activity or to a deeper sense of connection with a partner or partners.

In order to avoid comparing asexual experience against some kind of perceived norm, the word allosexual is used to describe someone who *does* experience sexual attraction. However, asexual and allosexual are not simple binary categories. There is a significant diversity within asexuality for which there are various commonly used descriptors. Demisexuality relates to somebody who may experience a very low level of sexual attraction but only within an already established and intimate relationship. Gray-asexuality identifies somebody who may experience some level of sexual attraction but so vaguely they may miss it. A split-attraction model is often used which distinguishes between romantic attraction (who one wants to snuggle or build a life with) and sexual attraction. Accordingly, asexuals (or 'aces') may describe themselves in terms of their romantic attraction using equivalent prefixes, hence homoromantic, heteroromantic, panromantic, biromantic or aromantic, or may fully embrace a split model with self-descriptions like ace/aro (asexual/aromantic). A useful glossary of terms used in asexual communities can be found at http://wiki.asexuality.org/Lexicon, but do note that the use of language is dynamic and constantly developing.

Though dated and considered a very tentative estimate, the best research so far indicates about one per cent of the population may be on the asexual spectrum (Bogaert, 2004), while in a more recent survey, ten per cent of LGBTQ youth identified as being asexual or ace spectrum (The Trevor Project, 2020). Still in its infancy, most research into asexuality has been in the disciplines of psychology and sociology, rather than counselling or psychotherapy. Recent research indicates some evidence for a relationship between asexuality and autism or neurodiversity (Yule et al., 2017), and asexuality and gender expansiveness, especially among young people (The Trevor Project, 2020). The incidence of mental health difficulties such as anxiety and depression are also higher in asexual people than in the general population (Borgogna et al., 2019).

When a client presents for therapy reporting no or low sexual desire, we may be tempted to take a history searching for the cause. Is this client a survivor of sexual abuse or assault? Are their hormone levels within normal range? Are they struggling to form relationships? While any or all of these may be part of their story, we should also keep in mind that this client could be on the asexual spectrum (and may not know it), and that there is no other cause.

Asexuality is sometimes referred to as 'the invisible orientation' – indeed, there is a book with this name (Decker, 2014). In many ways, there is nothing to 'see', no behaviour to observe that marks someone as asexual. In fact, asexuals will sometimes 'mask' their identity in order to fit in with society; I recall a lengthy discussion with a close friend about what I was looking for in a partner, setting the bar so high that such a person was unavailable. I could appear normal, but never find what I was looking for.

In order to better illustrate how asexuality may present in practice, various case vignettes are presented throughout this chapter. These are composites of real people. All names and other identifying features are changed in order to preserve confidentiality, but the situations and experiences are real.

Shame and internalised oppressions

Compulsory sexuality

All marginalised groups will experience oppression from those around them, pressure to conform, to be 'normal', to be like everyone else. When that experience is internalised, it turns into shame: "there is something wrong with me", "I ought not be who I am". Asexual people are marginalised and sometimes even pitied in a sexualised society which espouses such tropes as 'The 40-year-old virgin' and thinks that an active sex life is universal, or at least to be aspired to. Words used to describe people who don't have sex are either clinical or weighted with implicit denigration – 'chaste', 'celibate', 'prudish', 'repressed', while in conversations, there may be hints or suggestions that there's something wrong with them physically, mentally or emotionally which makes them 'undesirable'.

Sex is ubiquitous. Wherever you look, it is used to sell cars, advertise films, define success and entertain. It fills magazines, TV screens and books. Not so long ago, it was one of the things that defined liberation: free love. But for those for whom sexual desire and attraction are absent, it represents an anomaly, a part of 'normality' from which they feel excluded. A lesbian friend recently said to me that she often feels alienated in what she calls a 'hetero-normative' world. She talks of her friends who get married, raise families and live their sexuality publicly. For an asexual person, the 'hetero-normative' society of my lesbian friend goes one degree further and becomes a 'sexual-normative' world. Someone who doesn't experience what others call normal will likely remain silent and hidden.

There is a strong but subtle pressure to conform, to fit the mould. Even in the relatively under-sexed world of traditional organised religion, there is an implicit expectation of heterosexuality, marriage and procreation. In some religious teachings, marriage and childbearing form a part of the redemptive role of women, while the pressure to remain celibate until marriage assumes that sexual desire is present. Some go even further; on a website about a religious vocation, I found the following:

> What do you call a person who is asexual? Answer: Not a person. Asexual people do not exist. Sexuality is a gift from God and thus a fundamental part of our human identity. Those who repress their sexuality are not living as God created them to be: fully alive and well. As such, they're most likely unhappy.
>
> (Nantais & Opperman, 2010)

Poet Adrienne Rich (1980) showed that compulsory heterosexuality is not just the idea that most people are heterosexual. It is the sense that anything else is a deviation from a norm; society is structured to privilege those in heterosexual long-term relationships. Gupta (2015) and Przybylo (2016) echo Rich's idea and have written about compulsory sexuality; one doesn't have to look far to see, for example, tax advantages for those in committed relationships, single supplement charges for those holidaying alone, restaurant tables usually set for multiples of two diners. Most structures and assumptions work in favour of those in relationships, thus disadvantaging some asexual people and others not in relationships.

Minority stress

Minority stress around sexuality and gender is defined as the "negative impact of transphobic, homophobic and heterosexist cultural norms that spur the discrimination, bullying, marginalisation and stigmatisation of LGB&T people" (Nodin et al., 2015, p. 12). Asexual people are a minority within a minority and so suffer minority stress in double measure. With increasing acceptance in mainstream society for those who enjoy same-sex relationships, equal marriage and – from 2021 – equal access to civil partnerships in the UK, asexuals are still marginalised in LGBT spaces, remain invisible and, at best, are dismissed or ignored.

Deborah is 50 and has been single all her life, apart from one brief relationship as a teenager. She first heard about asexuality about 12 years ago. While a survivor of childhood sexual abuse, Deborah states very firmly that she isn't asexual for that reason. She describes finding herself, aged 13, in a relationship with an older man because she didn't pick up on the cues he was giving and then didn't know how to say no.

Deborah has revealed in therapy the deep levels of shame she carries. She feels ashamed because she hasn't "managed to find a boyfriend" when all her other friends have; she feels ashamed because she doesn't have a family or children; she feels humiliated because there must be something fundamentally wrong with her that no one has ever asked her out; she hides her loneliness, not wanting others to feel pity; she avoids social situations for fear of feeling out of her depth and having to answer intrusive questions.

With this and the other vignettes included in this chapter, you might want to reflect on what the story brings up for you and how you would imagine work-ing with the person depicted. To pick up on two points here, anecdotally, many asexuals will readily notice two people flirting with each other, but will often miss someone flirting with them. Statistically, asexual people are no more likely than the general population to have survived sexual abuse, although, of course, that still means that many will be survivors given the high rates of sexual abuse and assault, especially among women.

Relationships

We have few words to describe adult relationships: friend, close friend, best friend, partner, spouse, significant other. There is little nuance in these descriptors, and the use of phrases like 'just friends' or 'more than just friends' seems to devalue being a friend. Some asexual people use the terms QPR (queer platonic relation-ship) and QPP (queer platonic partnership) to describe non-romantic relationships, but these are not terms embraced by all.

Society deems that some relationships have more significance than others. Phrases like 'they're a friend' and 'they're my partner' carry different weights, and accordingly different prioritisation of time, resources, effort and emotional commit-ment. Many do not mention even important friendships, without being prompted, when asked about their significant relationships. Having recently embarked on a first 'partnered' relationship, one client noted just how many people have con-gratulated them, expressed their joy on their behalf as if this relationship above all others was the one that would make the difference to their life. Personally, I have more than half a century of deep, significant, rich and rewarding friendships which have never been celebrated or even noticed by others. We have all been deeply socialised within this value system, and I will admit to not having thought of my friendships as being as significant, valuable, or important as those friends' part-nered relationships. I have held back to my own, and their, detriment.

Beth, in her twenties, has grown up around queer friendship groups. She first heard of asexuality whilst still at school. Her motto was 'better weird than boring', and her school-based queer peer group maintain some con-tact albeit all now living further afield. Beth's family is also supportive but distant since she has moved cities for her job. Beth has come for therapy because she is lonely. She wants to move in with a friend for companionship but fears he would think she was leading him on.

Working with relationships is always the stuff of therapy. But consider Beth, who is not looking for a sexual partnership but for relationships that will meet different needs for intimacy. She states she is looking for friends, but in Beth's mind, those friendships couldn't be as important as another's 'partner'. One of the things Beth and I have done together is to explore ten different Greek words that signify love in some way in order to identify and celebrate existing friendships and to consider areas of lack.

- *Eros:* passionate, sexual love, the drive towards life and pleasure, aesthetic beauty.
- *Philia:* a deep friendship, soul mates, platonic but long-lasting.
- *Ludus:* playful love, games, conquests.
- *Agape:* selfless love, altruistic, unconditional.
- *Pragma:* long-standing, loving with the head, not the heart, mature.
- *Philautia:* healthy self-love.
- *Storge:* affectionate love, developing slowly from friendship, devotion.
- *Mania:* obsessive love.
- *Meraki:* creative love, doing or making something with love, wholehearted.
- *Xenia:* hospitality love, welcoming the other into our space.

All clients, not just asexual clients, need to be supported in developing breadth in relationships, but asexuality draws our attention to how significant those relationships can be without sexual contact. Dating apps are useful for some, but not so often for asexual people since there is a cultural presumption that subscribers are ultimately looking for a sexual relationship. Beth reported that she had signed up with several apps, 'outing' herself as asexual on one, and staying private about her asexual orientation on others. She told me that most of those who responded to her profile disappeared 'as soon as they knew that sex would never be on the table'.

Polyamorous or open relationships can be attractive for asexuals because, with multiple people involved in consensual dynamics, the pressure can be taken off an asexual person to meet their partners' sexual needs. In turn, this may reduce the anxiety of being side-lined or abandoned for withholding sexual intimacy while still having the closeness and security of commitment.

Coming out

Coming out for asexuals is as fundamental to being known as it is for those of other sexual orientations. The phrase 'coming out' has its origins in the idea of coming out of the closet (out of hiding and shame) and of taking pride in one's identity.

Carla was in her mid-twenties and told me she had arranged to meet someone for a drink having initially connected through a dating app. They had been communicating for a couple of weeks and Carla felt the relationship was going well so far. "Do I tell her I am asexual?" she asked in a therapy session. Previously she had identified herself as asexual on the app and had no responses, but removing reference to her sexual orientation (and otherwise identifying as biromantic) had elicited a very different response.

This dilemma can be bewildering for clients. Unless their sexuality is already otherwise known, to communicate this on a first date raises fears of being summarily rejected, and not communicating it raises fears of accusations of 'leading someone on'.

My personal experience of coming out, and that of many asexuals, was what can only be described as 'underwhelming'. I had been reading and exploring the notion of asexuality for several years, had begun to bring this to my therapy and decided I wanted to open up to a couple of close friends. One (an activist of a different sexual identity) responded, "Well, at least no one sends you hate mail", another (a GP) said, "You should get your hormones tested – you can get treatment for that", and a third offered, "So, you aren't having sex . . . neither are loads of people; get over it". I felt deflated, invisible and un-known.

It is true that no one sends me hate mail; nothing that I do (or rather don't do) offends anyone's moral codes. However, in a different kind of way asexuality offends society's generalised belief in the universality of sex as being a driving force, an erotic imperative. It is also true that not everyone is having sex; I empathise with the loss of those who would like to have sex, or who miss it having previously been sexual. However, that is not the same as being asexual.

The counselling literature tells us the coming out process is an important part of identity formation. Most models of identity formation acknowledge the importance of finding belonging, finding others who are like you and finding a tribe. There are gay, lesbian and queer bars and clubs that are relatively easy to identify in most larger towns and cities in the UK, but in order to find others who don't like toast, one doesn't go and stand next to a toaster! The largest asexual communities are to be found online, although participants in organisations like AVEN also arrange regional and local meet-ups, and it is useful to direct clients towards these to find peers. However, these gatherings are not for everyone, and it isn't always easy to find peers in the groups – I attended a meet-up and was the eldest by 25 years.

The coming out process for asexuals may have a different significance than for other GSRD (Gender, Sex and Relationship Diversities) identities. For some, it feels completely unnecessary, while for others, the need to come out emerges as a pushback on pressure from family and friends to 'find someone', an exploration of personal identity, or from the desire to find an asexual community (Robbins et al., 2016).

In this day and age, it would be unusual to arrive in adolescence and, given the nature of social media and of current educational programmes, not to be aware of the existence of same-sex attraction or gender expansiveness. Asexuality is, as we have seen, still often invisible and is rarely portrayed in media and films, let alone positively. It is still common for younger asexuals to arrive in early adulthood without a word that describes their experience; most youngsters report that they first learn about asexuality through internet searches.

Sex and consent

What is sex?

Famously, former President Bill Clinton declared, "I did not have sexual relations with that woman, Miss Lewinsky" (Waxman & Fabry, 2018). He subsequently admitted that it would depend on the definition of sexual relations. When working with clients of Christian faith, in preparing for marriage some will tell me that they don't intend to have sex before their wedding. But what do they mean?

There are many stories in this chapter of those who have engaged in sexual intimacy because they felt they should. One of the biggest questions that remains unaddressed, and one that is crucial for asexuals, is what is sex and what is not? What is it that someone doesn't want to engage in? Young people learn about sex and perceived sexual norms from school-based sex education, mainstream and social media and from watching pornography, which is freely accessible to them online. In all of these arenas, what is communicated is that real sex is about penetration of some kind and that the goal of sex is always orgasm. In this context, I am using the word 'sex' to describe activities that are erotically engaging or motivated.

Both cultural attitudes to sex (sex-positive, sex-neutral, sex-negative) and an asexual's own responses to sex (on a spectrum from aversion to positive) will affect how an individual deals with sexual contact in their relationships. For some, it is an accepted part of life together, perhaps not something they would seek out, but can be embraced in a similar way perhaps, as mowing the lawn or emptying rubbish bins. For others, there is a nightly endurance test from which there is little room to escape. The scope of attitudes that asexual people have towards sex could be summarised thus:

- Those who want nothing.
- Those who want some touch but not sexual touch.
- Those who want solo but not partnered sex.
- Those who are up for sexual touch for a partner but not for themselves.
- Those who might want to explore sexual/sensual touch for themselves.

All of these positions are equally valid.

Talking about sex and touch

It can be awkward or difficult for people to feel comfortable talking about sex, sensation and bodies within relationships but is essential where touch is part of intimacy. It is important to be able to communicate to a partner what touch feels good, and what does not. Talking about bodies in the abstract may be fine, but talking about one's own body is much harder. For some asexuals, there could be additional hurdles with which to contend. Someone who has not been in a sexual relationship may be more likely than others to lack the useful vocabulary for body parts; textbook terms can feel cold and clinical while adolescent 'behind the bike shed' language will feel juvenile. There may be a process to reclaiming parts of the body that have hitherto not felt significant or even owned. The therapeutic relationship can offer a safe space for supporting clients to gain some confidence with this.

Alongside those who have had sexual experience, there will be those who not only have not had a sexual experience but have only limited experience of touch of any sort. Holding back from sexual contact for some will mean holding back from other sorts of touch. Holding back from physical touch out of fear or avoidance of sexualised experience can mean that the brain doesn't know how to interpret signals associated with touch. For example, there could be confusion between pain, pleasure, tickling or just an overwhelming physical sensation that an individual needs time to become accustomed to. Some asexuals wishing to explore their sexual bodies and learn assertive and affirmative communication may find it helpful to find a safe massage therapist, or even a sexological bodyworker,[1] where touch is boundaried, one-way and always consensual, in order to discover what types of touch can be pleasurable.

Negotiating sexual contact

> Emily is now in her early thirties. She is in an open relationship, and her female primary partner knows she is ace/biromantic. She was previously in an abusive controlling relationship with a man, who told her she was bad for not giving him sex whenever he wanted it. Emily also dates others in a more casual way. She loves having sex with men, principally because she is happy seeing them satisfied, and feels good about herself to give them that gift. What she really longs for herself is the time 'after sex' when they can be skin to skin and cuddle, with no need for anything more. When I asked her if she could request that without having to go through the ritual of sex first, she said that it would be far too vulnerable to let someone know that was what she wanted. Our work together has included supporting Emily to own her likes and dislikes and to validate them in their own right, without needing to pay for cuddles with sex.

In the sexological literature, we can find various models of sexual arousal, most of which aren't particularly inclusive of asexuality and need to be reconsidered in this light. Working with asexual clients who are sex-positive, it is useful to help them identify aspects of their subjective relational experience that lead towards sexual contact being wanted. Some have described noticing an unusual sense of urgency in kissing, for example. Some have reported a subjective almost empathic connection with what their partner may be experiencing physically and acting on that. Some have told me about merely sitting with their disinclination to engage sexually, and supporting themselves towards a willingness to 'give love to their partner', and this being enough to overcome their reluctance. These may all be common experiences for allosexuals too, but for an asexual client, it is useful to help them identify what happens for them in sexual moments, to work with those moments rather than against them, if that is what the client wishes. JoAnn Loulan's Sexual Model (in Iasenza, 2020) is much more inclusive of asexual experience, even if it is not named as such. Loulan starts with willingness, which can be a precursor to desire, and has pleasure as a goal, rather than orgasm.

> Joseph and his wife, Sophie, who are in their mid-twenties, asked for support as Joseph realised he is asexual. They had been childhood sweethearts, and have now been married for eight years. Joseph is anxious that Sophie will not want to stay with him, and Sophie is anxious that Joseph will want to leave the marriage. As well as working with their anxieties, we have engaged in a process of using a "Yes, No, Maybe" list such as the one offered by Scarleteen (scarleteen.com) to facilitate conversations around what could be possible and what is now off the table. They have discovered that Sophie is just as satisfied with plenty of close skin-to-skin contact, and penetration using toys. Joseph is happy because he loves giving Sophie pleasure, but his body is less involved.

Consent

There is an unspoken pressure, often felt acutely by asexual people, that they should say yes to sex, at least sometimes. It is framed as compromise, meeting someone half-way, because the consensus is that you can always say no to a stranger, but not to your partner. Consider the following scenarios:

> Daisy (18) has never had a boyfriend before. In fresher's week at university, she is anxious to look 'cool and evolved' around her new friends, and after a party, ends up going back to David's room. They make out. He produces a condom and asks, "Are you up for this?" She allows it, not wanting to appear immature.
>
> Has Daisy fully, enthusiastically consented?
>
> Tom has been in a relationship with George for 15 years. They have shared a bed since moving in together. Tom has never enjoyed sex, but it is 'what they do'. He has increasingly been finding excuses not to have sex, but every so often agrees to it because he feels bad for George.
>
> Is Tom fully, enthusiastically consenting?

They are adults, and are making decisions knowing what they are choosing. There is no question here of any wrong-doing by their partners. However, if Daisy and Tom are asexual, then their understanding of consent may be compromised because of our common socialisation regarding the universality of sexual attraction. This is a hermeneutical injustice, which philosopher Miranda Fricker (2006) defines as:

> the injustice of having some significant area of one's social experience obscured from collective understanding owing to a structural prejudice in the collective hermeneutical resource.
>
> (p. 100)

A client once told me they and their partner had sex most Saturday mornings because it was when both were home without rush. My client soon came to dread Saturday mornings and longed for it to be over. What if the reason you don't want to have sex is because you don't enjoy it? Ever? The pressure to come up with reasons or excuses can be exhausting. There is a 'good enough' reason to not want sex: being asexual.

What if we were to qualify consent, and make it more nuanced? Could this help clients in both deciding and communicating *how* they consent, as well as *that* they consent?

John, late twenties, said to me: "I guess I never really consent to have sex and stuff, I just went with the flow. I never really asked myself if I wanted to do it". John had even wondered if he was trans since he believed he couldn't be a real man if he didn't want sex.

In order to fully consent to sexual contact, the nature of that contact should be agreed actively not passively. This requires two skills, which can be practised and developed in the counselling room and in other relationships. The first is checking in with oneself: "Is this something I *want* to do with this person, in this context, today?" Consent to self is a pre-requisite to consent given to another. The second is modelling and practising using the language of consent, such as asking clients: "Is it ok for you if we talk about . . ." or "How might you feel if . . .".

Libby, mid-twenties, told me: "I think that consent in all areas of a relationship is important. I will actually get consent from someone before venting about a problem to them, or asking them for help with something. You know, I'll say – I'm dealing with something, and it's hard, and here are some of the things that could be triggering about it; is it ok if I talk to you? Or – I want to ask you for a favour, but I first want to let you know that you can say no, and it won't affect our relationship".

For asexual people, the layers of shame around being different, a possible lack of sexual experience, and the lack of sexual desire or attraction can make it challenging to give active consent. Various models are available for teaching consent. One, by Planned Parenthood (plannedparenthood.org) uses the acronym FRIES for Freely given, Reversible, Informed, Enthusiastic, Specific consent. 'Enthusiastic' may be problematic in the context of asexuality so could be replaced by 'willing'. Betty Martin's 'Wheel of Consent' (2014) is another practical tool for clients to practise giving and asking consent for anything from simple touch to sexual contact and to both express desire and give permission.

Solo sex

Solo sexual activity (such as masturbation) is also different for asexuals. Some may not engage sexually on their own at all. Others enjoy sex alone because it feels pleasurable, relieves tension or stress, or find they have a libido which they prefer to take care of alone. The distinction between sexual attraction and libido, or sexual desire, is an important one as many asexuals will experience the latter but not the former. It is like knowing one is physiologically hungry, but the hunger is not being directed to any food in particular. Many asexuals would say that they masturbate, but it is to satisfy a physiological urge rather than to connect with any fantasies of a lover; for many, sex doesn't make sense in relation to other people.

Kink and BDSM

Some interesting research has been conducted drawing links between asexual communities and BDSM and kink (see Bisbey, Chapter 9, this volume). Some people enjoy kink and do not experience it as sexual but may enjoy receiving bodily sensations, learning intricate bondage techniques, dressing up or serving another. For those people, this kind of play could be more of a leisure, artistic or spiritual activity. It might include a sense of being part of a community of other kinksters where everyone enjoys different kinds of activities, but all are considered valid.

Those involved in the kink scene usually develop the capacity to communicate clearly about limits, boundaries and consent, which makes this world quite attractive to asexual people for its clarity and safety. It offers the possibility of intimacy and connection without genital sex being assumed as inevitable. Notwithstanding, some asexuals have been found to feel conflicted about having a kinky asexual identity. In one recent study (Winter-Gray & Hayfield, 2021), the following was reported:

> For some, there was dissonance in identifying as asexual while experiencing fantasies or sexual feelings or attractions. This created doubts and difficulties in managing their seemingly sensual (and perhaps sexual) self while occupying an asexual identity. For some of these participants, it seemed that their

asexual identity had not always coincided easily alongside their kinks and fantasies; hence this sense of a lack of congruence between asexuality and kink and fantasies seemingly created a sense of not being 'asexual enough'.

As therapists aiming to work competently with asexual clients, whether they identify as such or not, we can be effective in holding an open space for exploration of what kinds of intimacy and connection clients may find appealing.

Conversion therapy

A lack of interest in sex has historically been pathologised by mental health professionals to the extent that only in the most recent version of the *Diagnostical and Statistical Manual of Mental Disorders* (DSM 5, 2013) has asexuality been presented as an alternative explanation for low sexual desire.

> One client, Nicola (aged 35), gave an account of the journey she and her husband endured seeking a solution for her lack of sexual desire. Initially consulting their church leadership, they were referred to a sex therapist. Nicola recounted: "At first we were getting shown this whole page spread of willies . . . and then it was sort of like, all these people who feel ashamed of their body or whatever . . . and I thought I don't feel ashamed of my body, I like my body, I'm very happy with my body! That's not the problem! I mean, to be honest, I feel like even the sex therapist was out of her depth, that she hadn't encountered anyone asexual."

Presumably, the therapist's (and the pastor's) intentions were good, but both, acting out of ignorance, caused significant distress to Nicola and her husband. The Memorandum of Understanding on Conversion Therapy in the UK (MoU, 2022) is a document signed by all the leading medical/psy/therapy professional membership organisations, leading LGBT bodies and NHS England, Scotland and Wales. It makes clear that attempts to alter a person's gender identity or sexual orientation are unethical, potentially harmful and are not supported by evidence. The Memorandum states:

> For the purpose of this document, sexual orientation refers to the sexual or romantic attraction someone feels to people of the same sex, opposite sex, more than one sex, or to experience no attraction.

The Memorandum goes on to oblige signatory organisations to ensure that all practising members are adequately trained and briefed so as to cause no harm.

As a profession, I believe we are falling short of meeting these obligations. The National LGBT Survey (Government Equalities Office, 2018) shows that 10.1 per cent of asexual individuals have either been offered, or have had, conversion therapy to 'correct' or change their sexual orientation, which is a higher proportion than for any other sexual orientation.

As a profession, we have a responsibility to educate ourselves about asexuality, or we could be in danger of inadvertently colluding with attempts to change our clients' relationship with sex and sexual intimacy.

Summary

- Asexuality is a sexual orientation defined by not experiencing sexual attraction. It is often referred to as 'the invisible orientation'.
- It is not a choice or a failure of development. It does not need to be fixed.
- Sexual attraction, sexual desire and sexual behaviour are different processes.
- Asexuality describes a spectrum of experience; there is not a binary (allosexual/asexual) model, and asexuals will demonstrate a wide variety of attitudes to sexual contact.
- Asexuals are a minority within the GSRD minority, and finding a like-minded community can be a challenge.
- Asexual clients will bring the whole gamut of difficulties to therapy, as would any other client. However, some common stressors particular to asexuality are: being misunderstood, living within a society characterised by compulsory sexuality, erasure, loneliness and relationships being under-valued.
- Consent within the self is an important precursor to giving consent to anyone else.
- Therapists have a responsibility for self-education around asexuality to mitigate potential unwitting collusion with so-called conversion therapies.

Note

1 At the time of writing this chapter, COSRT deems unethical to suggest or refer to a sexological bodyworker.

References

American Psychiatric Association. (2013). *Diagnostic and Statistical Manual of Mental Disorders: DSM-5*. Arlington, VA: American Psychiatric Association.

Bogaert, A. (2004). Asexuality: Prevalence and associated factors in a national probability sample. *The Journal of Sex Research*, 41(3), 279–287.

Borgogna, N.C., McDermott, R.C., Aita, S.L., & Kridel, M.M. (2019). Anxiety and depression across gender and sexual minorities: Implications for transgender, gender nonconforming, pansexual, demisexual, asexual, queer, and questioning individuals. *Psychology of Sexual Orientation and Gender Diversity*, 6(1), 54–63.

Chen, A. (2020). *Ace: What Asexuality Reveals about Desire, Society, and the Meaning of Sex*. Boston, MA: Beacon Press.

Decker, J.S. (2014). *The Invisible Orientation: An Introduction to Asexuality*. New York: Carrel Books.

Fricker, M. (2006). Powerlessness and social interpretation. *Episteme: A Journal of Social Epistemology*, 3(1–2), 96–108.

Government Equalities Office. (2018). *National LGBT Survey*. https://assets.publishing.service.gov.uk/government/uploads/system/uploads/attachment_data/file/721704/LGBT-survey-research-report.pdf

Gupta, K. (2015). Compulsory sexuality: Evaluating an emerging concept. *Signs*, 41(1), 131–154.

Iasenza, S. (2020). *Transforming Sexual Narratives*. New York, NY: Routledge.

Martin, B. (2014). *Wheel of Consent*. https://bettymartin.org/videos/

MoU. (2022). *Memorandum of Understanding on Conversion Therapy in the UK – Version 2*. www.bacp.co.uk/media/11738/mou2-reva-0421.pdf

Nantais, D., & Opperman, S. (2010). *8 Myths about Religious Life*. https://sgfp.wordpress.com/2010/03/29/8-myths-about-religious-life/

Nodin, N., Peel, E., Tyler, A., & Rivers, I. (2015). *The RaRE Research Report: LGB&T Mental Health: Risk and Resilience Explored*. PACE. www.queerfutures.co.uk/wp-content/uploads/2015/04/RARE_Research_Report_PACE_2015.pdf

Przybylo, E. (2016). Asexuals against the Cis-tem! *TSQ: Transgender Studies Quarterly*, 3(3–4), 653–660.

Rich, A. (1980). Compulsory hetereosexuality and lesbian existence. *Signs*, 5(4), 631–660.

Robbins, N.K., Low, K.G., & Query, A.N. (2016). A qualitative exploration of the 'coming out' process for asexual individuals. *Archives of Sexual Behavior*, 45(3), 751–760.

The Trevor Project. (2020). *Research Brief: Asexual and Ace Spectrum Youth*. www.thetrevorproject.org/2020/10/26/research-brief-asexual-and-ace-spectrum-youth/

Waxman, O.B., & Fabry, M. (2018). From an anonymous tip to an impeachment: A timeline of key moments in the Clinton-Lewinsky scandal. *Time*. https://time.com/5120561/bill-clinton-monica-lewinsky-timeline/

Winter-Gray, T., & Hayfield, N. (2021). 'Can I be a kinky ace?': How asexual people negotiate their experiences of kinks and fetishes. *Psychology & Sexuality*, 12(3), 163–179. doi:10.1080/19419899.2019.1679866

Yule, M.A., Brotto, L.A., & Gorzalka, B.B. (2017). Human asexuality: What do we know about a lack of sexual attraction? *Current Sexual Health Reports*, 9, 50–56. doi:10.1007/s11930-017-0100-y

Suggested reading

Barker, M.J., & Richards, C. (2013). Asexuality. In *Sexuality & Gender for Mental Health Professionals: A Practical Guide*. (pp. 101–111). London: Sage.
A useful reference guide and a great starting point for further exploration. Contains some helpful questions for practitioner self-awareness.

Bogaert, A.F. (2012). *Understanding Asexuality*. Plymouth: Rowman & Littlefield Publishers.
A book at the crossover between academic writing and general reading, but not always popular with aces, for writing 'about us without us'. Explores some interesting questions about the place of sex in society.

Burgess, R. (2021). *How to Be Ace: A Memoir of Growing Up Asexual*. London: Jessica Kingsley Publishers.

An honest and sensitive graphic memoir, illustrated by Rebecca, of growing up through school and university while identifying as ace. Great for young people negotiating similar challenges (including anxiety and OCD), and for gaining an inside perspective of ace experience.

Cerankowski, K.J., & Milks, M. (Eds.). (2014). *Asexualities: Feminist and Queer Perspectives*. London: Routledge.

A book-length collection of research and critical essays on theories of asexual orientation; the politics of asexuality; asexuality in media culture; masculinity and asexuality; health, disability, and medicalization; and asexual literary theory.

Chen, A. (2020). *Ace: What Asexuality Reveals about Desire, Society, and the Meaning of Sex*. Boston: Beacon Press.

Written by an ace-identified journalist, this book is full of perspectives from diverse asexual people, demonstrating the breadth of the ace spectrum. Well-researched and very readable.

Decker, J.S. (2014). *The Invisible Orientation: An Introduction to Asexuality*. New York: Carrel Books.

Written by an asexual on how it is to be asexual. A great introduction for those exploring their identity as ace and those close to them.

Oseman, A. (2020). *Loveless*. London: Harper Collins Children's Books.

A novel for young adults on coming to an asexual identity and starting university. Insightful, warm, witty. Winner of the YA Book Prize 2021.

Chapter 5

Exploring erotic diversity in heterosexuality

Keeping a queer eye for the straight guys

Julie Sale

The paradox of straight diversity

You could be forgiven for wondering why there is a chapter on heterosexuality in a book on erotic diversity in GSRD people. Heterosexuality is cast as normative which, by definition, is the opposite of diverse. It is seen as the orientation against which erotic diversity is defined; monolithic, bland straights in one camp and manifold, kaleidoscopic queers in the other (Ward, 2020). Although currently attracting more interest (Ward, 2020; Dean & Fischer, 2020), heterosexuality is less frequently examined in gender and sexuality studies, and when it is, it is considered to be 'nasty, boring and normative' (Beasley et al., 2012); nasty due to imposed gender roles, patriarchy, and the prevalence of violence in heterosexual relationships, boring due to the emphasis on the biological imperative of reproduction and, by default, penis in vagina penetrative sex, and normative as in homogeneous, lacking in variety and imagination (Beasley et al., 2015; Ward, 2020). Western society divides sexuality into heterosexuals on one side and every other identifier on the other, assuming that 'sexuality and gender are only relevant . . . for people of marginalised sexualities and genders', when 'Actually, sexuality and gender are highly relevant – and linked to struggles – for normative groups such as heterosexual and cisgender people too' (Barker, 2019, p. 13). Heterosexuality is conflated with heteronormativity, leaving 'little room for any reflection upon the possibility that non-normative and even innovative opportunities might be intrinsic within the mainstream, dominant practices of heterosexuality' (Beasley et al., 2012, p. 23).

Safe and effective therapy practice with heterosexual clients requires both an analysis of the impact that heteronormative scripts have on straight people and a recognition of the variety of erotic expression within a heterosexual orientation. The potential for generating and perpetuating shame in therapy with heterosexual clients is high. An unexamined heteronormative perspective can be dangerous in a straight therapist's work with their straight clients. Think of a couple therapy scenario where one partner has a kink that the other takes exception to, or one has had an affair, or, heavens forefend, one has visited a sex worker, and it's easy to imagine that the purpose of the therapy can become 'straightening up' that

DOI: 10.4324/9781003260608-6

behaviour by bringing it back into line with heteronormative expectations, rather than creating space to explore wider erotic and relational needs. Although attention is given, quite rightly, to how straight therapists can work safely with queer clients (Tilson, 2021), consideration must also be given the other way around. A queer therapist holding a perspective that straight clients are privileged oppressors of minority sexualities at worse and have a 'sick and boring' sexual culture at best (Ward, 2020) runs the risk of developing antagonistic, patronising, or dismissing therapeutic dynamics with straight clients or avoiding straight clients altogether. Cultural competence, critical thinking, and scrutiny of bias are required to work safely and effectively with heterosexual *and* queer clients.

Let's get this straight – terms and conditions

Heterosexuality is defined as 'of, relating to, or characterised by sexual or romantic attraction to or between people of the opposite sex' and heterosexual as 'a person who is sexually or romantically attracted to people of the opposite sex' (Merriam Webster, 2021a). Although a term that is assumed to be 'as old as procreation, as ancient as the lust of the fallen Eve and Adam . . . essential, unchanging: ahistorical' (Katz, 1995.2007, p. 13), heterosexuality is, in fact, a relatively modern invention. The earliest known use of the word 'heterosexual' is in an article by Dr James G. Kiernan, published in 1892 (Katz, 1995.2007; Kiernan, 1892), and is used to describe 'perverted' rather than 'normal' sex. In this use of the word, Kiernan describes heterosexuals as people who had 'inclinations to both sexes', so the 'hetero' did not mean interest in a different sex, but rather an interest in both sexes, what would today be considered as bi-sexual (Katz, 1995.2007; Kiernan, 1892). The term 'hetero-sexual' appears in Richard von Krafft-Ebing's *Psychopathia Sexualis* in 1893 and is used to describe the perversion of desiring sex for pleasure rather than for reproduction (Katz, 1995.2007; Krafft-Ebing, 1893). The concept of sex being for pleasure was counter to the reproductive imperative that has dominated Western concepts of heterosex since the 1600s (Katz, 1995.2007), and was placed firmly in the deviant category by Krafft-Ebing. It isn't until Freud's concept of the 'libido' that the 'pleasure principle' narrative begins to develop, and the drive for satisfaction is considered to be more primary than the drive for propagation (ibid.). In 1923 heterosexuality makes its first appearance in the Merriam-Webster dictionary, some 14 years after homosexuality (described as 'a morbid sexual passion for one of the same sex') was included, and was defined as a 'morbid sexual passion for one of the opposite sex' (ibid., p. 92), reflecting the continued pathologisation of heterosexual pleasure. As Katz (1995) writes: 'The advertising of a diseased homosexuality preceded the publicizing of a sick heterosexuality' (1995, p. 92). By the end of the 1920s heterosexuality 'had triumphed as dominant, sanctified culture' (ibid., p. 83), and by 1934 the Merriam-Webster definition changes to one that is currently recognisable; heterosexuality is a 'manifestation of sexual passion for one of the opposite sex; normal sexuality' (ibid., p. 92).

Heteronormativity was introduced as a word by Marcus Warner in 1991 (Warner, 1991), building on second-wave feminism's critique of patriarchy and gender structures (Rich, 1980; Rubin, 1997; Wittig, 1997; Herz & Johansson, 2015). The Merriam-Webster dictionary defines heteronormativity as 'of, relating to, or based on the attitude that heterosexuality is the only normal and natural expression of sexuality' (Merriam Webster, 2021b). In addition to the 'normal' and 'natural' narratives of heterosex (Katz, 1995.2007; Beasley et al., 2012), heteronormativity as a term encapsulates lifestyle expectations of marriage, monogamy, reproduction, and parenting (Herz & Johansson, 2015; Robinson, 2016; Dean & Fischer, 2020). It references biological essentialist gender identities and roles (Ward, 2020) and defines sex as penis in vagina penetration (Katz, 1995.2007; Beasley et al., 2012).

Heterosexuality and heteronormativity are not synonymous (Beasley et al., 2015). Heterosexuality is a sexual orientation, and heteronormativity is a dominant social narrative. Being heterosexual does not automatically make one heteronormative (Beasley et al., 2015). As Ward states, 'straight people are not reducible to straight culture. Many straight people relate to their heterosexuality in dazzlingly feminist and queer ways' (Ward, 2020, p. 153). At the same time 'straight people can be very attached to being straight, both erotically and culturally' (Ward, 2020, p. 157), and heteronormativity does not always serve heterosexuals well as 'institutionalized, normative heterosexuality regulates those kept within its boundaries as well as marginalizing and sanctioning those outside them' (Jackson, 2006, p. 105).

Sexual diversity and heterosexuality

Opposite sex attraction is only one facet of heterosexuality (Dean & Fischer, 2020, p. xiv). The World Health Organisation states the following:

> Sexuality is a central aspect of being human throughout life and encompasses sex, gender identities and roles, sexual orientation, eroticism, pleasure, intimacy and reproduction. Sexuality is experienced and expressed in thoughts, fantasies, desires, beliefs, attitudes, values, behaviours, practices, roles and relationships. While sexuality can include all of these dimensions, not all of them are always experienced or expressed. Sexuality is influenced by the interaction of biological, psychological, social, economic, political, cultural, ethical, legal, historical, religious and spiritual factors.
>
> (WHO, 2006)

Within this broad concept of sexuality, erotic diversity within heterosexuality is inevitable. The work of Zoologist and early Sexologist Alfred Kinsey (Kinsey et al., 1948, 1953) revealed that a variety of sexual expressions within a heterosexual identity was not uncommon, even in conservative 1950s America, demonstrating that erotic diversity in heterosexual people is not a recent phenomenon. His reports recorded that married people (at the time by definition heterosexual) had same-sex sexual experiences, engaged in extra-marital sex, and enjoyed sexual responses to sado-masochistic stories and biting.

Heterosexual diversity, however, is often framed as straight people becoming more queer as if only queer people have broad and colourful sexual practices (Ward, 2020). As Beasley, Brook and Holmes state, 'The critical canon has almost always assumed that subversive-transgression in sexuality occurs only for queer sexualities, and that possibilities for a more progressive heterosexuality lie in the degree to which hetero practices drift to the queer' (Beasley et al., 2012, p. 7).

Heterosexuals can be kinky (Sprott & Berkey, 2015), sexually transgressive (Clement, 1990; Bell, 2006), and non-monogamous (Klesse, 2014; Barker, 2005; Wilt et al., 2018).

They have anal sex (Aguilar, 2017; Branfman, 2017; Wignall et al., 2019; McBride & Fortenberry, 2010), they pay for sex, and they are paid for sex (Smith & Mac, 2018).

The problem is that within the context of heteronormativity, erotic diversity can be socially vilified and professionally pathologised rather than celebrated, as it is in queer culture (Ward, 2020). Sex and Relationship Education (SRE) only became compulsory in schools in England in September 2020, and due to the coronavirus pandemic, schools were allowed to delay implementation until summer 2021 (UK Parliament, 2021). Diversity campaigners managed to ensure the inclusion of LGBT identities and relationships in the requirements (Terrence Higgins Trust, 2017), and the concept of consent is integrated into the curriculum (Department for Education, 2019). However, the word 'pleasure' is not used once in the Guidance, and the emphasis remains on the prevention of STIs and unwanted pregnancies (Department for Education, 2019). Although parents will no longer be able to withdraw their children from compulsory relationship education or classes on reproduction, they are still able to remove their children from sex education (Parentkind, 2021). Heterosexual people in heteronormative societies have very little access to basic education on sex and relationships, let alone nuanced thinking about sex and gender.

Although not so pronounced in 'post closeted culture' (Seidman, 2002; Dean, 2014), the division of society into straights and queers, each with separate cultures, social groups, rituals, and lifestyles, is still an aspect of life for some demographics, meaning that many straight people have no real contact with queer people. Queer people in a heteronormative society cannot avoid examining the social constructs of sex, sexuality, and gender as their lived experience doesn't match societal messages. Straight people with non-heteronormative sexual preferences, a basic level of sex education, limited exposure to critical thinking about sexuality, or access to a community of like-preferenced people are vulnerable to isolation, deep shame, and distress (New et al., 2021). They can act on sexual interests that are considered diverse in straight culture, such as bondage or anal sex, without proper education or preparation, increasing the risk of hurting themselves or their sexual partners (Kink Lovers, 2021). They present to therapy believing they are weird, and tragically, they could well be met with a therapist whose own het-eronormative socialisation inclines them to agree (New et al., 2021). Challeng-ing heteronormative narratives about sex and consequent socialised bias about non-heteronormative sexual expression is central to safe therapeutic practice with heterosexual clients with diverse sexual preferences.

Kinky straights

Darren is a cis-gender, heterosexual male client in his 30s. He is in a long-term relationship with Sally, and they are due to have their first baby in a few months' time.

Darren comes to therapy in a heightened state of distress. He tells you that he is turned on by nappies and baby changing products. He knows this started when he was 11 years old when his baby sister was born. He loved the sight, smell, and feel of a new nappy, the wipes, and the cream. Darren has masturbated whilst holding or wearing nappies or using baby changing products since then. The whole experience, when he is engaged in it, is pleasurable and soothing for him. He masturbates this way around once a month when Sally has a girls' night out.

As his baby's arrival gets closer, Darren is becoming more and more concerned. There will be baby changing products around the house, and he is afraid he will become turned on at the sight and smell of them in the presence of the baby or Sally. He is completely clear that he is not at all sexually attracted to babies, the thought revolts him, but he is scared that Sally might think he is. He has never told her about this turn-on as he feels sure she would not understand, and he has no desire to bring the preference into his partnered sex life.

Darren describes his sex life with Sally as great and both emotionally and sexually fulfilling. He has no history of childhood sexual abuse or other trauma. He describes his childhood as normal, and he has a loving relationship with his parents and sister. He has no mental health problems and felt reasonably ok about his solo sexual behaviours until Sally became pregnant.

Self-Reflection

Take a moment to sit with your thoughts and feelings about Darren. Be honest with yourself about the impact this case has on you. Consider the following questions:

- How does Darren's story affect you?
- What thoughts or fears does this case raise in you?
- Have you ever heard of this sexual preference before? How do you judge it?

- What does your therapy training tell you about this kind of sexual preference?
- Do you think you could work therapeutically with Darren, or would you be tempted to refer him on?
- If you want to refer him on, why?
- If you want to work with him, what would your approach be?
- Do you see any safeguarding issues connected to Darren's preferences?
- Did you assume there would be a trauma history that contributed to Darren's sexual preference? If so, what in your training alerted you to this possibility?

From a heteronormative therapeutic perspective, Darren's turn-on would potentially be considered strange and worrying. Why would a grown man be into baby changing products? Maybe he is a covert or suppressed paedophile? Is there a safeguarding issue? There is nothing quite like an association between sexual arousal and children to loudly set off a general therapist's safeguarding alarm bells. Their training may have told them that non-normative sexual expression is always connected to an adverse childhood event or trauma (Money & Lamacz, 1990), although there is no evidence that people with kink preferences have a greater incidence of trauma history than the general population (Kleinplatz & Moser, 2004). They might be inclined to persist in that belief despite Darren's assertion to the contrary, spending much of the therapy excavating Darren's past to find an attachment wound or suppressed sexual abuse memory. A general therapist might be drawn to an attachment-based formulation, conceptualising Darren's sexual interest in baby products as part of an adaptation to an attachment breach caused by the arrival of his baby sister (Holmes, 1993). A standard therapeutic approach to clients presenting with kink preferences that are consensual and lawful, but feel unwanted, is to work towards stopping or reducing the sexual practice, rather than the more effective approach of expanding an understanding of it and integrating it into clients' sense of their erotic self (Neves, 2021). If we replaced the word 'kink' with 'same-sex' in this scenario, the problem with abstinence-based approaches to kink sexuality becomes even starker (Sale, 2019).

Through a sexology and diversity aware lens, Darren's preference for nappies and baby changing products may be seen simply as part of his erotic template (Neves, 2021), what would be described as a kink or a fetish, established by the impactful sensory experience of the sight, smell, and feel of baby changing products at the point of his emerging sexual development. From what we know so far, it is the sight, smell, and feel of the products that turn Darren on, not the fact they are typically used for babies, although of course, this would need to be checked out. A kink-informed therapist would normalise Darren's preference and give him space to air his understandable concern about the baby products being more freely available around his home when his new baby arrives. The differences between the contexts of Darren's solo sex practices and the context of changing his baby would be explored, along with practical considerations, such as using different brands of products for each situation.

Although all of the major professional bodies are signatories to the Memorandum of Understanding on Conversion Therapy V2 (BACP, 2022), the risk of 'accidental conversion therapy' is significant with regard to straight clients presenting with kinky sexual preferences (Sale, 2019). The talking therapy profession does not have a great track record in the treatment of people with so-called atypical sexual preferences (Langdridge, 2018), with legal and consensual activities still meeting diagnostic criteria for 'disorders' (First, 2014).

If the success of the *Fifty Shades of Grey* books and films is anything to go by, interest in kinky sex is prevalent in heterosexuality (Sprott & Berkey, 2015). Studies suggest that kink is an aspect that is present in approximately 23% of the population in terms of fantasy and expressed in behaviour by between 10% and 15% of the population (Sprott & Berkey, 2015). A significant number of these people will identify as straight. We have a responsibility therefore to educate ourselves on kink practices in service to our heterosexual clients, many of whom will be outside of an established kink community.

Chapter 9 in this volume presents a framework for uncovering and addressing anti-kink bias and guidance on how to develop competence in working with clients with kink preferences. Shahbaz and Chirinos (2017) have developed a *Healthy BDSM Checklist* to assist therapists in the assessment of safety in kink-based behaviours, structured around the exploration of dimensions including consent, wellness, values, and identity. These resources are a great place to start to learn about kink.

Heterosexual anal sex

Javed is a British man of Indian descent. He has regular casual sex with white women, avoiding women from his Indian culture as they are 'wife territory'. The last time he had casual sex, the woman inserted her finger into his anus, and he had the strongest orgasm of his life. Although it was the hottest sex he had ever had, Javed is now very worried that liking anal penetration means that he might be gay, and he has approached you to 'get rid of the gayness in him'.

Tara often talks about her sex life in her therapy sessions, which on the whole appears to be positive and pleasure-driven. She starts one session by saying, 'this might be too much information but, seriously, I am so sick of men thinking they can just stick their dick up my arse without asking? What is it about men and anal sex? They are obsessed. I blame porn!' She tells you that it is typical these days for 'boys', as she calls them, to assume that 'girls' are all up for anal sex. She says she and her friends often find anal sex painful but feel they have to go along with it as 'he' is clearly enjoying it.

Heterosexual anal sex has been a part of straight erotic imagination and behaviour for centuries, with depictions of it found in art and artefacts 'since antiquity' (McBride & Fortenberry, 2010). Despite this, anal sex has, until relatively recently, largely been associated with gay men (Branfam et al., 2017; Wignall et al., 2019) and with sexual health risks (McBride & Fortenberry, 2010). Research estimates that around a third of heterosexual adults have engaged in some form of anal sex (Habel et al., 2018), making heterosexual anal sex common. The ubiquity of references to anal sex in popular culture and its prevalence in heterosexual pornography suggests that, like oral sex, it is gradually becoming less stigmatised (McBride & Fortenberry, 2010). The term 'pegging' was coined by Dan Savage in 2001, with the help of a survey of his column readers, to describe the act of a female penetrating a male anally with a dildo (Aguilar, 2017). Having a word that specifically describes heterosexual anal penetration neatly distances straight anal sex from gay sex, at once claiming its eroticism and establishing its straightness (Aguilar, 2017).

To throw an even queerer light onto anal sexual behaviour, data from NATSAL 3, (NATSAL, 2013), a nationally representative survey of British adults aged 16–74 conducted in 2010–2012, suggest that around 22% of men with same-sex sexual experiences in the previous year identified as heterosexual. Sexual behaviour and sexual identity are not always concordant; men have sex with men and identify as straight (Pathela et al., 2006).

Javed associates anal penetration with gay men and is not aware that it is a form of sexual expression that all sexualities and genders engage in. As his therapist, we can explain to him that his sexual response to receptive anal penetration is completely normal and does not influence his heterosexual identity or his masculinity, and we can guide him to question the logic of a part of human anatomy being exclusively the preserve of gay men.

Tara's experiences point to both the increased acceptability of anal sex in contemporary heterosex and to the lack of education on how to do it well. If the only source of education on anal sex is its performance in pornography, the importance of hygiene, preparation, relaxation, graduation, and, essentially, lubrication will likely be missed. Poor education on best practices of anal sex increases the chances of it being painful (Branfam et al., 2017; Wignall et al., 2019; McBride, 2017). As Tara's therapist, we can direct her to sources of information on how to better prepare for anal sex. A simple Google search on 'anal sex guide' lists 'about 151,000,000 results' of sites offering articles, videos, hints, and tips on safe and pleasurable anal sex.

We can also help Tara to question the unexamined heteronormative script that is influencing her attitudes to sex with straight men. Tara and her friends tolerate painful anal sex because their sexual partners enjoy it. Feminist writers have long pointed out the patriarchal basis of heteronormativity, its inherent misogyny, and prioritising of male pleasure over female safety (Ward, 2020). This session could be an opportunity to invite Tara to question the appropriateness of such an imbalanced attitude to sexual pleasure.

We could talk to Tara about active consent and perhaps introduce her to Dr Betty Martin's Wheel of Consent (Martin & Dalzen, 2021). This model gives us a framework for considering the dynamic dimensions of consent in the receiving and giving of touch. Uniquely in the consideration of consent, Martin's model distinguishes between who is doing the touching and who it is for, within four quadrants; giving, receiving, taking, and allowing. In the 'give' quadrant, a person is doing something for the pleasure of another, 'you look tired, would you like a back rub?' In the 'receive' quadrant, a person is having something done to them for their own pleasure, 'I would love a back rub'. In the 'take' quadrant, a person is doing something to another for their own pleasure, 'I want to touch you – may I rub your back?', and in the 'allow' quadrant, a person is having something done to them for the pleasure of the other, 'sure, you can rub my back for a while'. Each quadrant of the Wheel is acceptable within the boundary of consent. The model emphasises that it is not possible to truly give or receive consent without clarity in communication, intention, and action.

In terms of the Wheel of Consent, the men who are attempting anal penetration with Tara are operating in the shadow side of the 'take' quadrant. They are doing a sexual action to Tara for their pleasure without her express consent. Explaining the basic principles of the Wheel of Consent to Tara can help her to understand how to move from the non-consensual, passive acceptance of anal penetration to an informed 'allow' or 'receive' position.

Non-monogamous straights

Zack is a serial cheater. He has never been able to stay faithful to his wife of 24 years, Tia, much as he loves and respects her. He explains himself by saying that he can't resist flirting with women as it makes him feel alive. The flirting inevitably leads to an emotional connection and sex outside of his marriage. He has never considered leaving Tia, and he hates that his behaviour hurts her. He says he wouldn't mind if Tia had other lovers, so long as she didn't leave him. Tia is a psycho-therapist, and she thinks Zack has issues with commitment due to his parents breaking up when he was a young child, and his mother leaving him with his emotionally detached father. Zack and Tia have been in and out of couples therapy throughout their marriage, but Zack has not been able to change.

Lisa and Tan have enjoyed swinging since the start of their relationship. They take pride in their non-conservative attitudes to sex and are open about their swinging practices with their friends. Once a month they have a big night out in their local swingers club. Their rules are that they always stay in the same room, even when having sex with other people. On their last visit, Lisa left Tan to visit the toilet and, on the way back, was approached by a couple she had been flirting with earlier. She went with them into a private room to have sex without letting Tan know. Tan sees this as a serious breach of their agreement and feels he can no longer trust Lisa. They have not been to the club since, and they are arguing most days. They access couples therapy to see if they can work things out.

Cherry and Simon have been reading about polyamory. They have both always thought that loving only one person at a time makes no sense, but the idea of changing the structure of their marriage worries them. They seek out a couples therapist to explore the idea of consensual non-monogamy further and to work out if and how they could open their relationship to other sexual and emotional partners.

Monogamy is a central tenet of heteronormativity, perpetuated by the evolutionary anthropology narrative that pair-bonding evolved to ensure the safe rearing of our young (Fisher, 2017). Although deeply inculcated in the heterosexual conscious, the naturalness of monogamy is a contested premise, with the almost non-existence of monogamy in nature and the global prevalence of infidelity in human societies given as evidence that the 'practice or state of having a sexual relationship with only one partner' is perhaps not innate (Ryan & Jetha, 2010, pp. 134–137). Ryan and Jetha argue that monogamy is a social construct that developed with the advent of agriculturalism, which created a social requirement for property and paternity protection not necessary in a hunter-gatherer society (Ryan & Jetha, 2010). The last two decades have seen a building interest in the concept of consensual non-monogamy and polyamory (Anapol, 1997; Hardy & Easton, 1997:2017; Fern, 2020; Kauppi, 2021), challenging the idea that adults are only able to love one intimate partner at a time.

The unquestioned monogamy standard prevents heterosexual people from openly challenging its feasibility or honestly discussing their sexual and relationship needs with their partners. Weight is added to the monogamy imperative by the romance myth, the idea that one person can fulfil all of our emotional and sexual needs (Perel, 2007), resulting in secrecy, betrayal, and non-consensual non-monogamy, otherwise known as affairs.

By repeatedly having sexual relationships outside of his marriage to Tia, Zack is engaging in non-consensual non-monogamy. The influence of his childhood on his sexual behaviour is certainly worthy of investigation in therapy but so is an examination of the assumed monogamy principle on which the couple's heterosexual marriage is based. What if polyamory is more of a natural relationship style for Zack than monogamy? This perspective shifts the focus of the couple therapy to how Zack and Tia manage a mixed polyam/mono orientation rather than trying to fix Zack's unfaithful behaviour.

Lisa and Tan are engaging in consensual non-monogamy in their swinging practice (Wilt et al., 2018). The problems they are currently facing appear to be more about a breach of their relationship agreement than the swinging per se, yet they run the risk to be exposed to heteronormative couples therapy in which their swinging may be cited as the core issue.

Cherry and Simon are an increasingly common type of couple accessing sex and relationship therapy (Fern, 2020; Kauppi, 2021). They are curious about consensual non-monogamy and are looking for guidance from their therapist. Their challenge will be to find a couples therapist with sufficient knowledge of relationship diversity to support them, rather than question the appropriateness of their relationship choices.

Conclusion

Unexamined heteronormativity harms heterosexual people (Jackson, 2006). To free heterosexuals from the shaming straight jacket, heterosexual therapists need to examine how much of their perspective on sex and relationships is an uncritical absorption of heteronormative cultural scripts. Queer therapists can share their sexual diversity knowledge with, and extend their well-versed respect for diversity to, their straight clients. We need to remove our heteronormative lens when viewing heterosexual clients *and* queer clients. Through our sex-positive, pleasure-based, sexual diversity lens, we can see a more expansive and nuanced version of sexuality, one based on more than gender as the defining feature of orientation, and we can move our collective conscience to van Anders' vision of there being more similarity in sexualities than differences.

> I see a sexual diversity perspective as a stage in a sequence that focuses initially on sexual minorities as 'other' relative to an unstated normative backdrop, then recognizes that minorities are minoritized relative to majorities and focuses additionally on sexual majorities and minority-majority difference, and then understands that positionality is relative and dynamic, with sexualities existing within social locations in such a way that there can be heterogeneity within sexualities and commonality between them.
>
> (van Anders, 2015, p. 1187)

References

Aguilar, J. (2017). Pegging and the heterosexualization of anal sex: An analysis of savage Love advice. *Queer Studies in Media and Popular Culture*, 2(3), 275–292.

Anapol, D. (1997). *Polyamory: The New Love without Limits*. San Raphael: IntiNet Resource Centre.

BACP. (2022). *Memorandum of Understanding on Conversion Therapy in the UK. Verison 2*. Updated March 2022. https://www.bacp.co.uk/media/14985/memorandum-of-understanding-on-conversion-therapy-in-the-uk-march-2022.pdf. (Accessed: 22 August 2021).

Barker, M.J. (2005). This is my partner, and this is my . . . partner's partner: Constructing a polyamorous identity in a monogamous world. *Journal of Constructivist Psychology*, 8(1), 75–88.

Barker, M.J. (2019). *BACP Good Practice across the Counselling Professions 001 Gender, Sexual, and Relationship Diversity (GSRD)*. Lutterworth: BACP.

Beasley, C., Brook, H., & Holmes, M. (2012). *Heterosexuality in Theory and Practice*. New York: Routledge.

Beasley, C., Brook, H., & Holmes, M. (2015). Heterodoxy: Challenging orthodoxies about heterosexuality. *Sexualities*, 18(5/6), 681–697.

Bell, D. (2006). Bodies, technologies, spaces: On 'dogging'. *Sexualities*, 9(4), 387–407.

Branfman, J., Stiritz, S., & Anderson, E. (2017). Relaxing the straight male anus: Decreasing homohysteria around anal eroticism. *Sexualities*, 21(1–2), 109–127.

Clement, U. (1990). Surveys of heterosexual behaviour. *Annual Review of Sex Research*, 1(1), 45–74.

Dean, J.J. (2014). Straights. In *Heterosexuality in Post Closeted Culture*. New York: NYU Press.

Dean, J.J., & Fischer, N.L. (Eds.). (2020). *Routledge International Handbook of Heterosexualities Studies*. London and New York: Routledge.

Department for Education. (2019). *Relationships Education, Relationships and Sex Education (RSE) and Health Education: Statutory Guidance for Governing Bodies, Proprietors, Head Teachers, Principals, Senior Leadership Teams, Teachers*. https:// assets.publishing.service.gov.uk/government/uploads/system/uploads/attachment_data/ file/908013/Relationships_Education__Relationships_and_Sex_Education__RSE__ and_Health_Education.pdf (Accessed: 21 August 2021).

Fern, J. (2020). *Polysecure: Attachment, Trauma and Consensual Nonmonogamy*. Portland: Thorntree Press.

First, M.B. (2014). *DSM-5 and Paraphilic Disorders. Journal of the American Academy of Psychiatry and the Law*, 42, 191–201.

Fisher, H. (2017). *Anatomy of Love. A Natural History of Mating, Marriage, and Why We Stray*. London: WW Norton and Co.

Habel, M.A., Leichliter, J.S., Dittus, P.J., Spicknall, I.H., & Aral, S.O. (2018). Heterosexual anal and oral sex in adolescents and adults in the United States, 2011–2015. *Sexually Transmitted Diseases*, 45(12), 775–782.

Hardy, J.W., & Easton, D. (1997:2017). *The Ethical Slut, Third Edition: A Practical Guide to Polyamory, Open Relationships, and Other Freedoms in Sex and Love*. California and New York: Ten Speed Press.

Herz, M., & Johansson, T. (2015). The normativity of the concept of heteronormativity. *Journal of Homosexuality*, 62(8), 1009–1020.

Holmes, J. (1993). *John Bowlby and Attachment Theory: Makers of Modern Psychotherapy*. London and New York: Routledge.

Jackson, S. (2006). *Gender, Sexuality and Heterosexuality: The Complexity (and Limits) of Heteronormativity*. London, Thousand Oaks, CA and New Delhi: SAGE Publications.

Katz, J.N. (1995.2007). *The Invention of Heterosexuality*. Chicago and London: The University of Chicago Press.

Kauppi, M. (2021). *Polyamory: A Clinical Toolkit for Therapists (and Their Clients)*. New York: Rowman and Littlefield Publishers.

Kiernan, J.G. (1892). *Responsibility in Sexual Perversion*. Chicago: Medical Recorder May 1882.

Kink Lovers. (2021). https://kinklovers.com/resources/bdsm-education/ (Accessed: 21 August 2021).

Kinsey, A., Pomeroy, W., & Martin, C. (1948). *Sexual Behavior in the Human Male*. Philadelphia: Saunders.

Kinsey, A., Pomeroy, W., Martin, C., & Gebhard, P. (1953). *Sexual Behavior in the Human Female*. Philadelphia: Saunders.

Kleinplatz, P.J., & Moser, C. (2004). Towards clinical guidelines for working with BDSM clients. *Contemporary Sexuality*, 38(6), 1, 4–5.

Klesse, C. (2014). Polyamory: Intimate practice, identity or sexual orientation? *Sexualities*, 17(1/2), 81–99.

Krafft-Ebing, R. (1893). *Psychopathia Sexualis, with Especial Reference to Contrary Sexual Instinct: A Medico-Legal Study*. Philadelphia: F.A. Davis.

Langdridge, D. (2018). *Kink, Pathology and Perversion: A Critique* [Video file]. www.youtube.com/watch?v=IGDH_e80yls&feature=youtu.be (Accessed: 21 August 2021).

Martin, B., & Dalzen, R. (2021). *The Art of Receiving and Giving: The Wheel of Consent*. Oregon: Luminaire Press.

McBride, K.R. (2017). Heterosexual women's anal sex attitudes and motivations: A focus group study. *Journal of Sex Research*, 56(3), 367–377.

McBride, K.R., & Fortenberry, J.D. (2010). Heterosexual anal sexuality and anal sex behaviors: A review. *Journal of Sex Research*, 47(2), 123–136.

Merriam Webster. (2021a). www.merriam-webster.com/dictionary/heterosexual (Accessed: 17 August 2021).

Merriam Webster. (2021b).www.merriam-webster.com/dictionary/heteronormative (Accessed: 18 August 2021).

Money, J., & Lamacz, M. (1990). *Vandalized Lovemaps: Paraphilic Outcome of Seven Cases of Paediatric Sexology*. New York: Prometheus Books.

NATSAL. (2013). *Natsal-3*. https://www.natsal.ac.uk/natsal-survey/natsal-3 (Accessed: 21 August 2021).

Neves, S. (2021). *Compulsive Sexual Behaviours: A Psycho-Sexual Treatment Guide for Clinicians*. Oxon: Routledge.

New, C.M., Batchelor, C.L., Shimmel-Bristow, A., Schaeffer-Smith, M., Magsam, E., Bridges, S.K., Brown, E.L., & McKenzie, T. (2021). In their own words: Getting it right for kink clients. *Sexual and Relationship Therapy*, 36(4), 313–317.

Parentkind. (2021). www.parentkind.org.uk/Parents/Relationships-Education-and-Relationships-and-Sex-Education-RE- (Accessed: 21 August 2021).

Pathela, P., Hajat, A., Schillingher, J., Blank, S., Sell, R., & Motashair, F. (2006). Discordance between sexual behavior and self-reported sexual identity: A population-based survey of New York City men. *Annals of Internal Medicine*, 145(6), 416–425.

Perel, E. (2007). *Mating in Captivity, Sex Lies and Domestic Bliss*. London: Hodder and Stoughton.

Rich, A. (1980). Compulsory heterosexuality and lesbian existence. *Signs*, 5(4), 631–660.

Robinson, B.A. (2016). *Heteronormativity and Homonormativity* (pp. 1–3). The Wiley Blackwell Encyclopaedia of Gender and Sexuality Studies. Wiley: London

Rubin, G. (1997). *The Traffic in Women: Notes on the "Political Economy" of Sex*. New York and London: Monthly Review Press.

Ryan, C., & Jetha, C. (2010). *Sex at Dawn. How We Mate, Why We Stray, and What It Means for Modern Relationships*. London: Harper Collins.

Sale, J. (2019). *Are You an Accidental Conversion Therapist?* www.theinstituteofsexology.org/blog/are-you-an-accidental-conversion-therapist (Accessed: 21 August 2021).

Seidman, S. (2002). *Beyond the Closet: The Transformation of Gay and Lesbian Life*. New York: Routledge.

Shahbaz, C., & Chirinos, P. (2017). *Becoming a Kink Aware Therapist*. New York: Routledge.

Smith, M., & Mac, J. (2018). *Revolting Prostitutes. The Fight for Sex Workers' Rights*. London and Brooklyn, New York: Verso.

Sprott, R.A., & Berkey, B. (2015). Media review: At the intersection of sexual orientation and alternative sexualities: Issues raised by fifty shades of grey. *Psychology of Sexual Orientation and Gender Diversity*, 2(4), 506–507.

Terrence Higgins Trust. (2017). *Shh – No Talking: LGBT-Inclusive Sex and Relationships Education in the UK*. www.tht.org.uk/endthesilence (Accessed: 21 August 2021).

Tilson, J. (2021). *Queering Your Therapy Practice: Queer Theory, Narrative Therapy, and Imagining New Identities*. New York: Routledge.

UK Parliament. https://commonslibrary.parliament.uk/research-briefings/sn06103/ (Accessed: 21 August 2021).

van Anders, S.M. (2015). Beyond sexual orientation: Integrating gender/sex and diverse sexualities via sexual configurations theory. *Archives of Sexual Behaviour*, 44, 1177–1213.

Ward, J. (2020). *The Tragedy of Heterosexuality*. New York: New York University Press.

Warner, M. (1991). Introduction: Fear of a queer planet. *Social Text*, 9(4), 3–17.

Wittig, M. (1997). One is not born a woman. In L. Nicholson (Ed.), *The Second Wave: A Reader in Feminist Theory* (pp. 265–271). New York: Routledge.

WHO. (2006). *The World Health Report 2006: Working Together for Health*. Geneva: WHO.

Wignall, L., Scoats, R., Anderson, E., & Morales, L. (2019). A qualitative study of heterosexual men's attitudes toward and practices of receiving anal stimulation. *Culture, Health & Sexuality*, 22(6), 675–689.

Wilt, J., Harrison, M.A., & Michael, C. (2018). Attitudes and experiences of swinging couples. *Psychology & Sexuality*, 9(1), 1–16.

Chapter 6

Intersex-centred sex therapy and relationship counselling

Six commonly neglected concerns of intersex adults

Dr Y. Gávriel Ansara

Who are intersex people?

Intersex is an umbrella term to describe people with one or more of over 40 innate physiological characteristics. Although these characteristics are natural manifestations of human biological diversity, contemporary medical norms pathologise and marginalise people whose bodies do not fit popular definitions of strictly female or male bodies. Intersex characteristics can involve chromosomes, genitals, gonads, hormones, and aspects of reproductive anatomy, including features present at birth and innate characteristics that develop later in life, such as during puberty. Although some people's intersex characteristics may be identified at birth, intersex characteristics are often not discovered until later in life. Some intersex features are not externally visible at any stage of life. Contrary to stereotypes, it is not usually possible during regular social interactions to determine whether or not someone is intersex. This means you are likely to have met intersex people before without knowing it.

Respectful use of the term "intersex" is as an adjective, not a noun (i.e., "an intersex person", "person with intersex characteristics", or "person with an intersex variation", but not "an intersex", "an intersexual", or "the intersexed"). The adjective to describe a non-intersex person is endosex (i.e., "an endosex person"). Although some people prefer to describe their specific intersex characteristics, research suggests that intersex is the most preferred term among actual intersex people (e.g., Jones et al., 2016). Despite this documented preference, many endosex professionals and parents continue to promote pathologising language such as "Disorders of Sex Development" (sic), which many intersex people experience as inaccurate, offensive, and harmful. "DSD" language promotes negative bias by constructing intersex people as having disordered bodies that require medical intervention to "fix" – often without actual intersex people's informed consent. Despite efforts by some clinicians to keep the initialism of "DSD" while shifting to "*Differences* of Sex Development", this option still marginalises intersex people. It disregards scientific evidence of human biological diversity. "DSD" language is also closely linked with ongoing human rights violations against intersex people, so intersex people can experience endosex providers who use this terminology as emotionally distressing and unsafe.

DOI: 10.4324/9781003260608-7

One popular misconception about so-called "sex chromosomes" is that all people have either XX or XY chromosomes and that this genotype determines people's so-called "biological sex". This reductionist, unscientific ideology excludes people with intersex combinations such as XXY (Klinefelter's), XO (Turner's), and XXXY, XXXXY, and XYY (three Klinefelter's variants). Recent scientific findings show that chromosomes alone do not determine physiological sex characteristics as commonly assumed and that so-called "biological sex" is plastic and mosaic, not static, deterministic, or dimorphic (Ah-King & Nylin, 2010; Joel, 2021; Joel et al., 2015, 2020).

Sanz (2017) critiqued the Anglocentric/Eurocentric sex binary – the belief that there are two distinct and natural sexes, female and male – as an untested epistemological framework and rejected the scientific legitimacy of "biological sex" as "a circular network that reproduces itself precisely because it has no clear referent" (Sanz, 2017, p. 3). Despite its lack of scientific validity, this sex binary and the construct of "biological sex" continue to be invoked to justify human rights abuses against intersex people. Even in regions where attempting to change people's sexuality and gender to fit societal norms is criminalised, endosex medical professionals continue to inflict medically unnecessary and invasive psychological, hormonal, and surgical procedures on intersex people. These interventions, typically beginning during infancy and often continuing through adolescence and even into adulthood, are often justified due to heterosexist and ethnocentric assumptions about people's psychosocial needs. Later in this chapter, I explore some specific examples of coerced and involuntary surgical interventions imposed on intersex people.

Intersex inclusion or coercive queering?

For over 15 years, I have contributed to intersex advocacy, education, and outreach initiatives in local, national, and international contexts as a professional and community member. I testified at the historic Australian Senate Committee Inquiry on the involuntary or coerced sterilisation of intersex people in Australia. I helped to develop the mental health practitioner training for the Yellow Tick accreditation initiative. During that time, I encountered many nominally "queer" publications *about* intersex people *without* input from actual intersex people (see also Ansara, 2021, on reducing bias in professional communications). Numerous queer theorists and gender studies scholars have purported to advocate on intersex people's behalf without ever listening to – much less elevating – the communications of actual intersex people.

Given the reasonable mistrust with which many intersex people view these fields of study and the fact that many intersex people do not self-identify as "queer", some people in intersex communities are likely to ask what a book chapter on intersex people is doing in a "queer"-themed book. This chapter has been included *precisely because* nominally queer, endosex professionals and communities need to acknowledge that being subsumed under the umbrella of "queer" can feel profoundly alienating for intersex people.

Ansara (2010, 2015) explained *coercive queering* as a practice that delegitimises people's understanding of their genders and bodies by lumping people under a "queer" umbrella without their consent. Coercive queering functions at both experiential and structural levels. For intersex people, coercive queering enacts *endosexism*, a term to describe how endosex people and lived experiences are valued and prioritised. In contrast, intersex people and lived experiences are simultaneously devalued and erased (cf. Holmes, 2016). Coercive queering often involves the non-consensual objectification of intersex people's lived experiences, such as reducing intersex people to mere tropes and rhetoric in queer theory. Including this chapter in a nominally "queer"-themed book is a strategic and pragmatic resistance to intersex erasure and coercive queering that I hope will raise awareness among endosex therapists and provide intersex people with a useful self-advocacy tool that can be shared with endosex health professionals.

Scope of this chapter

Few therapeutic publications address the specific erotic, affectional, and intimate relationship needs of intersex adults. To address this gap, I focus on only a few relevant and neglected therapeutic themes frequently raised by actual intersex people and communities in these three dimensions of lived experience. I hope other publications will fill the remaining gaps.

Some key neglected concerns of intersex adults

The following are six key neglected concerns relevant to the erotic, affectional, and intimate relationship needs of intersex adults:

- Epistemic injustice.
- Endosexist norms and standards.
- Medical trauma, impeded interoceptive awareness, and iatrogenic alexithymia.
- Disclosure and stigma management.
- Shame, self-worth, and relationship capital.
- Barriers to erotic, affectional, and intimate relationship boundaries.

After discussing each neglected area of concern, I guide sex therapists and relationship counsellors on how to adapt their existing practices.

Concern 1: epistemic injustice

Identifying concerns

The term *epistemic injustice* (Fricker, 2007) has been applied to describe how inequitable access to knowledge production and communication can perpetuate the systemic oppression of intersex people (Carpenter, 2016; Hart & Shakespeare-Finch,

2021). Fricker (2007) delineated two forms of epistemic injustice: *Testimonial injustice*, which occurs when people's accounts of their lived experiences are discounted, disbelieved, or treated as less authoritative due to their marginalised status; and *hermeneutical injustice*, which refers to challenges people face when trying to understand and communicate their own lived experiences, due to these experiences having been excluded from the collective conceptual and linguistic resources of their society.

Identifying and meeting the sex therapy and relationship counselling needs of adults with intersex characteristics can be fraught and complicated, given the manifold internal diversity among this population. Both forms of epistemic injustice affect intersex people's ability to share and validate their own lived experiences. Carpenter (2016) identified two forms of hermeneutical injustice faced by intersex people: One form occurs through societal identity discourse that, by using identity-focused language, mischaracterises intersex human rights concerns as being about sexual orientation and gender identity instead of being about bodily autonomy. Coercive queering (Ansara, 2010, 2015) of intersex people is an example of this form of hermeneutical injustice. The second hermeneutical injustice is perpetuated through "a deliberate culture of secrecy" (Carpenter, 2016, p. 79) that ensures intersex people lack the vocabulary to make sense of their everyday lived experiences and histories, combined with discriminatory clinical language that denies intersex people and their endosex parents the opportunity to discuss intersex people's bodies outside of an endosexist deficit perspective.

Carpenter quoted Holmes's (2011) analysis showing that "silencing is precisely the point of the new terminology". Holmes's article critiqued a so-called "consensus" statement that medical professionals made *about* intersex people *without* prioritising any input from actual intersex people and blatantly disregarding the consensus among real intersex people and communities. Holmes explored how this statement functioned as a systemic barrier that stigmatised intersex people's bodies and denied intersex people the opportunity to determine authoritative descriptions of their own embodiment. Attempts by endosex professionals and professional bodies to elucidate intersex lived experiences are often similarly hindered by this combination of erasure, pathologising, and refusal to accept intersex people as the best authorities about their own bodies. Intersex people are also excluded from normative curricula (Brömdal et al., 2021) and from media representations of adults with erotic, affectional, and intimate relationship needs.

Many people with marginalised innate physiological characteristics cannot safely disclose details of their lived experiences in print. Among the intersex people who spoke with me about their erotic, affectional, and intimate relationship lived experiences for this chapter, Bonnie Hart was the only person who wished to be identified by name. All other representations are anonymised composites drawn from frequently recurring clinical circumstances to address ethical concerns.

Bonnie Hart (she/her) is an intersex woman, peer worker, advocate, content specialist, and social science researcher who has investigated how people born with intersex characteristics navigate the complex psychosocial and medical concerns involved in accessing safe healthcare and psychosocial services. Bonnie has served in leadership roles with Intersex Peer Support Australia (formerly the Androgen Insensitivity Syndrome [AIS] Support Group Australia [AISSGA]) and the Yellow Tick initiative, through which she has supported organisations and service providers to develop intersex-inclusive practices through delivery of training and policy review. Bonnie is also an original signatory of *The Darlington Statement* (2017), an intersex-led consensus statement developed by people from intersex communities in Aotearoa/New Zealand and the unceded Aboriginal lands colonially known as "Australia".

During our interview for this chapter, Bonnie and I discussed our shared insight that practitioner acknowledgement of epistemic injustice is pivotal to understanding the therapeutic needs of intersex people. Considering the many concerns that have been silenced and how much has remained unaddressed due to the exclusion of intersex people from processes of knowledge production about their own embodiment, Bonnie (25 March 2022, by Zoom video, audio recording only) explained that

> this is an onion. Where the centre of the onion lies is hard to determine because we are talking about populations of people who have limited access to knowledge about themselves, their bodies, and their experiences, and how to place those selves, bodies, and experiences within social, relationship, family, structural, clinical, and legal contexts.

Although people's sources of knowledge about sex and sex education vary widely by sociocultural factors, media representations are often influential. Given the disproportionate gap in representations of intersex people, endosex practitioners often fail to anticipate the devastating impact epistemic injustice can have on the erotic, affectional, and intimate relationship lives of intersex people.

In addition to intersex people's bodies being problematised, Bonnie noted that, in the absence of basic education to understand their bodies and experiences, "a lot of that responsibility comes back onto the person to have to know, advocate, and discuss these difficulties with whoever they're engaging with". This responsibility can be challenging to accept "if your body isn't stereotypically male or female, if you actually have an experience of those differences being pathologised earlier in life, and if discussions around sex exclude you, because you don't often know where you stand in that scenario".

Hart and Shakespeare-Finch (2021) shared some examples of epistemic injustice from *Our collective story* (2017), a collection of reflective writings developed during AISSGA Intersex Peer Support meetings:

> It was always a day filled with mixed emotions she couldn't quite name. . . .
> She didn't have the words to describe to her mother how this felt. Instead,

she wouldn't mention it, in the hope that this would minimise or erase what had just happened.

(p. 10)

They never told a lie about their body, not knowingly. How was it possible to tell the truth about your body without knowing what intersex was? What language is used to describe it?

(p. 10)

It wasn't until 10 years later she learnt the whole truth, that her "ovaries" were actually testes, and that she would discover a whole community of amazing people like her.

(p. 11)

These brief examples illustrate how epistemic injustice can affect intersex people's capacity to make sense of and communicate about their embodiment and lived experiences.

What can practitioners do?

The most helpful thing practitioners can do to address epistemic injustice is to treat intersex people as the best authorities about their lived experiences. Recognising people's authority as knowers about themselves is an essential component of intersex-centred care known as *cultural humility* (Tervalon & Murray-García, 1998). Whether loving parents, concerned partners, altruistic researchers, or well-intentioned health professionals, *no one* can adequately represent intersex people *without* listening to, prioritising, and elevating what actual intersex people wish to share. By practising cultural humility, practitioners can address testimonial injustice and begin to learn about and promote the in-group intersex community language needed to rectify hermeneutical injustice. Genuinely intersex-centred care means *only* intersex people themselves are communicating on their own behalf or with consensual communication support, without uninvited proxies or substitutes. For participants who find spoken words difficult, such as people with neurodivergent and/or disability-related needs, practitioners need to integrate alternative and augmentative communication options (also known as AAC; see Chan, 2022).

The absence of shared collective resources for making sense of and communicating one's intersex lived experiences in an endosexist society requires sustained clinical attention. When establishing therapeutic relationships with intersex people, sex therapists and relationship counsellors can explicitly acknowledge epistemic injustice. To rectify epistemic injustice, practitioners can do the following:

• Evaluate the extent to which people's current language feels affirming and accurate for them.

- Explore whether people are familiar with the intersex-affirming language to describe their own bodies and lived experiences.
- Connect people with intersex community resources that use affirming language to describe their bodies and experiences.
- Guide intersex people to develop their own affirming and accurate language to describe their bodies and lived experiences.
- Model the use of intersex-affirming language with therapy participants and in professional spheres when communicating with colleagues and professional bodies.
- Encourage endosex intimate partners of intersex adults to use the affirming language intersex people prefer for themselves.

Concern 2: endosexist norms and standards

Identifying concerns

Practitioners' use of endosexist conceptual frameworks in sex and relationship therapy disadvantages intersex people by treating endosex people as the standard reference point against which all people's bodies and experiences are evaluated. One widespread endosexist norm is invoked when therapists conflate people's sex characteristics with concepts such as "sexual orientation" and "gender identity". This conflation has resulted in the failure of human rights frameworks such as the *Yogyakarta Principles* to protect actual intersex people's human rights (Carpenter, 2020). When this conflation occurs, therapists misconstrue intersex as a matter of *identity* and can inaccurately evaluate intersex people as having confusion about their gender and sexuality when they do not. Intersex people have many different ways of describing their bodies and lived experiences. Intersex people can have any sexual orientation, including straight/heterosexual. Despite the continued misrepresentation of intersex people as a so-called "third gender", intersex characteristics are distinct from gender. Many intersex people have fixed, binary genders and identify unambiguously as women or men. Many non-binary and agender people are endosex. Unfortunately, the conflation of intersex people with non-binary gender erases the diversity of both intersex and endosex people's lived experiences and, in so doing, contributes to harmful public policy and legislation (see Carpenter, 2018). In addition, a national study from the unceded Aboriginal lands colonially known as "Australia" found that most intersex respondents (55.3%) did *not* consider themselves to be part of "the LGBTIQ community" and over a third (38.3%) reported that they did *not* consider participating in "the Australian LGBTIQ community" to be a positive experience (Hill et al., 2020). Even this small sample of intersex people highlighted that referring intersex people to intersex-specific community organisations is crucial.

The distinction between identity and embodiment for intersex people is vital for practitioners to grasp due to its *clinical* implications. For example, many intersex people who have achieved clarity about their sexuality and gender do not automatically have a comparable degree of clarity about their *embodiment*. They may seek thera-peutic support to help them to make sense of and communicate about their bodies, and to achieve erotic satisfaction alone or with other people. Endosex practitioners need to be aware that intersex people who have a well-developed understanding of their sexuality and gender and no struggle with their *identities* can still struggle to achieve a comfortable relationship with their *bodies*. Bonnie explained that

> even if you do have a binary gender, which most intersex people do, under-standing if you have some variations in your sex characteristics and how that information applies to you can be difficult, particularly if it's being talked about in binarised terms or heteronormative terms as well.
>
> This heteronormative view around the treatment model that people sub-scribe to and parents subscribe to presupposes a particular type of sexual orientation, presupposes what people would want to do with their bodies, and what will be important to them.
>
> (personal communication on Zoom, 25 March 2022)

Many endosex medical professionals still use endosexist standards like those Bonnie described to justify non-consensual interventions during childhood (Holmes, 2016; Davis, 2011). Endosexist standards can affect people's view of their own bodies, their erotic communication skills, and their erotic lives. The lack of open discussion with key attachment figures during puberty and the lack of intersex-inclusive sex education (see Brömdal et al., 2021) can inhibit the capac-ity of intersex people to discuss their erotic lives with therapeutic professionals, who may be accustomed to working with endosex people who have typically been given far more information about their own bodies.

What can practitioners do?

Practitioners working with intersex adults need to discuss people's intersex char-acteristics in terms of both their embodiment *and* their lived experience of the intrapersonal, interpersonal, systemic, and societal dimensions of that embodi-ment. Intersex-centred practice avoids relying on identity-based constructs created by endosex people (e.g., "coming out", "identity development", etc.) and prevents coercive queering by distinguishing between sexuality, gender, and embodiment. Clinicians can then initiate open conversations that many intersex adults have not had with parents and caregivers about their fertility and the erotic, affectional, and intimate relationship dimensions of their lives. Endosex clinicians will also need to examine and address their own endosex privilege and accountability for chal-lenging endosexist forms of systemic injustice.

By creating safe, affirming spaces for this exploration, clinicians can begin repairing ruptures caused partly by what Bonnie described as "the gold standard for clinical outcome, which is heterosexual intercourse". While engaging in these open conversations, practitioners can challenge endosexist norms and standards by ensuring that they discuss intersex characteristics as part of natural human biological diversity. This means not using endosex people as the standard reference point (e.g., not referring to endosex people and bodies as "normal" or "regular" people or bodies), as well as being careful to avoid pathologising language (e.g., "Disorders of Sex Development", "DSDs", or "intersex conditions").

Some key tasks early in therapy are to help people to develop an intersex-centred standard that uses intersex embodiment as the standard reference point and to find affirming and authentic ways to communicate about their bodies and lived experiences. When discussing partners, refer to endosex partners and intersex partners instead of only mentioning the sex-associated characteristics of the intersex partners or calling the endosex partners' bodies "normal" – this is offensive, as it implies that intersex people's bodies are abnormal. Applying intersex-centred language is particularly important when endosex partners struggle to understand and support their intersex partners. Attempts at "neutrality" in this context reflect the practitioner's unexamined endosex privilege, have an inequitable effect, and constitute collusion with endosex norms.

Concern 3: medical trauma, impeded interoceptive awareness, and iatrogenic alexithymia

Identifying concerns

The term *interoception* describes internal bodily sensations that include pain, temperature, hunger, thirst, and other important information about one's physiological condition. *Interoceptive awareness* is the conscious awareness of this information that can inform actions (Craig, 2003). Many intersex adults who have been denied safe opportunities to know their bodies and explore their erotic responses can struggle to develop interoceptive awareness. As Bonnie explained:

> I know from my personal point of view, I didn't ever really feel free to fall into my body and to actually openly explore my body and openly understand my body because there was so much that wasn't known, the body was pathologised before I even started to ask questions about what my body did. And then my body was changed. Irrevocably changed before I really understood what the implications of that were to be and how that would impact the way I felt about myself and the way I felt about myself in relation to other people.

Many people in intersex communities have described feeling unable to relate to their own bodies. Intersex people often report signs of *alexithymia*, a term that describes having limited or no ability to recognise or define the nuances of one's feelings and determine one's feelings and needs based on somatic stimuli. Research suggests that greater alexithymia is associated with lower interoceptive awareness (Berenguer et al., 2019). However, researchers continue to explore the nature of the relation between these two variables, and current evidence has established a correlational rather than causal relation. *Iatrogenic alexithymia* is a form of alexithymia caused by medical providers, such as the medical abuse and clinical culture of silencing and erasure to which many intersex people have been subjected.

Alexithymia is not a personal failing of intersex people. It is a reasonable adaptation and coping response to unreasonable treatment, such as the medical abuse and epistemic erasure to which intersex people are commonly subjected. Alexithymia can also affect people's ability to notice and identify what they are experiencing during an erotic encounter and to communicate their sensory and erotic desires to others. Alexithymia in sensory and erotic contexts can inhibit communication about one's own erotic and relational needs, which can in turn contribute to relational ruptures and impede people's capacity to enjoy a fulfilling erotic life.

Recent sexological research has documented how greater alexithymia and lower interoceptive awareness can be associated with lesser arousal, reduced lubrication, more difficulties in achieving orgasm, more dissatisfaction, more pain during erotic activities, and greater sexual distress for participants categorised as "female" (Berenguer et al., 2019). This research also showed that greater interoceptive awareness was associated with stronger desire in participants categorised as "female". A key finding of this research was that self-awareness of internal bodily states and emotions is pivotal to sexual functioning. Unfortunately, like many studies that focus on the nuances of adult erotic functioning and satisfaction in general, this study appears to have assumed participants' biology based on reported gender, omitted information on whether participant gender was assumed or self-reported, used biased phrases like "both sexes" and "opposite sex", and excluded adults with intersex characteristics. Unfortunately, researchers who consider intersex adults' erotic functioning and satisfaction often do so only tangentially to gather evidence to promote or critique medical interventions. Intersex-centred research will prioritise intersex people's functioning and erotic satisfaction.

Despite the research gap in this area, extensive anecdotal evidence from intersex communities illustrates how having one's body alternately demeaned and fetishised can make it challenging for adults with intersex characteristics to determine whether an erotic activity feels pleasurable, painful, or uncomfortable. One example that illustrates this effect came from Lina, an intersex woman who experienced medical abuse repeatedly while growing up, and who described feeling unable to discuss her body or communicate about her erotic needs and desires as a result. She felt these traumatic earlier experiences had damaged her ability "to know myself as an erotic being". The first images Lina saw of people with "bodies like mine" in books were

> these white hands with gloves on them coming into the sides of pictures of genitals. So the idea of hands near genitals, for me growing up, was linked to medical literature photography, which when I tried to learn about myself was the first and only image of people like me out there. For many years, I had to

do a lot of work to let people put their hands near my genitals because it was an association that was just not pleasurable. I also grew up with clinicians on a regular basis putting their fingers inside of my genitals.

(anonymous personal communication shared with permission)

Some intersex adults subjected to coerced and involuntary medical abuse during infancy, childhood, and/or adolescence experienced these intimate violations as societally sanctioned forms of child sexual abuse. In addition to psychological and emotional distress, intersex adults commonly report a range of physiological effects of this abuse, include scarring, painful urination, painful genital arousal, painful frontal enveloping (what in heteronormative and cisgenderist contexts is described in phallocentric terms as "penetration"), urinary incontinence, and little to no pleasurable sensation from genital contact (Jones et al., 2016). Some intersex people have expressed ambivalence or discomfort regarding any genital touch. Although some intersex people enjoy genital stimulation, practitioners need to be aware that this ambivalence or discomfort can stem from medical abuse. Many intersex adults subjected to medical trauma may avoid or become distressed by some or all forms of erotic activity that can trigger traumatic affective, cognitive, and sensory memory fragments and aggravate existing attachment injuries. People unable to identify and communicate their internal reactions during erotic activities due to impeded interoceptive awareness or iatrogenic alexithymia can experience re-traumatisation and increased dissociation.

What can practitioners do?

After establishing emotional safety, practitioners can communicate their awareness that many intersex people might experience difficulty with identifying and sharing how they feel in their bodies due to traumatic past medical experiences. By explicitly acknowledging the legitimacy of these experiences upfront, practitioners can establish a safer environment for later exploration of how impeded interoceptive awareness and iatrogenic alexithymia might affect intersex people's erotic lives and their capacity to articulate their erotic needs in therapy. Although narrative details of traumatic medical experiences are less likely to be shared before practitioners have earned people's trust, communicating one's receptivity to this topic can ensure practitioners establish an optimal therapeutic space for receiving such disclosures. Identifying the physiological effects of medical abuse reported by many intersex adults can also be essential to developing a viable therapeutic plan.

Many intersex people have described finding sex therapy and relationship counselling unhelpful when practitioners did not ask questions designed to help them find words to describe their erotic lives and challenges. For many intersex people, healing and recovery from medical abuse, stigma, and erasure may also involve seeking reparations and holding those responsible for these abuses accountable.

Addressing the impacts of medical trauma and iatrogenic alexithymia can be crucial to achieving desired outcomes in sex therapy and relationship counselling and can improve intersex people's erotic lives. Consider the following therapeutic concerns:

- Kumiko described to her therapist how she wanted to take sexy selfies to share with one of her partners, Yasmeen, but found herself unexpectedly distressed by seeing a picture of herself partially nude, as this triggered the memory of the medical photos that doctors had taken of her as a child and teenager without her consent or knowledge at the time.
- Ari noticed that they avoided genital contact with partners and felt uncomfortable with certain kinds of genital touch. When being touched genitally, they noticed that they often felt unable to ask for what they wanted. This resulted in an "orgasm gap", where they would touch their partners in ways that resulted in orgasms with relative ease, while Ari began to feel disgruntled and frustrated that their partners did not seem able to reciprocate. During conversations with their sex therapist, they realised that specific elements of the touch reminded them of the medical child sexual abuse they experienced during interventions to which they were subjected during childhood. Ari realised that these triggers made them feel small and silent, like the child they had been during these experiences.

In the many similar real-life situations that I have encountered as a therapist, participants achieved beneficial therapeutic outcomes only through addressing these concerns in terms of medical trauma, impeded interoceptive awareness, and iatrogenic alexithymia. There is no one-size-fits-all approach to helping people to recover from the impact of medical and societal trauma. A detailed clinical response is beyond the scope of this chapter. However, by integrating these concerns into routine investigations, practitioners can establish conditions conducive to addressing these key concerns.

Concern 4: disclosure and stigma management

Identifying concerns

Many intersex adults have had lived experiences of rejection, ridicule, and fetishisation by endosex partners. Medicalisation of intersex people's bodies can produce or increase loneliness and abandonment (e.g., Jones, 2022). Endosex partners often terminate intimate relationships upon discovering their partners are intersex. It is a common experience for intersex people to express anxiety and fear about disclosing their intersex characteristics to therapists. This hesitation is partly due to the many intersex people who have expressed dissatisfaction with endosex queer therapists' inability to conceptualise their lives beyond the limitations of identity-focused concepts like "coming out". This conceptual failure undermines therapists' capacity to support intersex people with figuring out to whom they could safely disclose their intersex characteristics, and how to manage their stigma about what many intersex people consider deeply personal and sensitive information that is poorly suited to the high visibility of a public pride parade or a "coming out" post on social media.

Disclosure can involve context-specific physical and emotional safety risks for intersex adults who identify as heterosexual and those who belong to conservative religious and cultural communities. Some religious and cultural communities are homosocial, with entirely gender-segregated spaces and events. In contexts where the socially constructed categories of sex and gender are conflated, disclosure of being intersex can result in an intersex person being ostracised, vilified, or rejected by the entire community. In addition to the violence by medical practitioners mentioned earlier, community environments governed by cultural traditions and religious laws can also be violent or hostile toward people known to be intersex. Where gender-specific traditions and laws determine what constitutes acceptable conduct, intersex people may face massive barriers to achieving equitable access to intimate relationships, social roles, and community activities. For therapists living in cultural contexts with fewer gender-based rules and restrictions, it is essential to avoid imposing ethnocentric assumptions or making blanket recommendations to either "come out" (sic) or leave the community entirely. Intersex people from minoritised cultural and religious communities can often feel unwelcome, both in intersex community spaces dominated by secular, Christianised, white Anglo cultural norms and in white Anglo-dominated therapeutic environments that do not recognise and address people's intersecting cultural and religious needs.

Some research suggests that intersex people may be more likely than endosex people to have disability needs. For example, Jones et al. (2016) found that 27% of intersex people reported having disabilities, while other studies found only 17% of transgender people and 18.5% of the broader Australian population reported having disabilities. Some intersex people with disability-related needs rely on support workers for basic functions such as feeding, toileting, and bathing. In this context, disclosure may raise existential threats about potential mistreatment or service denial, particularly when intersex people appear more likely than endosex people to be affected by intersecting forms of ableism.

What can practitioners do?

Practitioners need to educate themselves about intersex-specific cultural safety protocols and the existential and practical risks of self-disclosure when working with intersex people from racialised cultural backgrounds or religions and intersex people with disability needs. As the stakes of rejection from disclosure may be dangerously high, endosex practitioners need to educate themselves about the practical dimensions of a person's everyday life and reflect on their unexamined endosex privilege before developing a therapeutic response.

Concern 5: shame, self-worth, and relationship capital

Identifying concerns

Endosexist media norms about the "ideal" body and its capacities can limit intersex people's sense of having a "normal", functional, and physically desirable body. Consequently, many intersex people, particularly those subjected to medical abuse, grow up with an innate sense of being flawed and unattractive. For example, Declan was a sub who explained to the relationship therapist that he had wanted to engage in exhibitionist play with Marco, his endosex Dom. Even though it was Declan's fantasy to be paraded around the dungeon showing off his body for Marco, Declan had not anticipated the wave of shame and embarrassment that he experienced as a result of having learned that his genitals were hideously ugly and should remain hidden.

One intersex variation called hypospadias (singular and plural form) describes people's bodies that endosexist medical taxonomy describes as having the urethral opening situated on the underside of "the penis". According to this terminology, people with hypospadias are born with a urethral opening located somewhere between the area directly below "the penis and the scrotum". Infants with hypospadias are typically subjected to surgical intervention due to unsubstantiated claims that they will have psychosocial problems with standing urination and "penile penetration" later in life (Carmack et al., 2016). These medical claims contain unexamined ethnocentric, cisgenderist, endosexist, sexist, and heterosexist biases.

In many countries, it is widespread for endosex men to prefer urination while seated. For the past fourteen centuries, men from Muslim societies and cultures have preferred urination while seated (Nawab et al., 2006). Even in countries where prior sanitation options required standing urination, increased access to seated urination options can result in changing preferences. For example, Suzuki et al. (2022) found that 38.6% of Japanese endosex men urinated while seated, with 54.5% citing maintaining bathroom cleanliness as the reason for this preference. Given that standing urination had been a well-established norm among Japanese men only several decades earlier, this finding demonstrates the culture-bound and malleable nature of this supposedly essential biological norm.

Regarding medical claims that hypospadias causes adult sexual dysfunction, Carmack et al. (2016) noted that hypospadias is relatively common and that recent evidence suggests that many individuals with hypospadias do not experience the functional or psychosocial difficulties commonly claimed by endosex medical professionals. The researchers also explored evidence showing high rates of parental regret for hypospadias "repair" surgeries and noted that these surgical interventions have a substantial risk of adverse outcomes. The authors reviewed published outcomes data and conducted an in-depth analysis of typical rationales for hypospadias surgery, examining potential benefits, harms, and non-surgical alternatives. They found that "most childhood surgeries for hypospadias are performed for anticipated future problems concerning function and cosmesis, rather than extant physical and/or psychosocial problems that are adversely affecting the child's well-being" (p. 1047). Noting that surgery to address hypospadias "can be safely performed after an age of consent without increasing the absolute risk of surgical complications to an ethically meaningful degree" (ibid.), the authors concluded that such procedures should be performed "only if requested by the affected individual, under conditions of informed consent" (ibid.).

Although medical professionals justify surgical interventions for hypospadias as a supposed medical emergency requiring "repair" to provide "normal" function, people subjected to these non-consensual medical procedures have raised serious concerns about this practice. Orr (2019) explored how the violent medical abuse inflicted on intersex boys with hypospadias often resulted in shame, physical and emotional pain, trauma, and coercive reinforcement of hegemonic, hetero-masculine behaviour. Orr noted that this behaviour damaged these boys' sense of gendered belonging and turned the act of urination into a distressing and harmful experience.

The sense of shame many intersex people have internalised

> can significantly impact people's sense of self-worth, and place in the world, and also role in society. If people don't have access to clear role models of how to live with bodies that aren't typically male or typically female they'll rely on stereotypical role models to play out. And if you have low self-worth, and if you are, say, from my point of view, if I was a woman, a young woman growing up with a body that wasn't typically female, that didn't menstruate, that couldn't bear children, my perceivable relationship capital going into a heterosexual relationship was already at a deficit.
>
> (Hart, personal communication, interview conducted by Zoom, audio recording only, 25 March 2022)

This concept of "relationship capital" and intersex characteristics reducing one's worth as a potential intimate partner has far-reaching consequences that can increase the risk of intersex adults being subjected to coercively controlling partners. While preparing this chapter, I spoke with intersex people from multiple genders and sexualities who described how having their bodies stigmatised, problematised, and subjected to medical scrutiny from a young age had made them more susceptible to sexual abuse and consent violations from childhood through adulthood.

What can practitioners do?

After establishing a therapeutic relationship that feels safe and comfortable for intersex participants, explore whether they have concerns related to their relationship capital and whether this has been associated with shame or limited self-worth. Where relationship capital is a current issue, it can be beneficial to identify possible ways that intersex partners may feel they have felt coerced into accepting unfavourable conditions or boundary violations to offset their perceived deficits. It is important to notice and address situations in which intersex people appear habituated to mistreatment by endosex intimate partners due to perceived lack of relationship capital.

Concern 6: barriers to erotic, affectional, and intimate relationship boundaries

The ubiquitous and intersecting forms of epistemic injustice, endosexist norms, medical trauma, impeded interoceptive awareness, iatrogenic alexithymia, and societal stigma to which intersex people are often exposed can produce conditions unfavourable to the development of a sense of high self-worth. In this societal context, many intersex people have described the challenges they faced when trying to establish safe and affirming interpersonal boundaries. Despite substantial anecdotal evidence, intersex people continue to be neglected, under-identified, or entirely excluded from most intimate partner and domestic violence research. As Bonnie explained,

> I think from a therapeutic point of view, what's really dangerous for people with those types of lived experiences is often they are disconnected from peers. They don't have access to other types of narratives about how to be in relationships. So they fall into these relationships in order to get their intimacy needs met and their connection needs met, and these things happen to them in those relationships because they haven't got to practice speaking affirmatively about their bodies, they haven't got to ever explore how to enjoy a body as a natural, sensual, full thing.

A national study found that more than three-fifths (61.7%) of participants with an intersex variation had experienced insufficient authority over medical decisions about their own bodies, and over half (54.4%) had undergone an intersex-related medical intervention (Hill et al., 2020). Among those who had undergone this intervention, almost seven in ten (68%) occurred during childhood, and only 24% of those who had undergone intersex-related medical intervention reported having been mostly or completely able to give full and informed consent to this intervention (ibid.). Many intersex adults find that the repeated privacy violations to which they were subjected during childhood result in reduced capacity to assert their boundaries when confronted with similar boundary violations by endosex intimate partners. Bonnie described how this process occurred in her own past relationships. Due to the impact of having her boundaries violated by medical professionals while she was growing up,

> as a result, I felt less empowered to maintain my effective boundaries. I let myself, let my body be used as a currency to be able to maintain an emotional connection. And as a result, I experienced abusive situations, and abusive

relationships, and remained in those abusive relationships because I thought at a fundamental level, I probably deserved to be in that environment. And beyond that, I suppose I didn't have the worth to think that there would be another way of being in the world, because it hadn't been explained to me. And because often this, all of this dynamic that I'm talking about exists in a space where there is absolutely no psychosocial support offered to people. It's not offered at the very get-go, when people are making decisions in clinical spaces. And if it is provided in that space, it's really time-specific and discreet, and not the type of age-appropriate, longitudinal support that people need to be able to reassess situations as they develop and as their ideas develop around what their body is and what it's capable of doing.

Bonnie's experience highlights the long-term damage caused by health professionals' failure to treat her and her body as valuable and worthy of respect. Had they connected her with intersex-led community support sooner, Bonnie would have been able to meet other intersex people who could affirm her worth. Instead, the absence of supportive relationships that affirmed her body made her more susceptible to boundary violations in her intimate relationships and less able to identify and leave abusive relationships.

What can practitioners do?

Sex and relationship therapists need to consider how epistemic injustice, endosexist norms, medical trauma, impeded interoceptive awareness, iatrogenic alexithymia, and societal stigma may have affected intersex people's capacity to determine their limits, communicate those limits in the form of interpersonal boundaries, and respond to situations that endanger those boundaries. It may be valuable for clinicians to support people to develop their self-worth, gain skills in communicating their needs and limits, and identify and seek repair and accountability for attachment injuries and interpersonal ruptures.

Practitioners working with one or more intersex partners may need to explore options for improving communication about their erotic, affectional, and relational needs, desires, and boundaries. In addition, helping intersex people to access nonclinical spaces run by and for actual intersex people can provide the crucial peer support needed to acknowledge their own worth and establish safe and affirming erotic, affectional, and intimate relationship boundaries.

Conclusion

Intersex-centred practice means attending to the six neglected concerns discussed in this chapter: epistemic injustice; endosexist norms and standards; medical trauma, impeded interoceptive awareness, and iatrogenic alexithymia; disclosure and stigma management; shame, self-worth, and relationship capital; and barriers to erotic, affectional, and intimate relationship boundaries. By attending to these under-recognised concerns, sex and relationship therapists can gain essential therapeutic insights from intersex people's *own* wisdom and insights. By applying intersex-centred practice, sex and relationship therapists can support intersex therapy participants to achieve pleasure, satisfaction, and liberation in their erotic and affectional lives.

References

Ah-King, M., & Nylin, S. (2010). Sex in an evolutionary perspective: Just another reaction norm. *Evolutionary Biology*, 37(4), 234–246. https://doi.org/10.1007/s11692-010-9101-8

Ansara, Y.G. (2010). Beyond cisgenderism: Counselling people with non-assigned gender identities. In L. Moon (Ed.), *Counselling Ideologies: Queer Challenges to Heteronormativity* (pp. 167–200). Aldershot: Ashgate.

Ansara, Y.G. (2015). Challenging cisgenderism in the ageing and aged care sector: Meeting the needs of older people of trans and/or non-binary experience. *Australasian Journal on Ageing*, 34, 14–18. https://doi.org/10.1111/ajag.12278

Ansara, Y.G. (2021). Disrupting professional myths about "the mainstream": Diversity, inclusivity, and bias reduction are paramount in conventional publication standards. *Psychotherapy & Counselling Journal of Australia*, 9(2). https://pacja.org.au/volume-9-no-2-november-2021/

Berenguer, C., Rebôlo, C., & Costa, R.M. (2019). Interoceptive awareness, alexithymia, and sexual function. *Journal of Sex & Marital Therapy*, 45(8), 729–738. https://doi.org/10.1080/0092623X.2019.1610128

Brömdal, A., Zavros-Orr, A., lisahunter, Hand, K., & Hart, B. (2021). Towards a whole-school approach for sexuality education in supporting and upholding the rights and health of students with intersex variations. *Sex Education*, 21(5), 568–583. https://doi.org/10.1080/14681811.2020.1864726

Carmack, A., Notini, L., & Earp, B.D. (2016). Should surgery for hypospadias be performed before an age of consent? *The Journal of Sex Research*, 53(8), 1047–1058. https://doi.org/10.1080/00224499.2015.1066745

Carpenter, M. (2016). The human rights of intersex people: Addressing harmful practices and rhetoric of change. *Reproductive Health Matters*, 24(47), 74–84. https://doi.org/10.1016/j.rhm.2016.06.003

Carpenter, M. (2018). The "normalization" of intersex bodies and "othering" of intersex identities in Australia. *Journal of Bioethical Inquiry*, 15(4), 487–495. https://doi.org/10.1007/s11673-018-9855-8

Carpenter, M. (2020). Intersex human rights, sexual orientation, gender identity, sex characteristics and the Yogyakarta Principles plus 10. *Culture, Health & Sexuality*, 23(4), 516–532. https://doi.org/10.1080/13691058.2020.1781262

Chan, T. (2022, April 4). Position statement on autistic communication. *Reframing Autism Website*. https://reframingautism.org.au/position-statement-on-autistic-communication/

Craig, A.D. (2003). Interoception: The sense of the physiological condition of the body. *Current Opinion in Neurobiology*, 13(4), 500–505. https://doi.org/10.1016/S0959-4388(03)00090-4

Darlington Statement. (2017, March 10). *Darlington Statement*. https://darlington.org.au/statement/

Davis, G. (2011). "DSD is a perfectly fine term": Reasserting medical authority through a shift in intersex terminology. In P.J. McGann & D.J. Hutson (Eds.), *Sociology of Diagnosis*

(Advances in Medical Sociology, Vol. 12) (pp. 155–182). Bingley: Emerald. https://doi. org/10.1108/S1057-6290(2011)0000012012

Fricker, M. (2007). *Epistemic Injustice: Power and the Ethics of Knowing.* New York: Oxford University Press.

Hart, B., & Shakespeare-Finch, J. (2021). Intersex lived experience: Trauma and posttraumatic growth in narratives. *Psychology & Sexuality.* https://doi.org/10.1080/19419899 .2021.1938189

Hill, A.O., Bourne, A., McNair, R., Carman, M., & Lyons, A. (2020). *Private Lives 3: The Health and Wellbeing of LGBTIQ People in Australia.* ARCSHS Monograph Series No. 122. Melbourne, Australia: Australian Research Centre in Sex, Health and Society, La Trobe University. https://genderrights.org.au/wp-content/uploads/2020/11/Private-Lives-3-National-Report.pdf

Holmes, M. (2011). The intersex enchiridion: Naming and knowledge. *Somatechnics*, 1(2), 388–411. https://doi.org/10.3366/soma.2011.0026

Holmes, M. (2016). *Critical Intersex.* Oxon and New York: Routledge.

Joel, D. (2021). Beyond the binary: Rethinking sex and the brain. *Neuroscience & Biobehavioral Reviews*, 122, 165–175. https://doi.org/10.1016/j.neubiorev.2020.11.018

Joel, D., García-Falgueras, A., & Swaab, D. (2020). The complex relationships between sex and the brain. *The Neuroscientist*, 26(2), 156–169. https://doi.org/10.1177/1073858419867298

Joel, D., Berman, Z., Tavor, I., Wexler, N., Gaber, O., Stein, Y., . . . Assaf, Y. (2015). Sex beyond the genitalia: The human brain mosaic. *Proceedings of the National Academy of Sciences*, 112(50), 15468–15473. https://doi.org/10.1073/pnas.1509654112

Jones, C. (2022). The harms of medicalisation: Intersex, loneliness and abandonment. *Feminist Theory*, 23(1), 39–60. https://doi.org/10.1177/14647001211062740

Jones, T., Hart, B., Carpenter, M., Ansara, G., Leonard, W., & Lucke, J. (2016). *Intersex: Stories and statistics from Australia.* Cambridge, UK: Open Book Publishers. https:// hdl.handle.net/1959.11/18556

Nawab, B., Nyborg, I.L., Esser, K.B., & Jenssen, P.D. (2006). Cultural preferences in designing ecological sanitation systems in North West Frontier Province, Pakistan. *Journal of Environmental Psychology*, 26(3), 236–246. https://doi.org/10.1016/j.jenvp.2006.07.005

Orr, C.E. (2019). Resisting the demand to stand: Boys, bathrooms, hypospadias, and interphobic violence. *Boyhood Studies*, 12(2), 89–113. https://doi.org/10.3167/bhs.2019.120206

Sanz, V. (2017). No way out of the binary: A critical history of the scientific production of sex. *Signs: Journal of Women in Culture and Society*, 43(1), 1–27. https://doi. org/10.1086/692517

Suzuki, M., Shiratori, T., & Naito, A. (2022). Relevant predisposing factors for voiding in a sitting position among Japanese male adult patients. *Continence*, 2, 100030. https://doi. org/10.1016/j.cont.2022.100030

Tervalon, M., & Murray-García, J. (1998). Cultural humility versus cultural competence: A critical distinction in defining physician training outcomes in multicultural education. *Journal of Health Care for the Poor and Underserved*, 9(2), 117–125. https://doi. org/10.1353/hpu.2010.0233

Chapter 7

Trans sex and relationships

A practitioners' dialogue

Serge Nicholson and Ellis Morgan

Introduction

Ellis Morgan and Serge Nicholson met nearly two decades ago, at the start of their gender transitions. After many years of friendship, they both went on to train as therapists and now specialise in working with clients around gender identity issues. In this chapter, they recreate a dialogue that has evolved over their time as friends and colleagues about the nature of gender change, its impact on the sexual and relational lives of gender diverse people, and their approaches to trans affirmative therapeutic practice.

Ellis is a white, queer trans masculine person in his forties. He is a person-centred therapist specialising in working around gender identity.

Serge is a white trans masculine person in his sixties. He describes himself as a sight-disabled, polysexual, trans punk elder. He is a GSRD sex and relationship therapist, and a trans arts practitioner.

Reframing gender

ELLIS: Looking back, we met in the calm before the storm. It was the early 2000s, in London, and we could feel the beginnings of a gender revolution in the air. But reflecting now, I think we really had little sense of just how significant the gender revolution would be, or the social and political storm that it would cause.

SERGE: It's been an interesting time to live through, not only as a trans person but as someone stepping into therapeutic professional life working around issues of gender identity. It has really allowed me to appreciate so much of what is hidden beneath the surface of these social changes. Certainly, in the UK, many people have been able to move away from the tendency to see gender as a set of pre-fixed options, with people increasingly allowing themselves to find more accurate and nuanced ways of expressing who they are. But alongside this, we have also witnessed an extreme social pushback that is all about invalidating these identities.

DOI: 10.4324/9781003260608-8

ELLIS: If I had a mantra as a trans person and as a gender identity therapist it would be this – trans issues above all else are legitimacy issues. There's a reason why the most common trans pride slogans are 'Trans Men are Men', 'Transwomen are Women', and 'Non-Binary Is Real'. It's because this basic issue of legitimacy is so fundamental. Trans people have to lobby for their right to their identities, and continually fight against the tide of resistance. We know this of course – but what isn't always so obvious is what the realities of living with this legitimacy struggle look and feel like at the micro-level of trans peoples' lives.

SERGE: I think the important thing to grasp around gender legitimacy struggles is that they arise only if we insist on gender being something that's solid and immovably fixed in place. What it means for anything to be 'real' only exists so long as we keep it as an object, that can be proven, denied, stolen, or gifted. If we allow gender to be recognised rather as something we all *experience, make sense of and communicate* then we are in a territory where gender is something that everyone can own for themselves. I think for both of us, a helpful way of understanding how gender operates in these ways is to think of it as how we are personally and socially *framed*.

ELLIS: I agree. But this is a sensitive territory, so it feels important to say what our language of gender as a personal and social framing isn't; it isn't a statement that a trans or non-binary person's gender is merely imagined or 'socially constructed'. Gender is a very real personal *and* social experience. For therapists working with gender-diverse clients, this is particularly important to remember, as understanding and sharing the specificities of how our clients experience and frame their own genders is a crucial part of our work.

SERGE: It's interesting to be having this dialogue in the context of this Pink Therapy volume, because this conception of gender, as a way of being personally and socially framed, lands us squarely in the territory of what it means to work in a trans affirmative way. Looking at the evolution of Pink Therapy since its initial publication (Davies & Neal, 1996), we can see that the therapeutic world has played its own part in the gender revolution. Expanding the notion of Gay Affirmative Therapy to trans clients has had a transformative impact in lobbying for therapists to adopt a trans positive stance toward clients (e.g. Austin et al., 2017; Singh, 2016; Mckinney et al., 2020). Now, as we go forward, therapists need to be equipped with ways of hearing clients' own understandings of themselves, so that we can have a clearer picture of how the client needs to be affirmed.

ELLIS: To me it's clear that the way that our gender is framed affects every aspect of our experience – and when it comes to sex and relationships, this includes how we feel about our bodies, our desires, our ways of being intimate, and our relational dynamics. As therapists, this means our affirmative role with gender diverse clients stretches far beyond simply affirming a client's gender identity; we have to also understand how it permeates their whole life experience. So, let's begin our explorations of this.

Reframing sexuality

ELLIS: For me, there is a clear symbiosis between gender and sexuality. As you reframe the first, the other gets reframed simultaneously. What I have noticed in my own life, and in the lives of my clients, is that as the personal and social meaning of our gender changes, so too does the personal and social meaning of our sexuality.

SERGE: The image that comes to mind is a kaleidoscope. As you shift its position, the whole image changes.

ELLIS: Exactly. The *feel* and *meaning* of our sexuality can be significantly recast as part of our gender reframe. Much attention has been given in research to the impact that gender transition has on sexual orientation, with very mixed findings; from proposals that nearly half of us find our sexual orientation altered as we transition (Katz-Wise et al., 2016) to barely any of us at all (Defreyne et al., 2021). But that is not what I am pointing to here. Whether or not our sexual *orientation* changes, the cultural meaning of our sexuality can shift, and along with it our ways of experiencing and expressing it.

SERGE: Yes, there is something important that can be missed if we narrowly think of sexuality only in terms of the group of people we are attracted to. I think for example of a trans woman client who prior to transition had always been framed within her relationships as a heterosexual man, but post-transition has come to identify and express herself as a queer, female-attracted woman. Her *orientation* has not changed in the sense that she is still attracted to women, but her sexual *identity* has. How she wants to express herself sexually and be related to within her relationships with women has been wholly affected by her transition.

ELLIS: Though to complicate things a little, my practice also tells me that the span of our desire can also change as we transition, as new sexual identities become possible. An example that comes to mind is a trans man I worked with who prior to transition had identified as a butch lesbian and exclusively had sex with women, despite privately experiencing desire towards men. For him, sex with women within a butch-lesbian framing allowed him to keep hold of a relational sense of his masculinity, in a way that he felt would otherwise have been impossible. His eventual gender transition liberated what sex could mean for him and about him, enabling sex and relationships with men that did not feel inherently heterosexualising or femaling.

SERGE: I see this operating in many ways in my therapy practice too. Though I'm aware that shifting sexual identifications can often take a far less binary form. For many gender diverse people sexuality labels like gay, straight, or bisexual do not fit – we know this from our practice and our lives, and it's also well documented in research (e.g. McNeil et al., 2012; Ruberg & Ruelos, 2020). But this does not mean that less binary or queer-identified people don't experience a shift in their sexual meaning as they reframe their gender. I think for example of a non-binary client who has felt liberated precisely because they no longer feel they have to fit into conventional gender categories within sexual dynamics; they are now more able to carry their own sense of meaning within their relationships.

ELLIS: I would say that even for those trans people who do describe their gender or sexuality in more binary ways, there can still be a great deal of subtlety in what they mean about themselves when they use these binary terms. The trans man client I referred to who now felt able to have sex with men is a good example. He went on to describe himself as a gay man, but his therapeutic explorations involved unpicking what this meant for him. Being trans was such an important part of how he experienced his maleness that it coloured what being gay meant for him too.

SERGE: It's interesting how navigating these subjects can sometimes mean working so closely with what all these words mean for our clients – and sometimes conversely, it means working without reference to them at all. It is a common feature of the work I do, that I navigate people's sexual desires and experiences without any reference to these kinds of labels. They often become defunct, with the focus instead being on people's own unique contexts.

ELLIS: Quite – and this is true no matter how queer or conventional, binary or non-binary the person you are working with. For me, a central tenet of engaging deeply in work that explores gender identity is both to understand the power of all these categories that we might use to define ourselves – and to be ready to let them go. As the image of the gender kaleidoscope turns, and our gender diverse clients continue to nuance their own self meaning, we as therapists have to keep up with them, joining our clients where they are in that moment.

Exploring the reframed sexual self

ELLIS: For everyone, sexual and erotic encounters have the potential to powerfully expand our sense of ourselves. For gender-diverse people, this potential can be particularly important. Whether or not our gender-reframe involves medical steps to alter aspects of our physicality, we can still find ourselves assigning new meaning to our bodies. This new meaning can have important consequences on how we want to use our bodies, how we want them to be touched, and how we want them to be understood. By their very nature, gender transitions encompass a process of learning what the reframed self feels like within our shifted identity context – and sex, like all other parts of our experience, can feed into this learning process.

SERGE: For some of my clients I see this relearning of their sexual selves happening organically over time. Though for many others, I see it taking a more deliberate and practical form. For example, a trans masculine client has described to me how important it has been for him, even prior to his transition, to use sexual encounters with often hyper-masculine men as a way of learning about masculinity and male bodies. These encounters were a study-like experience for him, that provided an opportunity to find out how male bodies operate and how he could feel about himself in proximity to these forms of masculinity.

ELLIS: Another example of this kind of learning-through-sex that I sometimes hear about in my therapy room is through pornography and erotica. For some of my gender-diverse clients, these can provide an important opportunity to view and imaginatively engage with a wide range of bodies that they may not otherwise have access to. When considering the significance of this way of learning, it's helpful to be aware that prior to transition, trans and non-binary people are statistically far less likely to have experienced a diverse range of in-person sexual experiences than the general population (Bunenger et al., 2017; Marshall et al., 2020). Viewing pornography featuring trans people is sometimes more specifically used as an opportunity to imagine the potential for one's own transitioned body. Unfortunately, for trans feminine people in particular, this kind of trans-eroticisation has a long and problematic history of being pathologised (Serano, 2010). I frequently witness the internalised shame and confusion this produces as I accompany people in their processing of these experiences.

SERGE: The use of pornography need not be viewed as problematic. It is just one example of how researching adult sexual experiences can fuel this learning process – and there are many more ways besides. For some people, it might be through using dating or hook-up apps or other online platforms. For others, the exploration may encompass going to previously inaccessible spaces. I think of a trans masculine client whose learning experiences included going to gay male saunas. Similarly, it might involve accessing trans or queer specific spaces that provide safer opportunities for experimentation – I think for example of a trans feminine client immersing herself in the queer kink scene. Of course, for trans people like anyone else, accessing these experiences and spaces can simply be a way to meet people and fulfil our sexual desires. But in some contexts, they can also act as important sources of experiential learning that have the potential to shape our erotic self-knowledge and feed into the very core of our gendered sense of self. Recognising the power and significance of these experiences for our clients can consequently become an important aspect of our trans affirmative work.

Anticipating the challenges of reframing sexuality

SERGE: An important aspect of exploring sex and sexuality following a gender reframe can be facing down our fears or uncertainties around how transitioning will impact upon our desirability to others. We don't just learn about our desires for others within our new gender framing, we also learn about other people's desires for us.

ELLIS: It stands to reason that living as we do in a cis-centric social context, we are likely to anticipate some losses as well as gains as we reframe our gender. It's like playing a game of cards and having the card scoring rules suddenly change mid-game. What were previously strong aspects of your hand might now become weaker and vice versa. For example, a trans man with a small, slight stature might feel these features of his physicality to have been normatively 'rescored' to hold lower value in his post-transition context. Of course, our hopes are always that clients can come to embrace the positive value of their trans body, as part of a broader shift toward self-legitimacy. Along the way though, we may well witness them anticipating and experiencing this often frightening revaluing process. It's a powerful enough fear that it can hold people back from transitioning for years, or at all.

SERGE: What I find is that often we just don't know what situation awaits us as we transition. I think particularly of a number of young trans feminine clients I have worked with, in their twenties or early thirties, for whom attractiveness and dating are extremely important. They have a hope that transition could give them a life that includes feeling attractive and enjoying dating and relationships. But not being sure whether this will transpire can cause significant anxiety as they transition.

ELLIS: I'm conscious that for trans masculine people the pressures to be attractive can be quite different. It's not that there are no fears around this – conventional beauty standards impact on us all and have an especially huge impact on those also subject to the marginalising forces of racism and ableism. But I'm also aware there is a particular social stigma that trans feminine people experience when they aren't deemed by society to 'make the grade'. It's a point of difference that my trans feminine clients will often discuss with me. I can empathise with their fears and often their anger about the impact of the combined forces of our transphobic and misogynistic culture – but it is also important that they know I understand that the impacts of these on me as a trans masculine person are different.

SERGE: It feels especially important to acknowledge these differences with the rise of 'gender-critical' pushback against trans rights, which puts the safety of trans feminine people especially at risk.

ELLIS: Perhaps what isn't so immediately obvious is the way that transphobia in society affects non-binary people within their relationships and sexual encounters. Whilst more binary leaning trans men or women may be concerned with how their gender is being read and understood in a dating or sex situation, non-binary people have the additional stress of whether the very template of their gender is being recognised and respected. I think of a non-binary client who is exploring hook-up apps for the first time, and the central challenge they face is trying to ascertain whether their gender identity has been properly understood and taken seriously by the people they connect with. I think few of us would want to enter a sexual encounter with a person who was reading our bodies and our personhood in a way that was completely counter to our own.

SERGE: It's a key reason why many gender diverse people seek out other queer and trans people to date and have sex with (Williams, 2018). Quite apart from finding these people attractive in their own right, it can also provide a greater sense of security that you are being read and understood by partners in ways that feel accurate and fitting. If you have a queerer way of understanding yourself, you are also likely to have queerer ways of being able to understand others.

ELLIS: But not everyone wants to feel limited to having relationships with other gender diverse or explicitly queer people. What I hear from many clients is that they often find that putting themselves into more mainstream dating pools can feel like a lottery. And unfortunately, they aren't just imagining it; a relatively recent study showed that around 87% of people report that they wouldn't be prepared to consider a romantic relationship with a trans person (Blair & Hoskin, 2018). I find that a shocking statistic.

SERGE: It is a terrible reflection of our transphobic culture. But the picture it creates is not the whole story. There is also research that explores how a diverse and growing population of people now describe themselves as being exclusively trans-oriented (sometimes referred to as being 'skoliosexual') or explicitly trans-inclusive within their romantic and sexual desire (Tomkins, 2014). In my practice, I see that the growth of this trans-inclusive desire can make a huge difference to the self-esteem and range of relational possibilities that my clients experience.

ELLIS: I agree, that's fantastic. But we're in sensitive territory again, as I know the idea of trans-specific desire can make some trans people feel fetishised.

SERGE: Yes, but I think there is an important distinction to be made. Trans fetish-isation does exist, but to me, it's not really a desire for a trans person as such – it's a sexualisation of transness itself. It misses the person. The desire toward trans people that I am referring to might be better described as trans-attraction. It's a desire for someone *with* their gender diversity, as a cherished part of who they are.

ELLIS: I agree that there's a significant difference. In practice though, separating these from each other is a very nuanced and highly politicised matter. In particular I'm conscious that there are highly charged and varying opinions about who might appropriately describe themselves as exclusively trans-attracted or 'skoliosexual', with some trans people feeling that it can only ever be a non-fetishising sexual orientation when held by someone who is gender diverse themselves (see Jas, 2020). The implication of this perspective is that for a trans person to be exclusively attracted to other trans people is reasonable, based on their desire to be with another person of similar life experience, and someone who can understand them within their own cultural frame of reference. From the same vantage point however, if a cis person has the same trans-exclusive attraction, it is seen necessarily to be a desire *for* the trans person's difference, which for some can be experienced as othering and fetishising. Of course, not all gender diverse people take the view I've just described – many others welcome cis people's exclusive desires when they feel respectful and culturally sensitive. But taking stock of these differences of opinion demonstrates the issues of cis/trans power differentiation and the complexity inherent to the idea of trans specific attraction.

SERGE: Yes – and of course these varied perspectives are matched by the varied realities of trans people's relational lives. Many trans people enjoy a full and satisfying romantic and sexual life with partners who appreciate them for who they are, whilst for others, our transphobic culture can leave people feeling fetishised, rejected, unsafe, or alone. As we accompany our clients through this terrain, the understanding and affirmation they experience with us can be hugely significant, in bolstering their own sense of self-value and tending to the impact that such experiences have on them.

ELLIS: My hope is that, alongside this self-valuing, the possibility opens up for a growing sense of empowerment and agency, enabling clients to articulate and express their own sexual and romantic desires. For that to be effective, as therapists, we must learn to hear with a great deal of accuracy the ways that clients relate to themselves so that we can understand and affirm how this is reflected in their relational dynamics with others.

Reframing relationships

SERGE: Moving into our reframed sexual selves as part of a gender transition can present other challenges and opportunities when we are in existing relationships. And by 'relationships' I mean in the most inclusive sense; we might be in partnerships that are monogamous or non-monogamous, romantic or aromantic, sexual or asexual. They might be comprised of just two people or might be configurations of more.

ELLIS: Yes, as we reframe our gender, we may feel we need to reframe aspects of our existing relationships too. It can be uncertain territory, carrying the obvious potential for loss and discomfort. In my practice, I see that there are some common questions that transition raises for gender-diverse clients in this situation: how the relational dynamics with their partners might change or stay the same; how this will impact their shared physical intimacy; how they manage communication about these shifting dynamics; and whether they can resolve any tensions or conflicts. Partners of those transitioning can have their own specific concerns about what their partner's gender reframe means for their own sexual identity and for their social identity as a partnership. And of course, there may be worries about whether they will still find their partner attractive – and indeed if their partner will still be attracted to them.

SERGE: These are the kinds of questions that my clients and their partners often explore with me in relationship therapy – and for each relationship there is always a unique set of circumstances that create very different feelings and perspectives. In 2020 I was part of a systematic literature review of research on relationship satisfaction for transgender people and their partners. What was clear from surveying the research is that there is a bi-directional link between transition and relationship satisfaction (Marshall et al., 2020). What that means is that gender transitions impact upon people's relationships, but so do relationships impact upon people's experiences of gender transition. The positive or negative nature of these bi-directional influences very much depends on the particular relationship.

ELLIS: Indeed, a trans woman I worked with throughout her transition comes to mind as an example. She had been with her female partner for around five years when she began her transition. She had always been open with her partner about her feelings of gender incongruence, but nonetheless it was clear that her transition would result in some significant changes to their relationship. She described her relationship as one that was seemingly heterosexual to the outside world, though she and her partner lived with a sense of being queerly between sexual categories in their private relational world. My client's transition would change this significantly as she moved into a more explicitly female identity, moving both the private and public framing of their relationship into a female-female dynamic. My client's transition provided a catalyst for a deeper level of communication and honesty, strengthening rather than breaking down their partnership. In turn, this relationship hugely enriched her experience of transition, with both partners embracing a queer-femme framing of their relationship that hugely affirmed my client's female identity.

SERGE: Narratives like these bring me back to the imagery of our gender kaleidoscope. As our gender framing shifts, our relationship framing can shift too. For many, like your client, this can be experienced as a kind of *fitting into place*. Though for others there can be a queerer complexity to this when the relationship reframe results in partners having less conventionally compatible or seemingly mis-matching sexual identities. I think of a trans woman client and her cis male partner who I saw for relationship therapy. Prior to the trans partner's transition, both identified as gay men and were part of a gay male social group that provided them with an important sense of belonging. The potential difficulty was that whilst the trans feminine partner felt she needed to shed her gay male identity and move into a queer-feminine identity, it was very important to the male partner to retain his own framing as a gay man. Their resolution was to find a way of queerly *fitting out of place*; they allowed their relationship to exist between categories, whilst retaining their own respective sexual identities. Within my practice, seeing these kinds of mixed-orientation relationships is not uncommon.

ELLIS: Yes, I see this frequently too, but I'm also conscious that these queer solutions don't always work for people. Complications can arise when there are one or more partners for whom queerness of any form isn't a desired part of their relational framing. I think of a non-binary client, who is negotiating a relational reframing with their heterosexual cisgender male partner. When the partnership first formed, they both identified as heterosexual, but as my client has gradually come to express their non-binary gender, this heterosexual framing has become a difficult dynamic for them to exist in. For the cis male partner, however, heterosexuality is a central and non-negotiable part of his identity and his way of conceiving of their relationship. For this partnership, there is a seemingly insurmountable stalemate; whilst my non-binary client longs for this kind of relational queer 'betweenness', it simply does not present a workable solution for their partner. Like in all areas of life, sometimes there is no discomfort-free solution, and our work is to accompany our clients as they find a way forward that is likely to involve a sense of compromise or loss.

SERGE: There is also the practical matter of whether existing relationships can allow for explorations of emerging sexuality when this feels important. I think of a trans man client who has felt a strong desire to explore his sexuality post-transition to inform his reframed sense of self – but who finds it impossible to raise this with his cis-female partner whom he no longer shares a sexual relationship with, but who greatly values monogamy. His personal decision was to risk non-consensual non-monogamy.

ELLIS: What I can hear running as a thread throughout our reflections on clients transitioning in relationships is this; we have to be incredibly sensitive to the *meaning* that their relationships hold for them. In some partnerships, a gender transition signals a change in the ways some or all partners experience the meaning of the relationship, and this can unfold in many different ways: welcome or unwelcome, relationally compatible or incompatible. The challenge for us as therapists is to resist layering our own meanings onto their relationships and to hold ourselves open to hearing the very personal meanings they hold for them. This can more profoundly affirm and further deepen our clients' own sense of self within them.

Reflections on practice

ELLIS: Throughout this dialogue, the theme that we have been returning to again and again is that working therapeutically in a trans affirmative way requires paying careful attention to clients' understandings of their gender, sexuality, and relationships. Quite simply, to be affirmative in any meaningful way, we need to know what it is we are affirming. And that often means letting go of normative or fixed notions around gender and the kinds of bodies, desires, and relationships we imagine they might be accompanied by.

SERGE: At several points, I have been trying to share how many of the clients I work with come to have a more confident and positive self-valuing by adopting less restrictive, queerer conceptions of themselves. They come to question and loosen their normative ideas around what kind of body they ought to have, what kinds of desires they should experience, and the ways they should conceive of their sexuality and relationships. To my mind, in a society that remains structured around prizing cisgender and heterosexual people – as well as being white, male, and able-bodied – as trans and non-binary people we have no option but to let go of oppressive systems if we are to truly prize ourselves, and this can mean stepping into a queerer way of thinking. From a practice point of view, what this means is that therapists themselves need to be able to understand and embrace these queer values and perspectives, in order to recognise and affirm them within our clients.

ELLIS: Like you, in my therapy room I frequently witness clients rejecting normative standards, but this rejection doesn't always look overtly queer on the surface. Whilst I love seeing clients embrace a celebratory or assertive queerness, we mustn't believe this is the only or best way of relating to yourself as a gender-diverse person. Certainly, as therapists, we must not go the other way, and unwittingly dis-affirm our more binary or seemingly conventional clients.

SERGE: I absolutely agree, and I think our difference is only one of emphasis. I think my interest in overtly rejecting conventional, oppressive ways of thinking is rooted in my activism – but it is also very present in my practice because of the direct way I work as a sex and relationship therapist. For example, I will often engage with clients to help them connect with their bodies in ways that feel more congruent. I find that this work is most effective if I am upfront with my clients that this process of reconnection *is* radical, and requires giving ourselves permission to relate to ourselves in new and innovative ways.

ELLIS: I'm wondering what that can look like in practice?

SERGE: I have been working with a trans masculine client experiencing a long and distressing wait for medical assessment and diagnosis. We have been using guided body meditations to ease his immediate dysphoria during this time. These specifically aim to remap his relationship with his present embodiment and connect to the body that he is bringing into being. The body scan incorporates both mindfulness, using breathing techniques, and bringing loving kindness toward his present embodiment, that has served him well, even though it can be such a source of discomfort. In one session we expanded on this to explore and affirm his place within transgender history and culture. I guided him in bringing to mind a vast and diverse lineage of transgender kin that he is part of, drawing strength and resilience from a global community. In another session, the exercise became more introspective, as I helped him visualise the future body that awaits him and connecting to the fact that it is his flesh in the *here and now* that will form this future body. These exercises and others have brought comfort in the midst of gender dysphoria, and, I believe, have served also to communicate to my client my affirmation of his masculine identity and body, both as it is in the present, and in its future potential.

ELLIS: It's very interesting to see how our respective modalities influence our practice when exploring clients' gender identities. As a person-centred therapist, my emphasis is very much on being able to sense into and accompany my clients within their own experience and frame of reference. This doesn't mean that there isn't a challenge when I can see that a client is expressing internalised oppression – but for me this challenge is all about naming it, understanding it, and deeply empathising with the experience of it. I return in my thinking to Carl Rogers's way of articulating this paradox: it is only when I accept myself as I am that then I change (Rogers, 2004). We must facilitate our clients in fully recognising and accepting the ways in which they struggle to value themselves, if this is to finally release and change.

SERGE: I absolutely recognise the importance of empathy within our work – and even though my approach can be more directive, it also has to rest on deeply understanding a client's viewpoint and feelings. I'm aware though that we are now living in a time where this kind of empathic acceptance of gender diverse clients' understandings of themselves is increasingly challenged. Most recently, a paper published in the Journal of Medical Ethics has argued strongly against 'accepting' trans people's own feelings that transition is the right pathway for them, arguing instead that it is a clinician's ethical role to challenge such self-determinations (Lemma & Savulescu, 2021).

ELLIS: My central grievance with these arguments is that they set up a false dichotomy between whether as practitioners we *either* empathically accept a client's own view *or* offer exploration and challenge. In my work, what I see is it is only through offering a deeply trusting relationship, where a person is accepted exactly as they are, that they can bring all of their thoughts and feelings about themselves. It is from this point of openness and trust that they can then explore the potentially mixed or complicated feelings they might have about the prospect of transition. I feel certain that those clients I have worked with who ultimately decided not to transition would have struggled to come to this conclusion if they had sensed that my starting point as a therapist was one of scepticism about their own self-determinations.

SERGE: I think this is just one example of the impact of the historic positioning of gender incongruence as a mental health pathology. There is well-documented friction between the listing of Gender Dysphoria within ICD-10 to enable access to medical transition, and the social bias this creates in seeing trans people as in some way disordered (e.g. Butler, 2004; Drescher et al., 2012). The conversation we have been having here seems particularly important in this context; we are arguing for practitioners to centralise trans people's own ways of understanding themselves and to leave their own meanings and assumptions aside. I hope reading the accounts of clients we have provided here can contribute to this; but it is not enough in itself. We must continually expand our thinking through continuous professional development, exposure to trans people's voices and culture, and in choosing to take part in conversations like these.

Closing reflections

ELLIS: I think despite the differences in our modalities and life experiences, it is clear that we share a single viewpoint on this; working in an affirmative way requires more than a positive outlook toward trans and non-binary identities. We have to start from an understanding that we do not know what being trans, or being a particular gender means to the client in front of us.

SERGE: Exploring these meanings is an essential but delicate part of our therapeutic work. We need to exercise what Lucie Fielding (2021) has called ethical curiosity by following the client's lead. A common issue in this work is that we can let our curiosity run away with us – we can start to bring in our own assumptions about what will be relevant to our client's feelings around gender rather than focussing on what is relevant *for them*. For example, a classic error of this kind is therapists putting too great an emphasis on childhood gender experiences or feelings about genitals. For some trans people, neither of these might be particularly relevant to their feelings about their gender.

ELLIS: The reality is that no two gender-diverse clients will have the same way of conceiving of their gender or of the significance of their trans experience. These differences between people can have important implications for their sexual desires, identities, practices, and relationships (see Chapter 8). All these things become intricately affected by that kaleidoscopic picture we have been referring to. Part of our role as therapists is to hold the possibility open of how this changing picture works as an evolving self-configuration and to communicate its legitimacy. If the client feels profoundly secure in this legitimacy, they may then allow themselves to see all the parts of the picture that they may otherwise have found more difficult to integrate.

SERGE: What can feel like a paradox is that profoundly secure legitimacy does not mean securely *fixed in place*. It needs to be both secure *and* flexible. To allow for clients to be inconsistent, to feel differently about themselves from one week to the next, or from one vantage point to another. We have to allow for multiple self-meanings all at the same time and also be conscious that these may change.

ELLIS: It occurs to me that inside the mechanism of a kaleidoscope there are a number of mirrors arranged within a viewing tube. There is something that feels fitting about this as a metaphor for the work we have been describing throughout this dialogue. As therapists, the relationships we build with our clients can often act as a mirror, allowing them to witness their reflection within it. Perhaps in our work with clients exploring their gendered, sexual, and relational aspects of self – it is especially important to discard any expectations that the reflection that we see will be cast by a smooth, flat surface. Instead, we are likely to find ourselves looking through a kaleidoscope, reflecting multi-faceted and changing patterns. Only through recognising this can we legitimise and affirm *all* of what our clients show of themselves and can our clients in turn fully appreciate and value the picture that they see.

References

Austin, A., Craig, L.C., & Alessi, E.J. (2017). Affirmative cognitive behavioural therapy with transgender and gender non-conforming adults. *Psychiatric Clinics*, 40(1), 141–156.

Blair, K.L., & Hoskin, R.A. (2018). Transgender exclusion from the world of dating: Patterns of acceptance and rejection of hypothetical trans dating partners as a function of sexual and gender identity. *Journal of Social and Personal Relationships*, 36(7), 2074–2095.

Bunenger, S.L., Steensma, T.D., Cohen-Kettenis, P.T., & de Vries, A.L. (2017). Sexual and romantic experiences of transgender youth before gender affirmative treatment. *Paediatrics*, 139(3).

Butler, J. (2004). *Undoing Gender*. New York: Routledge.

Davies, D., & Neal, C. (1996). *Pink Therapy: A Guide for Counsellors and Therapists Working with Lesbian and Gay and Bisexual Clients*. Berkshire: Open University Press.

Defreyne, J., Elaut, E., Den Heijer, M., Kreukels, B., Fisher, A.B., & T'Sjoen, G. (2021). Sexual orientation in transgender individuals: Results from the longitudinal EMGI study. *Your Sexual Medicine Journal*, 33, 694–702.

Drescher, J., Cohen-Kettenis, P., & Winter, S. (2012). Minding the body: Situating gender identity diagnoses in the ICD-10. *International Review of Psychiatry*, 24(6), 568–577.

Fielding, L. (2021). *Trans Sex: Clinical Approaches to Trans Sexualities and Erotic Embodiments*. New York and London: Routledge.

Jas, Y. (2020). Sexuality in a non-binary world: Redefining and expanding the linguistic repertoire. *Journal of the International Network for Sexual Ethics and Politics*, Special Issue, 71–92.

Katz-Wise, S.L., Reisner, S.L., White Hughto, J., & Keo-Meier, C.L. (2016). Differences in sexual orientation diversity and sexual fluidity in attractions among gender minority adults in Massachusetts. *The Journal of Sex Research*, 53(1).

Lemma, A., & Savulescu, J. (2021). To be, or not to be? The role of the unconscious in transgender transitioning: Identity, autonomy and well-being. *Journal of Medical Ethics*, 1–8. doi:10.1136/medethics-2021-1037397

Marshall, E., Glazebrook, C., Robbins-Cherry, S., Nicholson, S., Thorne, N., & Arcelus, J. (2020). The quality and satisfaction of romantic relationships in transgender people: A systematic review of the literature. *International Journal of Transgender Health*, 21(4), 373–390.

McKinney, R., Desposito, M., & Yoon, E. (2020). Promoting identity wellness in LGBTGEQIAP+ adolescents through affirmative therapy. *Journal of LGBT Issues in Counselling*, 14(3), 176–190.

McNeil, J., Bailey, L., Ellis, S., & Regan, M. (2012). *Trans Mental Health Study*. www.treverseresearch.com/wp-content/uploads/2012/12/Mental-Health-2012.pdf

Rogers, C. (2004). *On Becoming a Person: A Therapist's View of Psychotherapy*. London: Constable and Robinson (first printed 1967).

Ruberg, B., & Ruelos, S. (2020). Data for queer lives: How LGBTQ gender and sexualities challenge norms and demographics. *Big Data and Society*, 7(1), 1–12.

Serano, J.S. (2010). The case against autogynephelia. *International Journal of Transgenderism*, 12(3), 176–187.

Singh, A.A. (2016). Moving from affirmation to liberation in psychological practice with transgender and gender non-conforming clients. *American Psychologist*, 71(8), 755–762.

Tomkins, A.B. (2014). "There's no chasing involved": Cis/trans relationships, "tranny chasers", and the future of a sex-positive trans politics. *Journal of Homosexuality*, 61, 766–780.

Williams, R.A. (2018). *T4T and Trans Separatism: The Politics of Radical Love*. https://medium.com/@transphilosophr/t4t-and-the-micropolitics-of-trans-liberation-357df39df017

Chapter 8

Sex in transition

From the medicalisation of transgender sexuality to the centrality of pleasure

Dr Annalisa Anzani and Dr Antonio Prunas

As Fielding (2021) recently argued, it is pointless to address the sexual well-being of transgender and gender-nonconforming (TGNC) people from a clinical perspective without being aware of (and necessarily challenging and deconstructing) the dominant narratives that have shaped the way in which mental health professionals have framed the erotic and sexual lives of TGNC people for decades.

These narratives have been present in the clinical and academic literature since the very introduction of gender-affirming treatments and have constituted the basis of the research studies that have been carried out ever since. The choice of research topics to focus on, the research paradigms and outcome measures adopted in follow-up studies, the assessment instruments, and the inclusion of control or normative groups against which the experiences of TGNC people were compared all followed this logic.

The early theorisations about transgender sexuality, from the 1950s onwards, created the basis for the overall pathologisation of the sexuality of TGNC people (Prunas, 2019), and these biases still remain deeply ingrained in clinicians and researchers and, sadly enough, TGNC people themselves.

These biased narratives have been masterfully summarised by Fielding in four main points:

- The "unimaginability" of trans bodies. According to this narrative, TGNC people are excluded from being objects of other people's desire and are also not imaginable as being able to experience sexual desire themselves. This implies the erasure of TGNC bodies and, at the same time, their fetishisation and objectification, with an impact in terms of internalised transphobia (i.e., the internalisation of negative messages) and difficulties in finding a sexual partner.
- Trans narratives are dominated by trauma and oppression, with an exclusive focus on disparities, morbidity, risk factors, stigma, and discrimination that may hinder, in the clinical relationship, the adoption of a sex-positive approach, and the exploration of a positive and satisfying relationship with the client's sexual self.
- A discourse centred on sexual losses refers to the assumption that being trans or starting a medical gender transition necessarily implies a sexual life that

DOI: 10.4324/9781003260608-9

is less than cis sexualities. This finds expression, for example, in the idea that hormone replacement therapy (HRT) determines a *loss* of sexual desire for trans women, as opposed to a *change* in erotic patterns.

• A clinical focus on sexual function: sexology, sex therapy, and sexual medicine have relied on paradigms that define goal treatments in terms of restoring "standard" functioning, rather than setting pleasure as the main aim of clinical interventions. Although such a focus on functionality and performance is limiting for *every* individual, regardless of their gender identity, it is particularly detrimental when exploring the sexual lives of TGNC people.

This chapter aims to review the scientific literature on the sexuality of TGNC people. We will start exploring early studies, highlighting their biases, and proceed to an overview of very recent contributions that tried to overcome those limitations. In particular, we will focus on four specific areas of sexuality (gender dysphoria and its impact on sexuality, sexual fantasies, sexual satisfaction and dissatisfaction, and fetishisation of TGNC individuals), examining recent contributions on each topic and deriving clinical implications to guide clinicians working with TGNC people.

Early studies

Research on the sexual experiences of TGNC people has been marked, for many years, by a heavily medicalised approach focusing on the impact of hormonal and/or surgical gender affirmation treatments on various aspects of sexuality.

These first studies followed a purely binary model and were entirely based on clinical samples recruited in gender identity clinics (Bartolucci et al., 2015; Wierckx et al., 2014). Because individuals presenting to gender identity clinics often report more distress regarding their bodies than trans individuals in the community (Jones et al., 2019), body-based distress may be considerably accentuated in clinical samples.

Another problem with the first generation of studies is that penile-vaginal intercourse is often considered the only potential sexual activity other than solo masturbation.

The first significant critiques of this strand of research came in 2015, with a groundbreaking article by Bauer and Hammond that highlighted the centrality of medical treatments in the study of transgender sexuality. The authors argue that ignoring the substantial group of trans people who do not desire to undergo medical treatments means adopting a cisgenderist and cissexist paradigm. Indeed, studies report that around 14% of trans women claim they do not plan to undergo any medical treatment or that the concept of medical transition does not apply to them, as well as 20% of transmen and 50% of non-binary (NB) individuals (Factor & Rothblum, 2008; Koehler et al., 2018; Scheim & Bauer, 2019).

Building on this critique, Bradford and Spencer (2020) note that, up to this point, the focus has been more firmly placed on the functional or problematic aspects of sexuality rather than sexual pleasure. Furthermore, pleasure has been viewed primarily as orgasmic capacity on a biological and mechanical level, rather than considering individuals' sexuality holistically.

Recent literature

In recent years, studies have emerged that seek to overcome these limitations, attempting to broaden the trans sexual experience.

Some studies have addressed the changes in sexuality that occur as a result of HRT. Indeed, gonadal hormones play an essential role in sexual well-being. Studies on HRT in trans men report marked changes following medical gender affirmation treatments. Physical changes induced by testosterone therapy include a change in body fat distribution toward an android pattern, increased total lean mass, and increased facial and body hair (Wierckx et al., 2014). Concerning changes related to sexuality, trans men report increased sexual desire that, in some cases, reaches hypersexuality (Rowniak et al., 2011). Also, a change in sexual practices is reported after HRT. For example, participants reported being more comfortable engaging in vaginal sex once they felt more substantial body congruence (Bockting et al., 2009). In general, bodily changes, particularly changes induced by HRT and top surgery, have been identified as factors increasing the sense of comfort in partnered sexuality in both trans masculine and NB people (Anzani et al., 2021a).

Regarding HRT in trans women, studies are scarce, and the effects on sexuality are often miscategorised as erectile dysfunction. Rosenberg and colleagues (2019) explored the physio-psychological changes that follow HRT for trans women. Most respondents report a positive and affirming experience with sexuality during the medical transition. The authors emphasise that a critical experience during hormone-induced body change is developing new erogenous zones, making other bodily districts besides the genitals the primary sources of sexual arousal and orgasms. From a physiological standpoint, participants describe breast development, skin softening, increased overall sensitivity, and a reduction in the capacity to develop and maintain an erection (Idrus & Hymans, 2014; Aguayo-Romero et al., 2015; Radix, 2016).

van de Grift and colleagues (2019) focused on understanding how sexual pleasure, sexual arousability, and sexual interest change after phalloplasty and metoidioplasty in trans men. In general, genital surgery for trans men leads to increased pleasure, sexual interest, and arousability. This outcome is more consistently reported by participants who underwent metoidioplasty; in contrast, phalloplasty makes penile sensitivity somewhat variable.

Other recent studies on genital surgery have been conducted in the area of vaginoplasty for trans women. For example, Milrod and colleagues (2019) studied the vaginoplasty procedure chosen by surgeons to operate on trans women (i.e., in terms of vaginal canal depth). The authors note that the choice of surgery often follows heteronormative expectations about how a vagina should look and function, rather than preserving sensitivity to sexual pleasure.

Gender/body dysphoria and sexuality

Gender dysphoria refers to the potential discomfort experienced when an individual's gender identity is different from what is expected based on their gender assigned at birth (American Psychiatric Association, 2013). Gender dysphoria is a multi-layered construct because it may be experienced either as body dysphoria, social dysphoria, or both. Body dysphoria refers to the relationship between the individual and their own gendered body, and it may lead to feeling uncomfortable with one's entire body or only specific body parts. Social dysphoria, in contrast, refers to the distress and discomfort that can be experienced as a result of how the person is perceived by society.

It is essential to recognize that gender dysphoria is not a universal experience for trans and NB individuals (Bouman et al., 2016; Byne et al., 2018), although, according to the dominant narratives, gender dysphoria has almost become a synonym for being trans.

The belief that TGNC people are disgusted by their own bodies and dissatisfied with their sex lives due to gender dysphoria has informed trans research, going unchallenged for decades. Early studies also conceptualised gender dysphoria dichotomously (i.e., the presence or absence), rather than using continuous measures, limiting the understanding of the specific ways TGNC people may be affected by it (Lindley & Galupo, 2020).

As a consequence, even now, body dysphoria is often used by clinicians as a monolithic, crosscutting term (Spencer et al., 2017), one invariably applied to all TGNC people, hindering clinicians from conducting a deep exploration of the specific meanings it holds for *that specific person*.

Indeed, not only is there a large variability across TGNC people in terms of the way body dysphoria is experienced, but differences can also be noticed at different times within the same individual as well.

The relationship with one's own body affects sexuality, and the perception of discomfort for certain parts of the body that may be involved in partnered or solo sex can have an impact on sexological well-being.

Recent studies have explored the impact of body dysphoria on sexuality in greater depth. The merit of this strand of research has been highlighting that:

1   The experience of body dysphoria in sex, particularly genital dysphoria, is not universal.
2   Trans people have an active sex life, despite their dysphoria.
3   Trans people can implement strategies to overcome body dysphoria in sex.

Anzani and colleagues (2021a) focused on the experience of trans masculine and NB individuals with their own bodies in sex. Body discomfort during sex emerged as a very relevant issue, but at the same time, participants described a variety of strategies to overcome body dysphoria during sex, which can be grouped into three main categories: avoidance, detachment, and pretending.

Avoidance strategies consist of covering or not using certain body parts that cause discomfort or may trigger dysphoria. In the experience of individuals who identify on a male identity spectrum, the area that frequently causes the most discomfort is the chest. The chest is often kept covered, wearing binders and/or a t-shirt during intimacy, or the partner is not allowed to touch the area. Similarly, when the genitals are the main area of discomfort, participants report keeping their underwear on or avoiding using that body part. Another form of avoidance involves hiding body parts or the entire body during sex by preventing their partner from seeing their naked body, by turning off the light or avoiding close physical contact with their partner.

Detachment strategies can be described as a kind of disconnection from the body during sexual activity that allows the individual to avoid discomfort. This disconnection may occur, for example, by devoting one's energy and effort to the partner's pleasure, rather than to one's own, in order to reduce body dysphoria (self-denial or self-forgetfulness).

Finally, pretending strategies include using imagination, actions, or language to experience sexuality as if the person had the desired body characteristics. These strategies include imagining one's genitals (or sex toys) as if they were and functioned as the genitals of the affirmed gender. For example, imagining the strap-on to be one's penis or stimulating one's anus by imagining it to be a vagina. For some people, this strategy helps overcome body dysphoria. For others, the difficulty connected with using sex toys makes it useless. Another form of simulation involves the use of language, for example, actively renaming[1] body parts in a way that is affirmative of one's gender identity.

Participants in the study also described a wide range of specific actions or lack thereof they took with their bodies when engaging in sexual activities. Some participants mentioned avoidance of sex altogether (around 12.5% of the trans masculine and NB participants), while some others only mentioned solitary masturbatory activity or mutual masturbation with a partner(s). Other participants engaged in specific partnered sexual activities or assuming specific sexual roles. Some participants mentioned kink and BDSM practices as an affirmative way to experience sex, or even set no limits on the use of their bodies in sex (11.6% of the total sample) (Anzani et al., 2021a). This last result is particularly significant in the light of old studies: although a subgroup of participants does establish some boundaries for their bodies during sex due to body dysphoria, a large group describes a broad spectrum of sexual activities and even an affirmative use of their entire body in sex.

As for trans feminine and NB individuals assigned male at birth, a recent study investigated the variables implied in engagement in sex, including body satisfaction, as well as social and contextual factors (Goldbach et al., 2022). The authors sought to identify predictors of various sexual outcomes, such as engagement in sexual experiences (receptive and insertive sex), pleasure related to sexual activity, pleasure related to intimacy, and finally, the importance of sexual activity. Interestingly enough and contrary to expectations based on common narratives, across all the models examined, transition status (i.e., hormone therapy) was not a significant predictor of any of the outcome variables. When demographics and contextual variables (i.e., body satisfaction, social dysphoria, and fetishisation) are taken into account, medical transition status appears to have no effect on trans feminine and NB sexuality.

Clinical implications

Celebrate sexuality

Clinicians should not assume that the sexual life of a TGNC client is necessarily non-existent or frozen because of the impact of body dysphoria or the fact that no medical intervention has taken place yet. The large majority of TGNC people are sexually active (regardless of their medical transition status), although they are less satisfied with their sexual life (Nikkelen & Kreukels, 2018) as compared to their cisgender counterparts: this finding leaves a great deal of space for sexological work with TGNC people. Clinicians who adopt the medicalised model often assume that medical transition is necessary to reduce gender dysphoria and that, in turn, reducing gender dysphoria is necessary to minimise sexual dysfunction (Coleman et al., 2012). Adopting this medicalised lens ignores how positive experiences associated with TGNC people (e.g., gender euphoria and identity affirmation) can influence medical transition decisions and sexual satisfaction. Also, research shows that TGNC people find effective (and sometimes creative) ways to share their intimacy with their partner(s). This repertoire of coping strategies can be expanded during consultations with the client by actively proposing strategies and techniques that other TGNC people find effective (as shown in the studies reviewed here) or working in group sessions or workshops.

Exploring body dysphoria

In exploring the sexual lives of TGNC people in a clinical setting, the assessment of body dysphoria is pivotal and requires an exploration of the following:

- If and to what extent body dysphoria is present.
- Which body parts or body areas are mostly responsible for distress/uneasiness/discomfort, keeping in mind that these may not necessarily include the genitals (e.g., the breast for trans masculine individuals or facial hair for trans feminine clients).
- Whether body dysphoria remains stable (accompanying the person every single day, with the same intensity) or changes over time and, in the latter case, which factors are implied in the fluctuations: these might include internal (i.e., mood), interpersonal (i.e., being called by the chosen name by family members or partners), and social[2] factors (i.e., being misgendered versus being recognised as one's own experienced gender).

• Changes in the intensity and in manifestations of body dysphoria can also occur as a result of age or of gender-affirming medical interventions (if applicable).

Finally, it is also important, while exploring body dysphoria and its impact on sexuality, to inquire about body parts the individual is satisfied with and comfortable using in sex. Focusing exclusively on difficulties and hurdles may be suggestive of a sex-negative approach, one often supported by the dominant narratives that were presented at the beginning of the chapter.

The use of sex toys for TGNC people

Sex toys can be very useful in sex counselling with TGNC people. Although all TGNC people can benefit from the use of sex toys (like most cisgender people), they can be particularly useful for experimenting and adapting to the changes brought about by hormone therapy or gender affirmation surgery. Within this perspective, autoeroticism can certainly be an important "gym", allowing the exploration of new methods of stimulation and pleasure that may be totally new (or significantly different) from those experienced previously.

Masturbation, carried out independently or mutually with a partner(s), even with the use of sex toys, can also be an intermediate step to become familiar with physical intimacy with the partner, set limits in the relationship, and find new ways to experience sexual pleasure.

Today, masturbation aids are available that are specifically designed by and for transgender people and aimed at reducing, containing, or overcoming dysphoria. This is possible by avoiding direct eye contact with one's own genitals (which can be a trigger for dysphoria) or using shapes or materials that are in line with the genitals of the gender with which one identifies. Many trans men also experience considerable relief from dysphoria through the use of penile prostheses.

Some devices are particularly suitable for transgender women or NB people assigned male at birth who experience discomfort with their genitals. In these cases, devices characterised by gender-neutral shapes (that do not refer to specific anatomical configurations), those that do not necessarily focus the stimulation on the shaft of the penis (shifting the focus to the anal area or perineum), or those that can be used while keeping the private parts covered with a sheet may be useful.

Be affirmative of other minority identities and non-normative sexual behaviours and practices (kink/BDSM, CNMs), as they are experienced by TGNC people as a way to affirm their gender identity in sex.

Sexual fantasies of TGNC people

The reasons to study sexual imagery in this specific target population are manifold. First, sexual imagery and fantasy are crucial aspects of human sexuality because they are associated with sexual arousal and response (Morin, 1995), and sexual fantasy can enhance (or inhibit) sexual responsivity and the willingness to engage in sexual activity.

Second, the dominant and long-standing medical narrative through which transgender identities have been historically conceptualised has led to a focus on specific components of their sexual lives (including sexual fantasies) as "markers" of an "authentic" transgender identity (Prunas, 2019).

For all these reasons, it is important to debunk myths about the sexual imagery of TGNC people by collecting their lived experiences and narratives from large samples of people with diverse gender identities and expressions.

Very recent contributions from our research group aimed at filling this gap in the literature by exploring the sexual imagery of NB people with a mixed-methods approach, using both qualitative and quantitative techniques (Lindley et al., 2020b; Anzani & Prunas, 2020).

Anzani and Prunas (2020) compared the sexual fantasies of cis men and women and NB people with a quantitative approach, making use of the Sexual Fantasy Questionnaire (SFQ; Bogaert et al., 2015). The results showed that, in contrast to cisgender men and women, NB people rated most of the fantasies included in the questionnaire as less sexually arousing. However, most of these fantasies are part of sexual scripts with strongly gendered connotations, and the lower propensity of NB individuals to consider those themes exciting may be due to a rejection of gender roles that those themes too rigidly incorporate.

In light of these limitations, Lindley et al. (2020b) adopted a bottom-up, qualitative research method investigating the sexual fantasies of NB people by means of an open-ended question. The results showed that NB participants' sexual fantasies rarely differed from those of cisgender participants. When differences emerged, NB participants described having a desire for different or both genitals, which would allow them to engage differently in sexual activity, a desire that may ultimately serve to affirm their identity.

Similarly, the way NB participants talked about non-normative identities or genitals differed from that of their cisgender counterparts. Cisgender participants spoke of a desire to have sex with transgender individuals, reducing them to their bodies or genitals (Mauk et al., 2013), whereas NB participants spoke about how they used their genitals in non-normative ways or how their non-normative identities impacted their sexual fantasies.

Finally, NB participants were significantly less likely to describe themselves as the object of another's desire. This could be the result of internalised transphobia, which, combined with high levels of body dissatisfaction (McGuire et al., 2016), could lead NB individuals to be less likely to fantasise about being another individual's object of desire. Additionally, cisgenderist conceptualisations of sex, which are pervasive in the assumptions of sexuality and sexual practice (Blumer et al., 2013), could influence NB individuals' view of their sexual desirability. Non-binary individuals may not be able to find reflections of societal sexual attraction toward NB identities and internalise this to mean that they, themselves, are not sexually desirable.

Clinical implications

Clinical use of sexual fantasy

Imagery-based techniques are a key component of the clinical toolbox of any sex therapist, and they are widely used to enhance sexuality and help overcome sexual difficulties, problems, and dysfunctions. Needless to say, such techniques, in order to be effective, should be accurately tailored to the specific client in consultation in order to avoid imposing a cisgenderist lens on the sexual imagery of gender-diverse clients.

Working on sexual self-esteem

It has been suggested that clinicians "cannot remain an impartial observer given the impact of minority stress in trans clients' lives" and that part of their mandate is to take an active role in countering the pervasive social messages that devalue trans sexuality (Spencer et al., 2017, p. 291). To do so, the clinician must help clients internalise positive and affirming messages about themselves and their sexuality by suggesting alternative trans-affirmative media, referring clients to sex-positive support groups, and engaging in community advocacy work.

Sexual satisfaction and dissatisfaction

The existing body of research used quantitative measures of sexual satisfaction to test the researchers' hypothesis on sexual satisfaction among TGNC people. However, as mentioned in the previous paragraph, this often consisted of assessing the capacity and willingness to engage in penetrative sex. Two more recent contributions (Lindley et al., 2020a; Lindley et al., 2020b) have broadened the view of sexual satisfaction and dissatisfaction among TGNC people by using qualitative methods to capture their direct experience, unconstrained by preconceptions and biases.

Regarding sexual satisfaction, Lindley and colleagues (2020a) highlighted aspects of interpersonal and intrapersonal contexts. On the one hand, partners were identified as key determinants of sexual satisfaction for the participants. Participants discussed how partners who understood their gender identity provided positive sexual experiences. This understanding found expression in respect for boundaries that participants had in place to protect themselves from experiences of gender dysphoria. Having a trans partner was also described by participants as a component of sexual satisfaction. Trans partners understood participants' experiences and were able to provide a safe space in which to engage with sex.

On the other hand, gender affirmation can result directly from the sexual behaviours enacted by the participants. Sex provides the opportunity to connect with their body and find pleasure in it, feeling desired and attractive. In some cases, sex even allowed participants to overcome gender dysphoria by focusing on pleasure; however, discovering which sexual activities were comfortable was an important step (Lindley et al., 2020a; Riggs & Bartholomaeus, 2018). Notably, although nearly half of the study participants had undergone HRT, very few of them mentioned that their satisfaction was related to medical transition.

The second study by the same research group investigated sexual dissatisfaction (Lindley et al., 2020a). In some cases, the findings mirror the previous ones; for example, the inability to find an accepting and affirming partner was reported as a factor in sexual dissatisfaction. In addition, the desire for different body parts and body dysphoria also contributed to sexual dissatisfaction, with some participants describing frustration with using prosthetics during sexual activity. Finally, some participants described anxiety when engaging in sex with new partners, questioning whether the other's interest was genuine or driven by a fetishistic drive. This fear, as discussed in the next paragraph, prevents them from participating in novel sexual encounters, contributing to sexual dissatisfaction (Lindley et al., 2020a).

Clinical implications

Key role of partners

The main implication of these findings is the key role of partners in contributing to the sexual satisfaction and dissatisfaction of TGNC people. Whenever possible, partners should be involved in the consultation with TGNC clients in order to explore strategies and behaviours that may contribute to (or hinder) a satisfactory sexual life for all the people involved. For instance, studies have shown that the active use of microaffirmations in romantic relationships may help TGNC individuals overcome negative internalised messages and feel worthy of love (Galupo et al., 2019; Pulice-Farrow et al., 2019). Also, TGNC individuals and their partners were shown to rely on several relational and practical resources to enjoy positive experiences with intimacy and sexuality (Siboni et al., 2021).

Sexualisation and fetishisation of trans and NB individuals

As mentioned in the previous section, one theme concerning TGNC people's sexual dissatisfaction was anticipatory anxiety regarding new potential sexual encounters and the fear of being fetishised by potential partners.

Serano (2007) describes the experiences of sexualisation and fetishisation of trans women as mainly directed to establish a power dynamic that subjugates trans (and cisgender) women to cissexist power.[3] The sexualisation of trans women stems from the erroneous assumption that they undergo genital surgery to be more attractive to (cisgender straight) men and be penetrated. According to this perspective, the bodies of trans women would only serve the sexual satisfaction of men.

Spencer and colleagues (2017), in a comprehensive study, explored the lived experiences of fetishisation in trans feminine, trans masculine, and NB individuals.

The authors found, in their qualitative analysis, that, in most cases, fetishisation was perceived as a negative experience that took the form of the sexual objectification of transgender bodies.

Individuals' experiences of fetishisation were frequently described as objectifying and dehumanising, in which people felt as if they were not seen as "real people" but rather as mere sexual objects.

The few participants who described fetishisation as positive framed the experience of fetish as a part of their kink sexual practice. Others considered fetishisation to be the expression of genuine sexual attraction to transgender identities, with a positive effect on their self-esteem. In other words, it seems that some TGNC people internalise the message that personal worth can only come from their sexual attractiveness. One very important new finding to highlight from the study is that fetishisation experiences are not exclusive to trans feminine individuals; rather, they are also frequently reported by trans masculine and NB individuals.

Clinical implications

Psychological effects of objectification

Objectification theory (Fredrickson & Roberts, 1997) states that sexual objectification experiences may lead to "self-objectification"; that is, women eventually internalise the concept of themselves as sexual objects and consistently monitor and measure their bodies against dominant cultural standards of beauty (Moradi, 2010). This internalisation process may bring about body shame and increased anxiety, which are very frequently reported among trans women (Moradi, 2010). Also, previous studies have identified a link between the sexualisation of trans women and a higher propensity to risky behaviours, especially in sexual situations. The need to receive gender affirmation from their male sexual partners may lead trans women to increase their willingness to engage in risky sexual behaviour and jeopardise their self-efficacy to negotiate condom use and/or substance use during sex (Sevelius, 2013).

Working on sexual assertiveness

The socially held assumption that they are undesirable to cisgender people (Fielding, 2021) may lead TGNC individuals (youths in particular) to show gratitude whenever they become the object of sexual interest from others and, therefore, be less able to negotiate limits and boundaries (Bartholomaeus & Riggs, 2017). These dynamics have enormous implications in terms of consent and may place the TGNC person at risk of experiencing sexual harassment and violence.

Always adopt a trauma-informed approach

Experiences of sexual trauma and victimisation are frequent in TGNC people, and up to half of TGNC people report they have been sexually assaulted at some point in their lives (James et al., 2016). Such rates are even higher for TGNC people of colour and those who have done sex work, been homeless, or have a disability. The impact of traumatic experiences (particularly sexual trauma) on several aspects of sexual functioning and well-being (i.e., sexual desire, sexual dysfunctions, and intimacy) is well known (McCarthy & Farr, 2011) because such experiences affect an individual's feelings, associations, and implicit memories regarding touch, trust, safety, and power (Zoldbrod, 2015).

Stigma toward partners of TGNC people

It is important to keep in mind that academic research has long pathologised attraction to TGNC people, attempting to probe into the reasons why some people (cisgender males in particular) may be attracted to TGNC partners. In most cases, the variables examined in such studies were clinical in nature in order to test *a priori* hypotheses in that direction (e.g., Hsu et al., 2016). This line of research has even led some researchers to classify this attraction as an overt form of paraphilia (Laws & O'Donohue, 2008).

This stigmatising attitude has important implications for the everyday lives of TGNC people looking for a partner. Blair and Hoskin (2019) report that, in a large sample of heterosexual, lesbian, gay, bisexual, queer, and trans individuals, 87.5% claimed that they would not consider dating a trans person. Cisgender straight men and women were the groups most likely to exclude trans persons from their potential dating pools.

Another relevant implication is that stigma against partners of TGNC people may end up generating conflicts and hardships in the relationship. This may happen, for instance, when the cisgender partner of a TGNC person is not willing to disclose the identity of the partner to their family of origin. These issues have been conceptualised as "couple-level minority stressors" (Frost et al., 2017), and they are experienced by individual partners or jointly by the couple as a result of the stigmatised status of their relationship. However, couple-level minority stress has most commonly been studied in gay couples, and more research is needed to explore its impact on the lives of TGNC people.

Dating

Fear and avoidance are reported on the part of TGNC participants as a common reaction whenever they feel fetishised. Avoidance of sexual and sentimental relationships due to the fear of being fetishised could be particularly problematic for TGNC individuals because romantic relationships are an important resource and protective factor for the health of TGNC people (Galupo et al., 2019; Meier et al., 2013; Pulice-Farrow et al., 2019). From this perspective, the role of mental and sexual health professionals is to help TGNC individuals walk the fine line between appreciation and fetishisation. Also, clinicians should be aware that the minority gender identity of the person may well interact with other marginalised identities (e.g., ethnic minority, disability, age) within an intersectional perspective. Finally, the search for a partner can expose TGNC people to negative experiences of invalidation and discrimination: a study by Anzani and colleagues (2021b) showed that social media and dating apps are common venues for both experiences of fetishisation and microaggressions.

Notes

1 Needless to say, the clinician should refer to those body parts accordingly.
2 Although gender dysphoria is often considered an intrapsychic variable (the relationship of a person and their own body), recent contributions (Lindley & Galupo, 2020) have suggested that it can be conceptualised as a proximal stressor within the Minority Stress Model because it involves the internalisation of social experiences. This remark has important implications in the area of sexuality because sexual encounters are, by all means, social encounters between two or more people entangled in gendered expectations (Simon & Gagnon, 2003; Lindley et al., 2020a). Thus, partnered sex can be a particularly triggering activity for gender dysphoria.
3 It is essential to distinguish sexualisation from being the object of sexual desire. The latter serves short- and long-term goals, such as achieving sexual satisfaction and pleasure or building a long-term relationship (Buss, 1998; Zawacki et al., 2009). Sexualisation, in contrast, establishes a power dynamic through actions such as catcalling, sexualised images passed on in the media and the role played by trans women in pornography (Serano, 2007).

References

Aguayo-Romero, R.A., Reisen, C.A., Zea, M.C., Bianchi, F.T., & Poppen, P.J. (2015). Gender affirmation and body modification among transgender persons in Bogotá, Colombia. *International Journal of Transgenderism*, 16, 103–115.
American Psychiatric Association. (2013). *Diagnostic and Statistical Manual of Mental Disorders* (5th ed.). Washington, DC: American Psychiatric Press.
Anzani, A., Lindley, L., Prunas, A., & Galupo, P. (2021a). "I use all the parts I'm given": A qualitative investigation of trans masculine and nonbinary individuals' use of body during sex. *International Journal of Sexual Health*, 33(1), 58–75. https://doi.org/10.108 0/19317611.2020.1853300
Anzani, A., Lindley, L., Tognasso, G., Galupo, M.P., & Prunas, A. (2021b). "Being talked to like I was a sex toy, like being transgender was simply for the enjoyment of someone else": Fetishization and sexualization of transgender and nonbinary individuals. *Archives of Sexual Behavior*, 50(3), 897–911.
Anzani, A., & Prunas, A. (2020). Sexual fantasy of cisgender and nonbinary individuals: A quantitative study. *Journal of Sex & Marital Therapy*, 46(8), 763–772.
Bartholomaeus, C., & Riggs, D.W. (2017). *Transgender People and Education*. New York, NY: Palgrave Macmillan. https://doi.org/10.1057/978-1-349-95309-7
Bartolucci, C., Gómez-Gil, E., Salamero, M., Esteva, I., Guillamón, A., Zubiaurre, L., Molero, F., & Montejo, A.L. (2015). Sexual quality of life in gender-dysphoric adults before genital sex reassignment surgery. *The Journal of Sexual Medicine*, 12(1), 180–188.
Blair, K.L., & Hoskin, R.A. (2019). Transgender exclusion from the world of dating: Patterns of acceptance and rejection of hypothetical trans dating partners as a function

of sexual and gender identity. *Journal of Social and Personal Relationships*, 36(7), 2074–2095.

Blumer, M.L., Gávriel Ansara, Y., & Watson, C.M. (2013). Cisgenderism in family therapy: How everyday clinical practices can delegitimize people's gender self-designations. *Journal of Family Psychotherapy*, 24(4), 267–285.

Bockting, W.O., Benner, A., & Coleman, E. (2009). Gay and bisexual identity development among female-to-male transsexuals in North America: Emergence of a transgender sexuality. *Archives of Sexual Behavior*, 38(5), 688–701.

Bogaert, A.F., Visser, B.A., & Pozzebon, J.A. (2015). Gender differences in object of desire self-consciousness sexual fantasies. *Archives of Sexual Behavior*, 44(8), 2299–2310.

Bouman, W.P., De Vries, A.L., & T'Sjoen, G. (2016). Gender dysphoria and gender incongruence: An evolving inter-disciplinary field. *International Review of Psychiatry*, 28(1), 1–4.

Bradford, N.J., & Spencer, K. (2020). Sexual pleasure in transgender and gender diverse individuals: An update on recent advances in the field. *Current Sexual Health Reports*, 1–6.

Buss, D.M. (1998). Sexual strategies theory: Historical origins and current status. *Journal of Sex Research*, 35, 19–31.

Byne, W., Karasic, D.H., Coleman, E., Eyler, A.E., Kidd, J.D., Meyer-Bahlburg, H.F., Pleak, R.R., & Pula, J. (2018). Gender dysphoria in adults: An overview and primer for psychiatrists. *Transgender Health*, 3(1), 57–70.

Coleman, E., Bockting, W., Botzer, M., Cohen-Kettenis, P., De Cuypere, G., Feldman, J., . . . Zucker, K. (2012). Standards of care for the health of transsexual, transgender, and gender-nonconforming people, version 7. *International Journal of Transgenderism*, 13(4), 165–232.

Factor, R., & Rothblum, E. (2008). Exploring gender identity and community among three groups of transgender individuals in the United States: MTFs, FTMs, and genderqueers. *Health Sociology Review*, 17(3), 235–253.

Fielding, L. (2021). *Trans Sex: Clinical Approaches to Trans Sexualities and Erotic Embodiments*. London: Routledge.

Fredrickson, B., & Roberts, T. (1997). Objectification theory. *Psychology of Women Quarterly*, 21(2), 173–206.

Frost, D.M., LeBlanc, A.J., de Vries, B., Alston-Stepnitz, E., Stephenson, R., & Woodyatt, C. (2017). Couple-level minority stress: An examination of same-sex couples' unique experiences. *Journal of Health and Social Behavior*, 58(4), 455–472.

Galupo, M.P., Lomash, E., & Mitchell, R.C. (2019). "I love you as both and I love you as neither": Romantic partners' affirmations of nonbinary trans individuals. *International Journal of Transgenderism*, 20(2–3), 315–327.

Goldbach, C., Lindley, L., Anzani, A., & Galupo, M. P. (2022). Resisting trans medicalization: Body satisfaction and social contextual factors as predictors of sexual experiences among trans feminine and nonbinary individuals. *The Journal of Sex Research*, 1–12. https://www.tandfonline.com/doi/abs/10.1080/00224499.2021.2004384

Hsu, K.J., Rosenthal, A.M., Miller, D.I., & Bailey, J.M. (2016). Who are gynandromorphophilic men? Characterizing men with sexual interest in transgender women. *Psychological Medicine*, 46(4), 819–827.

Idrus, N.I., & Hymans, T.D. (2014). Balancing benefits and harm: Chemical use and bodily transformation among Indonesia's transgender waria. *International Journal of Drug Policy*, 25(4), 789–797.

James, S., Herman, J., Rankin, S., Keisling, M., Mottet, L., & Anafi, M.A. (2016). *The Report of the 2015 U.S. Transgender Survey*. https://transequality.org/sites/default/files/docs/usts/USTS-Full-Report-Dec17.pdf

Jones, B.A., Pierre Bouman, W., Haycraft, E., & Arcelus, J. (2019). Gender congruence and body satisfaction in nonbinary transgender people: A case control study. *International Journal of Transgenderism*, 20(2–3), 263–274.

Koehler, A., Eyssel., J., & Nieder, T.O. (2018). Genders and individual treatment progress in (non-) binary trans individuals. *The Journal of Sexual Medicine*, 15(1), 102–113.

Laws, D.R., & O'Donohue, T.O. (2008). *Sexual Deviance: Theory, Assessment, and Treatment*. New York, NY: Guilford Press.

Lindley, L.M., Anzani, A., & Galupo, M.P. (2020a). What constitutes sexual dissatisfaction for trans masculine and nonbinary individuals: A qualitative study. *Journal of Sex & Marital Therapy*, 1–18.

Lindley, L.M., Anzani, A., Prunas, A., & Galupo, M.P. (2020b). Sexual fantasy across gender identity: A qualitative investigation of differences between cisgender and non-binary people's imagery. *Sexual and Relationship Therapy*, 1, 1–22.

Lindley, L.M., & Galupo, M.P. (2020). Gender dysphoria and minority stress: Support for inclusion of gender dysphoria as a proximal stressor. *Psychology of Sexual Orientation and Gender Diversity*, 7(3), 265.

Mauk, D., Perry, A., & Muñoz-Laboy, M. (2013). Exploring the desires and sexual culture of men who have sex with male-to-female transgender women. *Archives of Sexual Behavior*, 42(5), 793–803.

McCarthy, B., & Farr, E. (2011). The impact of sexual trauma on sexual desire and function. *Sexual Dysfunction: Beyond the Brain-Body Connection*, 31, 105–120.

McGuire, J.K. (2016). Body image in transgender young people: Findings from a qualitative, community based study. *Body Image*, 18, 96–107.

Meier, S.C., Sharp, C., Michonski, J., Babcock, J.C., & Fitzgerald, K. (2013). Romantic relationships of female-to-male trans men: A descriptive study. *International Journal of Transgenderism*, 14(2), 75–85.

Milrod, C., Monto, M., & Karasic, D.H. (2019). Recommending or rejecting "the dimple": WPATH-affiliated medical professionals' experiences and attitudes toward gender-confirming vulvoplasty in transgender women. *The Journal of Sexual Medicine*, 16(4), 586–595.

Moradi, B. (2010). Addressing gender and cultural diversity in body image: Objectification theory as a framework for integrating theories and grounding research. *Sex Roles*, 63(1), 138–148.

Morin, J. (1995). *The Erotic Mind: Unlocking the Inner Sources of Sexual Passion and Fulfillment*. London: Headline.

Nikkelen, S.W.C., & Kreukels, B.P.C. (2018). Sexual experiences in transgender people: The role of desire for gender-confirming interventions, psychological well-being, and body satisfaction. *Journal of Sex & Marital Therapy*, 44(4), 370–381.

Prunas, A. (2019). The pathologization of trans-sexuality: Historical roots and implications for sex counselling with transgender clients. *Sexologies*, 28(3), e54–e60.

Pulice-Farrow, L., Bravo, A., & Galupo, M.P. (2019). "Your gender is valid": Microaffirmations in the romantic relationships of transgender individuals. *Journal of LGBT Issues in Counseling*, 13(1), 45–66.

Radix, A.E. (2016). *Medical Transition for Transgender Individuals: Lesbian, Gay, Bisexual, and Transgender Healthcare*. Berlin: Springer International Publishing.

Riggs, D.W., & Bartholomaeus, C. (2018). Transgender young people's narratives of intimacy and sexual health: implications for sexuality education. *Sex Education*, *18*(4), 376–390.

Rosenberg, S., Tilley, P.M., & Morgan, J. (2019). "I couldn't imagine my life without it": Australian trans women's experiences of sexuality, intimacy, and gender-affirming hormone therapy. *Sexuality & Culture*, 23(3), 962–977.

Rowniak, S., Chesla, C., Rose, C., & Holzemer, W. (2011). Transmen: The HIV risk of gay identity. *AIDS Education and Prevention*, 23(6), 508–520. https://doi.org/10.1521/aeap.2011.23.6.508

Serano, J. (2007). *Whipping Girl: A Transsexual Woman on Sexism and the Scapegoating of Femininity*. Berkeley, CA: Seal Press.

Sevelius, J.M. (2013). Gender affirmation: A framework for conceptualizing risk behavior among transgender women of color. *Sex Roles*, 68(11), 675–689.

Scheim, A.I., & Bauer, G.R. (2019). Sexual inactivity among transfeminine persons: A Canadian respondent-driven sampling survey. *The Journal of Sex Research*, 56(2), 264–271. https://doi.org/10.1080/00224499.2017.1399334

Siboni, L., Rucco, D., Prunas, A., & Anzani, A. (2021). "We faced every change together": Couple's intimacy and sexuality experiences from the perspectives of transgender and non-binary individuals' partners. *Journal of Sex & Marital Therapy*, 1–24.

Simon, W., & Gagnon, J.H. (2003). Sexual scripts: Origins, influences and changes. *Qualitative Sociology*, 26(4), 491–497.

Spencer, K.G., Iantaffi, A., & Bockting, W. (2017). Treating sexual problems in transgender clients. In Z. Peterson (Ed.), *The Wiley Handbook of Sex Therapy*. Chichester, West Sussex, UK: John Wiley & Sons Ltd.

van de Grift, T.C., Pigot, G.L., Kreukels, B.P., Bouman, M.B., & Mullender, M.G. (2019). Transmen's experienced sexuality and genital gender-affirming surgery: Findings from a clinical follow-up study. *Journal of Sex & Marital Therapy*, 45(3), 201–205.

Wierckx, K., Van Caenegem, E., Schreiner, T., Haraldsen, I., Fisher, A., Toye, K., . . . T'Sjoen, G. (2014). Cross-sex hormone therapy in trans persons is safe and effective at short-time follow-up: Results from the European network for the investigation of gender incongruence. *The Journal of Sexual Medicine*, 11(8), 1999–2011.

Zawacki, T., Norris, J., Hessler, D.M., Morrison, D.M., Stoner, S.A., George, W.H., . . . Abdallah, D.A. (2009). Effects of relationship motivation, partner familiarity, and alcohol on women's risky sexual decision making. *Personality and Social Psychology Bulletin*, 35(6), 723–736.

Zoldbrod, A.P. (2015). Sexual issues in treating trauma survivors. *Current Sexual Health Reports*, 7(1), 3–11.

Chapter 9

Examining therapist bias when working with kink

Dr Lori Beth Bisbey

Kink, BDSM and fetish have been highlighted in popular media over the past 20 years. Many activities that were once so taboo that they were rarely talked about on mainstream television are now commonly mentioned. As a result, more people who have engaged or regularly engage in these activities are seen in therapy, counselling and coaching settings. Despite this, psychology, psychotherapy and counselling courses rarely cover these areas as part of training on relationships. Miller and Byers (2010) found that only 1/3 of a sample of 183 clinical and counselling psychologists had taken a sexuality related course during their graduate training. Surveys of practising psychologists paint an even more concerning picture with less than 1/2 to 1/3 of participants reporting any sexuality training (Reissing & Giulio, 2010; Miller & Byers, 2009, 2010) despite providing a variety of sexual health care services as part of their therapy with clients.

Those clinicians who do have training in sexuality as part of their courses often don't have training that covers gender, sex and relationship diversity. Clinicians who have not been personally exposed to gender, sex and relationship diversity often have no more knowledge about these practices and orientations than what they see in popular culture. This lack of knowledge leads to ineffective treatment at best and damaging treatment at worst. Even 'kink aware' therapists often have very limited knowledge about kink, fetish and non-monogamy.

The training clinicians do get in working with GSRD clients rarely includes any supervised practice. Supervised practice improves a clinician's clinical skills, case management, knowledge in specialist areas as well as supporting reflective practice. It is essential to help therapists identify and deal with their own feelings, countertransference, bias or issues and process these so they don't interfere with the client's progress in therapy. When I talk with therapists about working with people who practice kink or fetish, I recommend supervision from an experienced GSRD therapist who has been working with kink and fetish and preferably someone who has personal experience of these areas as well.

DOI: 10.4324/9781003260608-10

Defining kink and fetish

A simple definition for kink is sexual desire that is out of the ordinary. The most common kinks are desires for intense sensation of some kind and/or include a consensual exchange of power where one person agrees to lead and the other agrees to follow. For more detailed descriptions of kink, I recommend *The New Topping Book* and *The New Bottoming Book*, both by Dossie Easton and Janet Hardy (2001a, 2001b, Greenery Press) and *SM101* by Jay Wiseman (1997, Greenery Press).

Historically, a fetish is an object that was revered or worshipped. Eventually, diagnostically, a fetish (as in the most recent *Diagnostic and Statistical Manual of Mental Disorders 5* – Fetishistic Disorder) became something (an object or part of the body) that is necessary for sexual arousal. A person with a fetish cannot be aroused without the object of their fetish being present. For example, for someone who fetishises leather, it must be present for them to be aroused and to reach orgasm. The word *fetish* has entered the popular vernacular and now is used to mean something (or someone) that a person intensely desires. In this usage, it doesn't have the connotation that the object (or person) is either sexually arousing or necessary for sexual arousal. Fetishistic disorder is one of the paraphilias, disorders associated with atypical sexual desires and behaviours. The DSM-5 clearly states that most people with atypical sexual interests do not have a mental disorder.

In order to have a disorder, a person must:

- Experience distress about their interest (not merely resulting from disapproval of society).
- Have a desire or engage in a behaviour that causes distress, damage, injury to another – from people who cannot consent or are not giving consent.

Despite these qualifiers, it is not unusual for clients who do not meet these criteria to be treated as though they have a disorder because of the bias of the therapist. Many therapists believe that sexual behaviour that deviates from the norm is indicative of psychological issues, and the further from the norm the kink or fetish is, the more likely it is that the client will have their sexual behaviour identified as pathological by the therapist.

Clinical experience highlights that the kinks and fetishes that are usually most challenging for therapists who are not personally involved or who have not worked with a wide variety of GSRD clients are the following:

- **Water sports**: sexual play involving urine and urination.
- **Scat or hard sports**: sexual play involving faeces and defecation. Many therapists feel disgust at these types of activities and communicate this disgust non-verbally and sometimes unconsciously to clients. They don't understand how someone would feel arousal around these activities and highlight them

as pathological assuming that these activities by their nature degrade the person participating. They also cite the risks of disease inherent in this type of sexual activity, even though the risks vary widely depending upon the actual activity.

- **Humiliation**: sexual play involving humiliating a person or being humiliated by a person. This can include human toilet, name calling, objectification – having the person be an object like a table or footstool, forced feminisation (having a man dress in women's clothing, speak like a stereotypical woman, perform in the perceived female role sexually and often making fun of them as they do), chastity devices, amongst other activities. The bias is that people who enjoy these activities have low self-image or degrade themselves. Many therapists see this type of activity as symptomatic of deeper issues and inherently pathological. As a result, they see it as essential to 'treat'.

- **Consensual non-consent scenes** may involve rape, torture, interrogation. These are scenes where the person who is in the 'victim' role negotiates limits and asks the person who is the 'perpetrator' to do what they want within those limits. They often ask the person not to stop, even if they insist that a limit has been reached. In most kink and BDSM scenes/play, a safe word or gesture (or both) is agreed between the person who is the top (giving the experience) and the person who is the bottom (receiving the experience). This is a phrase, word or gesture that when it is expressed during a scene, stops the action completely. It is always meant to be something that would not normally come up in the course of a scene. Many people use a traffic light system: Green is "more please". Amber is "slow down or back off a bit". Red is "stop now". Gestures are also agreed in case the person is unable to speak because they are in a mental state that makes talking difficult or because they are gagged (as some people enjoy using gags as part of their kink).

  - In consensual non-consent scenes, sometimes people negotiate not to have safe words or gestures. It is then up to the top to assess whether things need to be slowed down or stopped. In other types of scenes, the bottom can call a stop to the action at any time. It is primarily in consensual non-consent that they agree not to have that level of control.
  - Therapists tend to be concerned about people being vulnerable and coerced into this type of scene and being physically and psychologically injured or abused. They become concerned about the validity of someone consenting once rather than giving enthusiastic ongoing consent. Consensual non-consent can be used by abusive partners as a way of doing what they wish without any concern for the health and safety of their partner. Unscrupulous dominant partners can put this phrase in negotiated agreements with submissive partners, having the submissive agree to consensual non-consent as part of the relationship ongoing. This is then used as an excuse when something they do is perceived as abusive. The submissive is reminded that they agreed to consensual non-consent and so the

behaviour is 'not abusive'. These things need assessment when someone presents with this relationship, but not all relationships that involve consensual non-consent are abusive. In most cases, both parties understand that ongoing enthusiastic consent is necessary for the relationship to be healthy. The dominant partner creates a safe space where the submissive partner can express upsets, needs, desires, difficulties without fear of reprisal and things can be negotiated on that basis. The dominant also makes sure that there is a regular check in with the submissive to make sure that everything is acceptable and running smoothly.

- **24/7 power exchanges or Total Power Exchange**: Many therapists feel that any type of ongoing power exchange is a recipe for abuse. They express concerns about coercion, around whether people are enacting pathology from their families of origin, concerns about controlling behaviour, whether people have agency and the ability to choose. What therapists often don't realise is how much personal work and negotiation goes into these agreements and how often people re-negotiate these agreements. People who engage in these relationships frequently communicate more often than those in more traditional relationships. They cannot make assumptions as each relationship is different. People in more traditional relationships often assume that each other understands the rules of the relationship the same way.
- **Blood play**: concerns include the possibility of permanent injuries and/or marks, disease transmission, the 'meaning' of this type of play. Some therapists look at blood play as a form of self-harm. Please note that according to the law in England and Wales, people cannot consent to self-harm, so though people may consent, it is still not considered to be legal.
- **Breath play**: concerns are first and foremost the dangerousness of the play. Some therapists see this as a passive suicide method and believe that people who are taking this level of risk are a clear danger to themselves, or the ones who are restricting their partner's breath are a clear danger to others.
- **Race play**: concerns are often about potential abuse (either as the giver or the receiver).

For almost all areas, concerns are that what a person is doing is either acting out trauma in a repetition compulsion or an attempt at mastery. Many therapists are concerned this is not being done consciously and the person may well take poor risks because they are unaware of their motivation and acting from history rather than making conscious choices. However, this can be an issue when people are involved in non–kink-related relationships as well. It is not unusual for people to act out their familial relationships in their adult romantic ones. As for all people, attachment styles formed in childhood carry over to choices made in adulthood when people have not explored these in some type of therapeutic setting.

For everything under the sun, there is someone who is sexually turned on by it. It may seem strange to the therapist, but part of the job is creating a safe space where someone can explore the things that turn them on even if these are very unusual. In my clinical experience, the more negative focus on a particular desire sometimes the more likely the person will become fixated on that desire.

Recent research highlights that therapists working with people from the kink, fetish and BDSM communities need to be careful of bias and negative judgements (Kelsey et al., 2012; Bezreh et al., 2012). The most common biases highlighted clinically and in research include the following:

- Kink/BDSM/Fetish are paraphilias and should be diagnosed as such whether or not they cause the client significant upset and/or difficulties in any areas of their lives, and therapy to 'cure' the paraphilia needs to be the priority.
- Kink/BDSM/Fetish are unhealthy and/or dangerous, and therapy to rid the client of these is the priority.
- Kink/BDSM/Fetish desires have most likely arisen as a result of abuse in childhood or, if not abuse, an incident or series of incidents in childhood. The corollary to this is: There is always value in 'figuring out' where these desires came from. There is often a belief that once the reasons are discovered, the person will no longer have the desires.
- Women who are submissive in relationships are vulnerable and likely subject to abuse. Related to this: The belief that being masochistic and/or submissive is pathological, and people who enjoy masochism or submission are vulnerable and need help to leave these relationships and/or stop this behaviour and change their sexual desires. A corollary is: These people are not able to give valid consent and/or don't have agency as a result of these desires and practices.
- People who are dominant and/or sadistic in their sexuality are abusive and/or controlling in the rest of their lives. A related belief is: People who identify as sadistic and/or dominant are likely to be psychopathic or sociopathic.
- People who are kinky/have a fetish/practice BDSM are more likely to have some diagnosable mental illness than the general population.
- The belief that these sexual practices and desires are at the root of any problem that the client presents with – whether they come in for sex or relationship work or for other issues.

These biases are applied to LGBTQIA++ people as well as heterosexual people. Some of these biases may not be conscious. Until the areas are explored, the clinician may not be aware of their own bias. In the next section, I provide a framework for uncovering these biases and addressing them as well as judgements.

Biases and blind spots

Banaji and Greenwald (2013) explore hidden biases in their book *Blind Spot: Hidden Biases of Good People*. They speak to the bits of information we gather on social groups that we store in our unconscious and that manage to guide some of our behaviour. We are unaware that these biases are impacting upon our behaviour and can be surprised when we discover they are there.

When it comes to sex and sexuality, obvious biases are very common. When a person encounters someone who has an obvious bias, they can either challenge the bias and educate the person or choose to avoid interacting with the person. Many clients find themselves in the position of being educators for their therapists around kink and fetish instead of being able to educate the therapist about their personal relationship to kink and fetish.

But as Banaji and Greenwald (2013) highlight, asking someone about their biases rarely produces accurate results. This is not necessarily because of dishonesty per se but rather because many of our biases live in the blind spot. In their book, they introduce the original Implicit Association Test and then one relating to race. Implicit measures have proven to correlate with bias moderately, and there is quite a bit of research demonstrating that scores on these tests can predict biased behaviour as well as attitude. Adaptations have been used to measure implicit bias in sex offenders who are paedophiles, attitudes to homosexuality, race, and a wide variety of other challenging areas. For the latest variety of adaptations, Harvard has an Implicit Associations Project ongoing that can be found at https://implicit.harvard.edu (Harvard Implicit Associations Project: Project Implicit. https://implicit.harvard.edu/implicit/)

In the course of my work, I have found it useful to create an adaptation that measures attitudes towards kink and fetish. I will detail the way the test works after I have given you a chance to take the test, so if you want to take it yourself, please do it now (see Figures 9.1 and 9.2).

Please take test A first, then test B.

The test you completed more quickly and with fewer mistakes highlights your bias. Often people are surprised as they see themselves as neutral. Yet implicit association tests highlight biases.

How does an implicit association test help us to understand our biases? In its simplest form, concepts we associate with positive words are concepts we are partial to. Those we associate with negative words are those we have a negative bias towards. We will complete a test more quickly and with fewer mistakes when words are paired 'correctly'. If I have a bias against kink or fetish, I would naturally pair terms with unpleasant or negative words. If I have a positive view of ordinary sex, I would naturally pair terms with pleasant or positive words.

If you completed test A more quickly, you have a positive bias towards kink and fetish. If you completed test B more quickly, you have a negative bias towards kink and fetish. Please note that these tests do not cover all kinks and fetishes, so it is possible that your results are specific to the kinks and fetishes named only. However, I tried to use a range of kinks, fetish and a range of usual sexual activities so that the test was more likely to pick up bias.

Implicit associations may seem a simplistic concept, and biases around sex can be complex and layered. However, this can be a useful tool to help identify bias that isn't conscious and to help clinicians start to unpack layers of bias relating to kink and fetish.

The Implicit Association Test Kink & Fetish
Dr Lori Beth Bisbey, 2021.

Test A
For kink/fetish activities and pleasant words, mark in the box to the left.
For everything else (ordinary activities and unpleasant words), mark in the box to the right.
Start at the top left and go from top to bottom, doing all the items in order.
Then do the second column. At bottom right, record the elapsed time in seconds and the number of mistakes.
Do it as quickly as you can without making mistakes.

Tick if kink/fetish		Tick if ordinary activity	Tick if pleasant word		Tick if unpleasant word
⬡	Rimming	⬡	⬡	Holding hands	⬡
⬡	Happy	⬡	⬡	Sadness	⬡
⬡	Missionary position	⬡	⬡	BDSM	⬡
⬡	Angry	⬡	⬡	Funny	⬡
⬡	Master/slave	⬡	⬡	Oral sex	⬡
⬡	Hateful	⬡	⬡	Latex/Rubber	⬡
⬡	Water sports	⬡	⬡	Sick	⬡
⬡	Gloomy	⬡	⬡	Sweet	⬡
⬡	Kissing	⬡	⬡	Threesome	⬡
⬡	Joyful	⬡	⬡	Awful	⬡
⬡	Cuddling	⬡	⬡	Massage	⬡
⬡	Love	⬡	⬡	Delicious	⬡
⬡	Bondage	⬡	⬡	Leather sex	⬡
⬡	Poison	⬡	⬡	Disgusting	⬡

Figure 9.1 The Implicit Association Test Kink & Fetish: Test A

Source: Bisbey (2021).

Another method to highlight bias is the exposure method. Exposure can be via written erotica, films, pornography, documentary, podcasts, classes, non-fiction writing or attending events in person (and observing). I recommend a systematic approach to exposure that involves the clinician working through a list of fetishes and kinks and gaining exposure to each one. When exposed, the clinician observes their own responses and completes reflective exercises to highlight any bias present. It is important to vary the type of material used for exposure in order to dig into the layers of potential bias.

The Implicit Association Test Kink & Fetish
Dr Lori Beth Bisbey, 2021.

Test B:
For kink/fetish activities and unpleasant words, mark in the box to the left.
For everything else (ordinary activities and pleasant words), mark in the box to the right.
Start at the top left and go from top to bottom, doing all the items in order. Then do the second column.
At bottom right, record the elapsed time in seconds and the number of mistakes.
Do it as quickly as you can without making mistakes.

Kink/fetish or unpleasant words		Ordinary sex or pleasant words	Kink/fetish or unpleasant words		Ordinary sex or pleasant words
◯	Rimming	◯	◯	Holding hands	◯
◯	Happy	◯	◯	Sadness	◯
◯	Missionary position	◯	◯	BDSM	◯
◯	Angry	◯	◯	Funny	◯
◯	Master/slave	◯	◯	Oral sex	◯
◯	Hateful	◯	◯	Latex/Rubber	◯
◯	Water sports	◯	◯	Sick	◯
◯	Gloomy	◯	◯	Sweet	◯
◯	Kissing	◯	◯	Threesome	◯
◯	Joyful	◯	◯	Awful	◯
◯	Cuddling	◯	◯	Massage	◯
◯	Love	◯	◯	Delicious	◯
◯	Bondage	◯	◯	Leather sex	◯
◯	Poison	◯	◯	Disgusting	◯

Elapsed time in seconds:
Mistakes:

Figure 9.2 The Implicit Association Test Kink & Fetish: Test B
Source: Bisbey (2021).

As bias can be unconscious, it can be useful to video record the therapists' reactions to each exposure activity. This will pick up facial expressions and body language that the person may not be fully aware of and give further clues to bias.

Once you have uncovered biases, challenging them as you would a fixed idea is a useful way to shift them. Often bias is a result of conditioning (societal and familial) and a lack of information.

When working with therapists who are not kink knowledgeable (have no lived kink experience and little experience with healthy sexual relationships that contain kink and fetish), the idea that kink and fetish are inherently deviant and therefore unhealthy is the most common bias I come across. In a recent workshop on kink, the vast majority of the therapists suggested that all humiliation kinks come from traumatic experiences and are efforts to master the trauma. The suggestion was that humiliation kinks are not ever simply a deviation from the norm and that, unlike kinks involving masochism, they are always a result of an inappropriate connection drawn in a childhood that contained bad parenting at best and abuse at worst. As a result of these beliefs, the bias for most of the therapists was that the kink needed to be cured or one that only remained in fantasy and that more 'normal' behaviours needed to be encouraged.

Some of the therapists wanted to focus on helping the client to make the connection between the incident or incidents that sparked the humiliation kink and the kink itself and then to analyse those incidents and relationships. Others wanted to come at these incidents from a behavioural perspective and try to break the link between the kink and the original incident, hoping that this would extinguish the sexual response to the humiliation. Very few therapists considered that there was little value in trying to get rid of these kinks and that the time would be better spent helping clients to accept their desires and find healthy ways to express them. Very few therapists considered that the client might not be coming to therapy to work on their desires and that diverting the purpose of therapy might be inappropriate.

One major problem in trying to 'treat' these sexual desires is that treatment for sexual desires (designed to eradicate the desire) is notoriously ineffective. Even when treatment is recommended because the desire causes potential legal consequences (like exhibitionism if one were to get caught, for example), treatment with psychotherapy is usually a minimum of two years and often medication is also used, especially if the behaviour has compulsive elements to it. After all this treatment, the outcome is still poor. So trying to 'cure' a desire that is only causing guilt or shame is a losing game (Dehlin et al., 2015; Council on Scientific Affairs, 1987).

Often attempting to find the incidents that helped to sexualise behaviour and objects that are not usually sexualised is nigh on impossible. People can search for triggering incidents and not find any or find so many as to make uncoupling the desire from the incidents extremely difficult. This type of treatment is long term and often very expensive, and in the end the outcome is far from guaranteed. The research so far is very spotty and mostly single case studies or is focused on paedophilia which is not a kink as the object of desire cannot consent. Some research found that behavioural treatment that uses aversion reinforcement combined with medication worked for people as long as the package was tailored to the individual arousal pattern but that booster sessions were necessary for those who had long standing desires (Kilmann et al., 1982). It should be noted that almost all the research has been on offenders and not addressed the desires that most people present with therapists.

As long as there is consent and the behaviour is not harmful to self and/or others (harm being defined as more than causing shame and guilt, which can be ameliorated), then the better treatment option is to help the client accept their desires and find healthy and safe ways to embrace them, which may include indulging in fantasy or reality or both.

There are a variety of biases that can be examined. They include the following:

Availability bias: Just because information is easily available and repeatedly visible doesn't mean it is accurate. This one is the 'everyone knows' bias. For example, for a long time everyone knew that people were 'born submissives' and that submissives experienced joy from service in all areas of their lives. In reality, many people who choose to submit are dominant in other areas of life.

Social media and Google make the availability bias a stronger one. Researching the facts needs to involve a deeper search than just a Google search. Sources of information must be vetted as well as the information itself to determine if something is a fact.

To combat the availability bias, facts and sources of facts should be regularly checked in a thorough manner. A person needs to ask themselves if they believe something just because they have heard it all over the place.

Confirmation bias: The tendency we have to only hear/pay attention to information that confirms our current beliefs. Social media has created huge areas where confirmation bias is an issue. The more you watch certain types of content, the more they are served to you until you may never hear a dissenting viewpoint and not even realise you are not hearing one. You might assume that this is because one doesn't exist or because you are correct.

In order to combat this bias, a person must actively seek out varied viewpoints. Classes for professional development can help to combat this bias as can professional clinical supervision.

The ostrich effect: avoiding triggers and/or hiding from facts you find difficult or anything that might cause confrontation. If you are doing this, you won't expose yourself to your biases or information that might trigger you.

This is where on-going personal work becomes so important to being an excellent therapist. The Ostrich Effect is defeated by dealing with triggers and learning to face facts that might cause some conflict with others. Learning to handle conflict professionally also helps with this bias. It is acceptable to disagree. People can learn to be comfortable enough with ambivalence to honour viewpoints different from their own while still maintaining their own views.

Over justification: People have a tendency to over justify their own beliefs in order to shore them up. These beliefs are often based on our own experience even when our own experience is limited. People want to believe in the health and accuracy of their sexual choices so may not consider that sometimes a choice which for others is positive may not be healthy for them. If a therapist is kink knowledgeable, they may have to be careful they don't swing too far in the direction that all kink is healthy and that a person should always be helped to accept their kinks and find healthy ways to enjoy them. In some circumstances, a kink or fetish may not be healthy. A kink or fetish may be healthy in some relationships but not in others. For example, for someone who was sexually abused and doesn't yet know how to choose safe partners, a rape kink may well be dangerous rather than a way of attempting mastery. If they don't have the skill to make a good choice, then the kink can lead to further abuse. In these situations, it may be appropriate to treat the trauma, get rid of the triggers, then help the client learn the skills needed to make a good relationship choice, and then finally examine where the kink fits in.

Anchoring in your own beliefs: This leads to jumping to conclusions. While being anchored can be helpful, it can also lead us to jump to conclusions about others based on our own bias. This bias is evident when people have not explored much outside of their own belief systems. A person may jump to conclusions based on their own experience before they have the details of the client's experience. Even people who have the same kink and like to experience it in the same way will interpret things differently. How kinks and fetishes are played out in relationships will vary from person to person and from relationship to relationship. Focussing on gathering the details before forming any conclusions will combat this bias.

Overconfidence bias: This is the tendency to be overconfident about the ability to generalise from our own experiences. We see our experiences as representative. Making sure to explore outside of our comfort zones helps to combat this type of bias.

Conscious and unconscious biases

There are two sets of biases to tackle: our assumptions (conscious bias) and our unconscious bias. To overcome conscious bias or our assumptions we can do the following:

1   **Listen** to the views of others, and stories of others' experiences. Experience of our colleagues, our clients. Check facts and read about the sexual activities your clients are presenting to you. It is a good idea to learn enough so that we can then ask our clients about their experiences without asking them to teach us about kink and fetish as a whole. *Different Loving: The World of Sexual Dominance and Submission*, written by Brame et al. (1996), is an excellent book to use as a resource to learn more about these sexualities.
2   **Observe** behaviour, situations and your own reactions. This was mentioned before.
3   **Clarify** and ask intelligent, respectful questions. Make sure to seek wide views from others. Talk with other professionals. Consider joining a peer supervision group with other therapists who work with people who practice kink and fetish. Seek professional supervision from a GSRD (gender, sex, relationship diversity) trained therapist.

Working on unconscious bias is more difficult. Earlier I highlighted implicit associations which demonstrate some of the unconscious biases we hold about kink and fetish. Banaji and Greenwald (2013) point out that we use different parts of our brains to address things similar to us and things different from us. We internalise stereotypes and judge trustworthiness in mere seconds usually based on little more than expressions, facial features and tone of voice. Unconscious bias influences all of our judgements about trustworthiness, character, potential and abilities.

Let's return to one of the most common biases held about people who are involved in kink and fetish activities: "Women who are submissive in relationships are vulnerable and likely subject to abuse". Related to this is the belief that being masochistic and/or submissive is pathological and that people who enjoy masochism or submission are vulnerable and need help to leave these relationships and/or stop this behaviour and change their sexual desires. A corollary: These people are not able to give valid consent and/or don't have agency as a result of these desires and practices. The idea that women who are submissive in relationships are vulnerable is relatively modern. Prior to the 1950s, women were counselled to be submissive to their husbands; submissiveness in a woman was seen to be a positive trait. Many people who engage in relationships with a negotiated power imbalance negotiate a 1950s style relationship which is now seen as a kink. Despite this, the bias is now that women, particularly those who submit to men, are vulnerable to abuse and cannot really give valid consent to engage in submission and any of the sexual practices that surround this power exchange. People who have embraced a feminist ideology believe they have embraced an ideology that champions choice for women and empowerment for women that leads to more choice. However, there are choices that are frowned upon within this system, and the choice to submit is one such choice. The bias is so strong that abuse and lack of mental capacity are often inferred when kink and fetish are involved.

In order to work on changing this bias, we can use the five steps recommended by Banaji and Greenwald (2013):

1   **Acknowledge the potential for bias**. Be open to the fact that all of us have biases and many of these are unconscious.
2   **Be wary of first impressions**. As well as first ideas about any concept. With the bias described earlier, we would seek to deconstruct the idea that a person who is submissive sexually is automatically vulnerable to abuse. We could note that some people are vulnerable to abuse whether or not they engage in kink or fetish, whether or not they are sexually submissive, and others are not particularly vulnerable to abuse even when they are sexually submissive, even when they engage in kink or fetish.
3   **Learn about stereotypes**. We can learn about stereotypes as it relates to kink, fetish and BDSM. There is a stereotype that says women are submissive and masochistic because of experiences of childhood abuse. There is often some truth in a stereotype, but it is often not even close to the whole truth. In this

case, some women are submissive and masochistic because of experiences of childhood abuse, and some of them have problems as a result of this. Others do not have problems as a result of this abuse. Still others are submissive and masochistic without having experienced any abuse in childhood. The largest number of women who are submissive and masochistic have not experienced abuse in childhood (at least according to current research; research on issues to do with sexuality and sexual practice is notoriously difficult as many people do not wish to divulge to a professional even in a virtually anonymous questionnaire).

4   **Broaden your focus by looking at many different types of instances of the thing for which you have a bias**. Look at men who are submissive to see if they are vulnerable as well as looking at women. Examine why there are differences between groups.

5   **Expose yourself to novel information and experiences**. This is the best way to combat unconscious bias: Keep learning.

Add these steps to challenging any bias you find as you would a fixed belief. Look for evidence (and beware of the confirmatory bias as you do). List other possibilities to the bias. Then seek out further information from publications, podcasts, educators, colleagues and supervision.

Power exchange dynamics (authority transfer dynamics)

This is an area where many therapists have a bias that gets in the way of helping their clients. It is often easy for therapists to challenge their own bias in relation to particular sexual kinks (like water sports or impact play, for example) but harder when the kink is relationship based and highlights an alternative relationship structure.

There are often concerns raised about consent when people are engaging in power exchange dynamics anywhere in their relationships other than 'just' in the bedroom. Issues around on-going consent, grooming and domestic abuse are often presented without much evidence as to why this should be a concern in all situations or for that individual client. The largest concerns are raised when CIS gender female clients engage in a power exchange with CIS gender male clients where the female is in the submissive role. Some even suggest that it is not possible for a woman to choose to submit to a man because society conditions her into that role so she cannot truly consent. This line of thought reduces a woman's agency to nothing simply because she is choosing the most normative of the kinks. It assumes that she has not done any personal work, examining her own desires and her own mind and that she has simply been led along by conditioning and unconscious bias. It is insulting to women who choose this relationship style. This is particularly so when the same people espouse the innovative choice of men who submit to women. I have had clients who were told that all other forms of power exchange are a choice but that the perceived heteronormative power exchange is not. (Perceived because even when a woman submits to a man, it does not necessarily mean that the couple is heterosexual.)

All relationships contain power dynamics. The difference with practitioners of BDSM is that their power dynamics are fully negotiated. Conventional marriages contain power dynamics. The most common dynamic still remains the man as the breadwinner who financially supports the family and the woman as the caretaker who emotionally supports the family. In these relationships, there is a division of labour and a division of power, and many of these relationships are not egalitarian in the slightest. In many, the men hold the power because they have primary access to the main means of agency in our society: money. In some, women hold the power through the use of their bodies and the provision or denial of sexual and intimate contact. Frequently these relationships are not only not negotiated, but the expectations and rules are all unspoken. The couple makes assumptions on the basis of normative acculturation and often forget that each culture has different ideas of normative behaviour, expectations and rules and that we learn different variations of the expectations and rules depending upon our specific family circumstances as reflected in our upbringings.

My clinical experience highlights that heteronormative couples often simply buy the monogamous relationship package containing a bunch of rules and expectations and assumptions that they have not examined. This is the Disney 'And They All Lived Happily Ever After' package. Aside from the fact that life is not static – we don't reach a point of happiness and stay there but rather have moments of happiness interspersed with moments of difficulty – this package inculcates all sorts of bias aside from heteronormativity.

Couples don't consider if these expectations match or if they suit them as a couple or even as an individual. As a result, many relationships run into difficulty because so much of the workings are seen as the magic of attraction, the magic of soul mates, and little attention is paid to the skills needed to build and maintain a long-term successful (happy) relationship. Therapists have an important role to play in helping people to examine these assumptions and expectations and helping them to learn the emotional, communication and social skills necessary to create their relationships and maintain them so they are healthy and happy.

If you look at my last paragraph, you can see at least one assumption I have suggested about what a successful relationship looks like. I referred to 'long-term' relationships. But not all short-term relationships are unsuccessful, and not all long-term relationships are successful. This is a bias that comes from the culture I grew up in. I highlight this to show how insidious our biases can be as therapists and how important it is for us to acknowledge and examine them. I might still believe that long-term relationships are more successful. However, if I acknowledge this, I do not need to pass this bias on to my client, or I can tell my client that this is my bias.

For some people, their sexual orientation is defined by a power dynamic. Sexual orientation describes who we are attracted to. Traditionally, this was limited to gender, so the axis was from heterosexual to homosexual. Sari Van Anders developed Sexual Configurations Theory. In *Beyond Sexual Orientation: Integrating Gender/Sex and Diverse Sexualities via Sexual Configurations Theory* (2015), she spoke about needing a theory of sexuality that came closer to what people actually experienced. People define their attractions by gender, by the types of sexual activity they enjoy (kink/BDSM), by whether they are very sexual or are not sexual (asexual) and by whether they are monogamous through to polyamorous (like to have sexual relationships with only one person or sexual relationships with more than one person). This model allows people to describe their orientation in much more detail. While orientation can change over time, it doesn't change by trying to change it. There are many people who see their power dynamic as their orientation. They are attracted to people who are dominant or who are submissive or who like to switch and gender doesn't really matter. When therapists try to 'cure' these people of their desire for a power exchange relationship, they are trying to change the person's orientation. They are giving the message that their attraction pattern is somehow disordered and unhealthy.

Being able to think in terms of sexual configurations and the intersections of various attractions helps therapists get rid of unconscious bias and be more neutral when working with clients who have sexualities that involve kink and fetish.

Jane came to therapy stating she and her partner, sam, were having problems with their power exchange dynamic. The problems started when they moved in together. Jane and sam were in a long distance Dominant/submissive relationship for 10 years. They saw each other four times per year for a week or two at a time, and spoke every day via text, phone or video chat. Both said they were clear about their roles. Jane said that when they moved in together, sam found reasons to avoid the daily tasks and rituals that they had in place for many years. They began to call her Jane instead of Ma'am or Mistress. She described feeling that sam was treating her as an equal instead of as their Dominant. Jane wanted help to become more comfortable in the relationship again and more comfortable with herself as the Mistress.

We explored the parts of her life that were unseen when sam didn't live with her, and she identified areas where she felt out of control: the way she managed her finances, the way she communicated with her adult child. She felt that seeing her in roles where she wasn't in control may have caused sam to lose respect for her, to see her in a more ordinary, equal light. They never spent time together when outside of holiday time. When they were together, sam was responsible for cooking, cleaning, and taking care of Jane. This was fine when on holiday. However, sam worked 12–14 hour days once they lived together and didn't have the energy to cook, clean or look after Jane. Jane realised that when sam didn't do these tasks, she felt they were not fulfilling the submissive role.

> In talking about this relationship, Jane highlighted feeling conflicted about being seen as the Mistress on a 24/7 basis because she felt Mistresses should be in control in all aspects of their own lives. She struggled with the places where she felt that she wasn't in control and couldn't master her own feelings, thoughts, and behaviours.
>
> The initial work centred on helping Jane to accept her ambivalence about having a dominant role all the time, helping her to unpack her view that dominance means being always strong, always in control of one's life and being able to take the lead in all areas. She uncovered significant shame around the parts of her life that were messy and around a desire to give up control for some of the time and take on a more submissive role.
>
> Further work centred on helping Jane resolve the shame she felt, accept her own ambivalence as well as accept the dominant and submissive parts of herself. Once finished, she decided to ask sam to come to couples therapy with her so they could explore a dynamic based on her new knowledge about herself.

In 2019, new clinical guidelines were published for working with people presenting with kink and/or BDSM. These can be found here: www.kinkguidelines.com/the-guidelines

For more clinical examples, I recommend: *Ortmann, D.M and Sprott, R.A. (2013) Sexual Outsiders: Understanding BDSM Sexualities and Communities. Plymouth UK: Rowman & Littlefield.* Hoff, G., & Sprott, R. (2009). Therapy experiences of clients with BDSM sexuailties: Listening to a stigmatized sexuality. *Electronic Journal of Human Sexuality*, 12.

References

American Psychiatric Association. (2013). *Diagnostic and Statistical Manual of Mental Disorders – 5 (DSM-5)*. Washington, DC: American Psychiatric Association Publishers.

Banaji, M., & Greenwald, A. (2013). *Blind Spot: Hidden Biases of Good People.* New York, NY: Delacorte Press.

Bezreh, T., Weinberg, T., & Edgar, T. (2012). BDSM disclosure and stigma management: Identifying opportunities for sex education. *American Journal of Sexuality Education*, 7(1).

Brame, G.G., Brame, W.D., & Jacobs, J. (1996). *Different Loving: The World of Sexual Dominance and Submission.* New York: Villard.

Council on Scientific Affairs. (1987). Aversion therapy. *JAMA*, 258, 2562–2566.

Dehlin, J., Galliher, R., Bradshaw, W., Hyde, D., & Crowell, K. (2015). Sexual orientation change efforts among current or former LDS church members. *Journal of Counselling Psychology*, 62(2), 95–105.

Easton, D., & Hardy, J. (2001a). *The New Topping Book.* San Francisco, CA: Greenery Press.

Easton, D., & Hardy, J. (2001b). *The New Bottoming Book*. San Francisco, CA: Greenery Press.

Harvard Implicit Associations Project: Project Implicit. https://implicit.harvard.edu/implicit/

Kelsey, K., Stiles, B., Spiller, C., & Diekoff, G. (2012). Assessment of therapist's attitudes towards BDSM. *Journal of Psychology and Human Sexuality*, 4(3), 1–13.

Kilmann, P., Sabilis, R., Gearing, M., Busktel, L., & Scovern, A. (1982). The treatment of sexual paraphilias: A review of the outcome research. *The Journal of Sex Research*, 18(3), 193–252.

Kolmes, K., Stock, W., & Moser, C. (2006). Investigating bias in psychotherapy with BDSM clients. *Journal of Homosexuality*, 50(2–3), 301–324.

Miller, S., & Byers, E. (2009). Psychologists' continuing education and training in sexuality. *Journal of Sex & Marital Therapy*, 35(3), 206–219.

Miller, S., & Byers, E. (2010). Psychologists' sexual education and training in graduate school. *Canadian Journal of Behavioural Science*, 42(2), 93–100.

Ortmann, D.M., & Sprott, R.A. (2013). *Sexual Outsiders: Understanding BDSM Sexualities and Communities*. Plymouth, UK: Rowman & Littlefield.

Reissing, E.D., & Giulio, G.D. (2010). Practicing clinical psychologists' provision of health care services. *Professional Psychology: Research and Practice*, 41(1), 57–63.

van Anders, S.M. (2015). Beyond sexual orientation: Integrating gender/sex and diverse sexualities via sexual configurations theory. *Archives of Sexual Behavior*, 44(5), 1177–1213.

Wiseman, J. (1997). *SM 101*. San Francisco, CA: Greenery Press.

Chapter 10

Treating anodyspareunia in MSM

Dr Bartosz Grabski

Introduction

Anal sexuality: a short historical background

Anal intercourse between men has been practised across different cultures and historical periods. It received more prominent social visibility and recognition in ancient Greece where anal intercourse between mature men and ephebes was ascribed pedagogic value in which virtues and wisdom of older lovers were passed onto the younger betrothed. As opposed to this apparently affirming attitude to anal sex between men, in many other cultures, as well as in the realms of the Western world across the following centuries, anal intercourse, not only between men, was strongly tabooed and prohibited (Imieliński, 1989). It has been pretty recently since what was treated as perverted in Western culture has become acknowledged and accepted as a valid form of sexual relations between people, but one cannot assume the process is complete, and taboo, misconceptions, and homophobia still shape the attitudes toward anal sex.

Men having sex with men sexual problems in classifications and research

The role of formal classifications, like DSM or ICD systems in sexology, is controversial. One can argue that they are *sine qua non* for undertaking any clinical treatment ("no disorder, no treatment"); others point to the danger of unnecessary medicalisation and rectification of diagnostic categories, which can actually blur the accurate identification of mechanisms underlying problems people experience in their sexual lives (Tiefer, 2012).

Leaving aside this controversy, the diagnosis is a reflection of the current mainstream thinking in sexology and is often required due to formal causes. As to the former question, the striking fact is that the currently available systems, i.e. DSM-5, ICD-10, and ICD-11, do not contain any category nor a specifier which would address sexual problems or disorders specifically experienced by gay men (WHO, 1992, 2018; APA, 2013).

Doi: 10.4324/9781003260608-11

What is more, the scientific literature on the topic is scarce, as reflected by a recent critical review and dominated by studies centred around STIs (sexual transmitted infections) (Mijas et al., 2021). However, the constantly growing body of scientific studies and clinical writings have explored what is considered to be hallmark features of MSM (men having sex with men) sexuality and also sexual problems these men may experience. Issues such as minority stress and homophobia (Meyer, 2003), characteristics of gay men's sexual milieu (in which potency and sexual performance are highly valued contributing to performance anxiety and comparison with other men), greater relational diversity (with more common single status) have been highlighted (McNally & Adams, 2001; Sandfort & de Keizer, 2001; Grabski & Kasparek, 2017).

As to the question of specific problems, attention has been paid to gag response on oral sex (Paff, 1985) and pain on anal sex (Rosser et al., 1997).

Sexual anal pain or anodyspareunia attempts at conceptualisation

The first comprehensive work on anal sexuality and its problems developed from the pleasure- and health-oriented perspective in an exquisite book by Jack Morin first issued in 1981. The book was revised by the author several times, and the fourth edition from 2010 is still available (Morin, 2010). Not only does this extensive piece of work provide a wide and multifactorial context for anal sexuality, including socio-cultural, anatomical, physiological, and biomedical aspects, but the author proposes an original approach to developing healthy and pleasurable anal sexuality which can serve both the clinicians and people seeking assistance.

Problems experienced by MSM on anal intercourse were then brought to light in 1997, when Rosser et al. (1997, 1998) postulated the existence of a "novel" sexual dysfunction that they called "anodyspareunia" and conducted a series of studies on its prevalence and correlates, and proposed specific diagnostic criteria that mirrored those for dyspareunia in the DSM classification.

This approach had its value, as it drew attention to what had been a neglected area of clinical scrutiny, but the validity of establishing this new sexual diagnostic category has been questioned (Hollows, 2007).

The term *anodyspareunia* will be thus used pragmatically across this chapter to denote any pain or physical discomfort associated with receptive anal intercourse, irrespective of the underlying mechanisms and contributing factors, which are a source of concern for a man and might benefit from clinical assistance. This approach is purely symptomatic and as such will encompass a vast array of possible factors contributing to pain ranging from lack of education and experience to specific anorectal diseases, all of which will have to be thoroughly assessed in the diagnostic process.

Anodyspareunia

Prevalence

The only study conducted in the representative sample of MSM on anodyspareunia indicated that out of 1190 men, 32% fulfilled criteria of mild, 17% of mild to moderate, 4% of moderate, and 2% of severe anodyspareunia as defined by the use of the adapted version of the Female Sexual Functioning Inventory (FSFI) (Vansintejan et al., 2013). The other studies that used composite scores for severity and frequency of pain measured on Likert scales indicated that around 12.5% (Rosser et al., 1998) to 14% (Damon & Rosser, 2005) of MSM may suffer from anal sexual pain, which could be clinically significant. Comparable results were achieved by Grabski and Kasparek (2020); in their study, 77.7% of men that engaged in anal receptive intercourse experienced some degree of pain. In 44.3% of men the pain was little, in 23.6% moderate, in 7.6% strong, and 2.2% judged it as very strong. The studies differ in methodologies; no standard measure with established diagnostic thresholds or accepted diagnostic criteria exists, but the results give a general overview on the prevalence of the phenomenon. Its clinical significance however, needs to be further elaborated.

Contributing factors

As with all sexual difficulties, factors that contribute to anodyspareunia can be of psychosocial or biomedical nature. The existing scientific data is rather sparse and unanimous. Researchers pointed to the role of internalised homophobia and stage of coming-out; perceived depth and rate of thrusting, and size of penis entering anus; specific anal health problems; not using poppers; younger age; less frequent sex with partner and lower number of sex partners; not being in steady relationships and having casual sex partners; not using lubricant and not massaging anal sphincter before anal sex; as well as performance anxiety, which all were either more often reported by men experiencing anodyspareunia or were related to sexual anal pain either in bivariate or multivariate analyses in the existing studies (Grabski & Kasparek, 2020).

Practitioners such as Jack Morin (2010) point to the central significance of the lack of relaxation and see it as the basis for pain-free, fulfilling anal experience.

Taking a practical stance, chronologically and functionally speaking, the contributing factors can be grouped into predisposing (those which make a person vulnerable to developing a problem, e.g., lack of knowledge), triggering (those which lead to its appearance, e.g., forced penetration and inadequate lubrication), and maintaining (those which make the problem persist, e.g., fear of penetration; Hawton, 2004; Althof et al., 2010, cited in Tripodi et al., 2012, pp. 114–116). The proposal for a practical conceptual framework rooted in a generic cognitive-behavioural model with inclusion of varied nature of operational factors is depicted in the Figure 10.1. The model pragmatically assumes interrelations

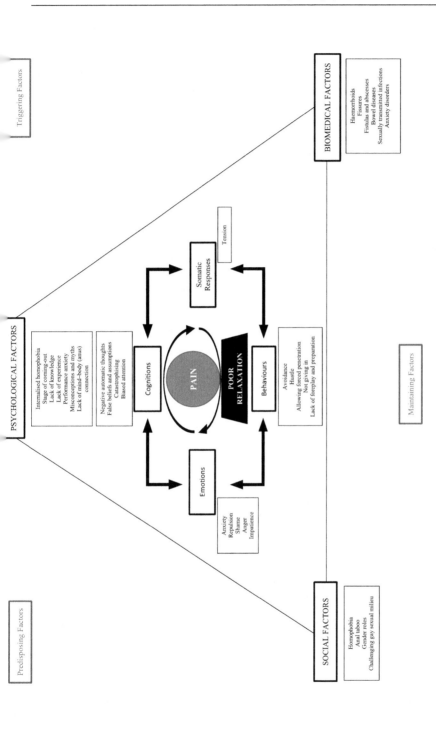

Figure 10.1 A conceptual framework of anodyspareunia as rooted in the generic cognitive-behavioural model, summarising varied nature and chronology of contributing factors

Sources: Althof et al., 2010; Beck, 2011; Grabski and Kasparek, 2020; Hawton, 2004; Morin, 2010.

between cognitions, emotions, somatic responses, and behaviours, which all can create a vicious circle fuelling the problem of pain. All factors, being either psychological (e.g., internalised homophobia), socio-cultural (e.g. anal taboo, gender roles), or bio-medical (e.g., haemorrhoids, fissures) which may contribute to poor relaxation will have to be taken into account at assessment and addressed when present at treatment.

The working of this conceptual proposition in a clinical case of a young gay man is presented here. The proposed framework may assist clinical assessment and be helpful in planning the scope and range of clinical interventions.

A gay man, now 34 years of age, grew up in a conservative catholic family with a history of self-hatred and attempts at self-cure in adolescence. The family was pretty strict and absorbed rules, order, an inflexible value system and excessive emotions control. Although the client seems to have accepted his sexual orientation and adopted at least a basic positive gay identity, he developed and maintained a rigid personality style with little connection to his emotions and body. His first receptive anal intercourse was uncomplicated and pain-free. It was with his first boyfriend, who was much more sexually experienced and happened spontaneously with some accompaniment of alcohol and a high level of desire and excitation. He just let it happen but had no knowledge of how to prepare or how to relax. In his second relationship, the problem of anodyspareunia began to emerge. It had been a long-lasting stable and exclusive relationship rather free of friction and excessive conflict. Both men had limited knowledge of the importance of adequate preparation (e.g., finger-anal play/massage, lubrication) and used face cream to reduce friction instead of a brand lubricant (as a result of the embarrassment of buying one and insufficient knowledge). They believed that intromission pain is a part of the game but will wear off in time. The client's partner had a big penis and although tried to be sensitive, they both believed that the intromission movement needed to be steady and consequently the pain needed to be endured. The results were mixed. Some of the attempts were successful, but some had to be interrupted because of pain and discomfort. This led the client to feel intimidated and inferior as well as making unfavourable comparisons with other men ("I cannot do this", "Other guys do it with ease", "I am no good"), negative automatic thoughts and catastrophising ("I will fail again", "It will hurt again"), when approaching intercourse with tension and anxiety. Avoidance of anal engagement developed in time. The process also triggered thoughts and feelings of inadequacy about men's sexual relationships with other men ("They were right, there is something incompatible between two men", "It is not normal") and about anal sex in particular ("It is unnatural, which is why it hurts"). He started to be afraid of the dire consequences but relied on a very vague image of rectal anatomy and physiology, imagining some sort of inaccessible dark body part, which gets traumatised and the blood is mixed with impurities, which fill the rectum. In time he developed bleeding haemorrhoids which, on one hand, contributed to pain but, on the other, supported his belief system.

The problem can be understood as a result of a complex interplay of psychosocial (e.g., internalised homophobia, lack of knowledge, misconceptions and myths, personality style and lack of mind-body connection, challenging gay social milieu) and biological (haemorrhoids) factors which exert their influence over a period of time with some playing the predisposing (e.g., personality, lack of education, homophobia), some triggering (e.g., penis size, lack of preparation, going too fast), and some maintaining (e.g., avoidance, expectations of pain, unchallenged belief system, haemorrhoids) roles. A vicious circle also develops, which can be understood as a self-fuelling process in which cognitive (e.g., "It will hurt again", "I will fail again", "It is not normal", It is unnatural"), emotional (e.g., anxiety, tension), somatic (tension/lack of relaxation), and behavioural (e.g., forced penetration, avoidance) processes interact to maintain and intensify the pain.

Clinical management

Assessment and diagnosis

As with other sexual concerns a comprehensive history taking creates the basis for a good assessment (Wincze & Weisberg, 2015).

Physical assessment by a trained physician, preferably a proctologist, should always be included whenever history, symptomatology, or course of the problem cast any doubts on the existence of a physical problem. One could even argue that due to the possibly disastrous consequences of some undiagnosed anal health conditions, for example, anal cancer, such an assessment should always be included in the diagnostic process and should precede any psychotherapeutic/behavioural treatment plan. Cooperation with an open-minded and "LGBT-friendly/informed" physician would be a reasonable solution as visiting a proctologist without earlier reassurance can be a source of immense stress and lead to avoidance (intersection of minority stress and anal taboo).

Clinical data to be obtained on assessment and relevant questions are juxtaposed in Table 10.1.

Table 10.1 Information to be gathered during history taking

Data and questions	Possible clinical significance
Was it the first attempt at anal intromission?	Lack of basic knowledge and experience.
What did the attempt at penetration look like (foreplay, massage of the anal sphincters, lubrication, forced or hurried intromission, depth and rate of thrusting)?	Technical mistakes when approaching anal sexuality.
Were previous attempts also painful? How frequent and how intense is the pain? What is the nature of the pain (type, location, duration)? Is there any relation to partner, place, circumstances, sexual position, sexual technique?	Elaborating pain characteristics can be helpful in the assessment of the intensity of a problem and possible aetiology or contributing factors.
Is this a problem? If so, for whom? What is the nature of a problem? What is the motivation for seeking consultation right now? What is the motivation to engage in anal sex at all?	If no problem, why look for treatment? If not for a client, then does he want to engage at all? If for a partner only, what does it say about the relationship dynamics?
Level of desire? Other sexual difficulties? Performance anxiety?	Lack of desire may contribute to poor relaxation. Erectile problems or premature ejaculation may be the only motivation to engage in anal sex to avoid embarrassment. Performance anxiety ("not being a good bottom") can impede relaxation.
Partner (causal, stable)? Feelings towards the partner and relationship dynamics?	For some, casual encounters may impede relaxation. Power struggle, fusion, attractiveness of a partner, and other typical relational dynamics may influence any sexual performance.
Knowledge (basic anal/rectal anatomy and physiology, importance of the preparation for sex)?	Clients should know how the anus, the rectum, and the pelvic floor are built, and how they can influence muscle tone and promote relaxation.
Pre-existing beliefs (cognitive representation of the problem)? Attitude toward anal sexuality?	Misconceptions, false beliefs, half-truths about anal sexuality and its problems are to be expected.
Sexual identity/orientation? Attitudes toward homosexuality?	If straight, then motivation for engaging in anal sex with other men may be worth exploring? Does it make fun? Is it desired? Sexual orientation mismatched will impede desire and genuine motivation for engaging in anal sex. Internalised homophobia is rather to be expected, and it has the potential to interfere with sexual performance and satisfaction.

Data and questions	Possible clinical significance
How the problem has been approached so far?	Previous attempts at self-help can shed light on a client's cognitive representation of the problem and possible mechanism and contributing factors.
Reaction to the problem of a client and of the partner (partners)?	This can be a source of much useful information, e.g., performance anxiety, cognitive representation of the problem, motivation to engage and for change, pressures, distancing, or support from the partner.
Any concurrent or existing symptoms (e.g., bleedings, discharge, itching, pain outside anal penetration)?	This warrants the decision to seek proctologist's consultation and be of diagnostic value, e.g., bleedings in haemorrhoids but also in gastrointestinal cancer.
Concurrent general and local medical or psychiatric problems? Substances use/abuse?	Poor general health, local medical conditions, and psychiatric conditions, including substance abuse, may influence sexual performance and satisfaction and also directly involve the anus or the rectum being a source of pain. Some substances used for anal intercourse may increase the risk of trauma.

Clinical interventions

As the nature of most of the problems in sexual life is diverse and contributing factors will range from simple lack of education to a complex interplay of multiple factors as highlighted previously, so should be the range of clinical interventions. The summary of key components in the recommended stepwise clinical approach to the management of sexual concerns is known as the PLISSIT-model (Annon, 1976, cited in Reisman, 2012, pp. 248–249). It consists of components which gradually intensify clinical interventions moving from basic but highly important issues like building therapeutic alliance and psychoeducation to the more complex clinical care, like individual or couple therapy. The model as applied to anodyspareunia is presented in Table 10.2.

Goals

The ultimate outcome goals of clinical interventions are the elimination of anal pain and increased sexual satisfaction with anal sexuality. The major instrumental outcome goal or treatment target is the promotion of relaxation. Other key goals are as follows:

1   Provision of factual knowledge.
2   Challenging misinformation and false beliefs.

3 Decreasing the influence of taboo and internalised homophobia.
4 Increasing mind–anus connection and inclusion of anal area into holistic positive self.
5 Promotion of anal health and elimination of anal health problems.
6 Promotion of mental health.

Table 10.2 The PLISSIT model applied to anodyspareunia

Component		Description and example
P	Permission	• Clinician must be ready to discuss the problem of anodyspareunia with a patient. • Patient must be assured that he can safely discuss all his concerns with a clinician. • Accepting milieu should be built and all healthy (accepted, consensual, not psychologically or physically harmful or contributing to the problem of anodyspareunia) behaviours affirmed and continued.
LI	Limited Information	• Misinformation and false beliefs should be clarified and challenged, and factual knowledge on basic anal anatomy, physiology, and essentials concerning painless, pleasurable anal sex should be provided in a tailored manner.
SS	Specific Suggestions	• These may concern specific information on relaxation techniques, favourable positions, validation of no need to hurry, lubricants, foreplay and preparation, participation of a partner, self-exploration and self-experience exercises, and elements of sensate-focus approach.
IT	Intensive Treatment	• Highly individualised therapy for more complex issues should be provided, e.g., individual or couple therapy, targeting deeply rooted problems (e.g., internalised homophobia, personality, psychiatric disorders, relational difficulties).

Source: Elaborated upon Annon (1976), in Reisman (2012, pp. 248–249).

Promotion of relaxation

Letting go seems more generally to be a premise for satisfying and uncomplicated sex (Weiner & Avery-Clark, 2017). It seems even more so for sexual encounters involving penetration and anal penetration in particular. All factors contributing to increased tension in the anal and perineal area should be addressed or eliminated, and all factors that increase the capacity for relaxation enhanced.

Provision of factual knowledge

Factual knowledge on anatomical construction of the anus, the rectum, and the pelvic floor is essential. A client not only should be aware of how these body parts are built, but also be informed and instructed how he can exert his volun-tary (direct) or indirect control over the muscle tone in this area. Contracting and relaxing muscles of this region is the ability that has to be then practised in self-experience homework assignments. A client should get familiar with the basic relevant facts, which are summarised next (Reicher & Łasiński, 1992; Morin, 2010; Birnbaum, 2017; Felt-Bersma, 2017).

The entry to the anus is protected by two adjacent muscular rings – the sphincters. The external sphincter is built of stria muscle tissue which means it has the ability of voluntary contraction and can be freely controlled. The internal sphincter consisting of smooth muscle is the same tissue which constructs internal organs and vessels and is under the control of the autonomous nervous system. It cannot be voluntarily contracted. Both muscles guard the entrance to the anus and need to be relaxed to allow smooth intromission of the penis.

The anus and the rectum rely on the so-called pelvic floor muscles closely functionally linked to the external sphincter. Their excessive tension will impede relaxation of the whole area and thus pain-free intromission. Pelvic floor muscles are also subject to voluntary control.

As the awareness of a capacity for contraction of both the external sphincter and pelvic floor muscles is generally insufficient, clients will benefit from direct instruction on how to contract these muscles. As the contraction and relaxation are pair-bond, the same concept as in Jacobson's relaxation training (Davis et al., 2019) may be applied. The instruction for the client to replicate the action of stopping the urine flow will contract the pelvic floor muscles and the external sphincter. When kept for several seconds and then released, the relaxation should then follow. Clients can be encouraged to practise these contractions/relaxations on a daily basis. Use of touch of the perineal area and the external sphincter should be encouraged to enhance the awareness of the muscle tone and a sense of control. Also, the other methods of influencing muscle tension, e.g., Schulz autogenic training (Davis et al., 2019), could be tried out so that a client can choose the one which suits him best. In this approach, images of the heaviness of the pelvic floor would be expected to promote relaxation thereof.

The rectum is not a straight tube but consists of two major curves. The first is particularly pronounced, and it is produced by a holding muscle, the pubo-rectal sling (muscle), which supports the rectum. As the sling is one of the mechanisms of faecal continence, on penetrating the anus, it will contract, even more, exacerbating the curve and making the insertion painful or difficult. The sense of bowel movement or need to defecate may also follow. A client will need to become acquainted with this phenomenon and learn to re-interpret the sensation. Mindful succumbing to these sensations without the threat of imminent defecation and the use of self-evoked and guided images of the relaxation of the sling and lessening of the rectal curve should be practised. Adjusting sexual position, e.g., using a classical missionary, may also flatten the curve and decrease pressure against the rectal wall. Other sexual positions, like doggie or squatting on, may also be advantageous for some, as they help to maintain a sense of control over the rate and depth of penetration.

As the contraction/relaxation of the internal anal sphincter is outside the direct voluntary control, the only way of influencing its function leads rather through consciously recognising its current state/tone and building the behavioural/reflexive bridge between its status and the self-produced narrative or imagery that reflects this status. This is actually similar to the biofeedback method, and as stated by Jack Morin, the "body is already equipped with a supersensitive biofeedback device [. . .] – your finger" (Morin, 2010, p. 63). A client should be instructed to insert his finger into his anus, feel and observe the changing tone of the internal sphincter and when it is getting relaxed, and produce images of the muscle getting relaxed and/or narratives describing the muscle status, like "I am getting relaxed now". The rationale here would be to produce a conditioned response of the sphincter to imagery or verbal clues. This exercise will require time and practice, and the penetration must not be forced and the sphincter's own rhythm respected.

The anal canal is partially covered with skin that can be found around the entrance of the anus (so-called anoderma) and the rest of it with the mucous membrane. Although the latter produces some mucous discharge, it is rarely sufficient to promote smooth frictional movements without irritation. As it will reflexively produce defensive tension, the use of lubricant is highly recommended to promote relaxation and a pain-free anal experience. Clients should be taught about different qualities of accessible lubricants and encouraged to use them amply (see Table 10.3 for short reference).

Table 10.3 Basic types of lubes – a quick reference

Type	Pros	Cons	Additional remarks
Water-based	Slippery texture Condom-safe Easy to clean up Toy-friendly Cheap and widely accessible	Short-lasting with the need to re-apply regularly Usually contain preservatives which can be allergenic	Have some cooling down properties which may be preferred by some users
Oil-based	Slick and slippery texture Extremely long-lasting Cheap and widely accessible	Condom-unsafe Latex toy-unfriendly Stain sheets Mineral oils (e.g., Vaseline, baby oil) may dry up mucosa Vegetable oils may have allergenic properties and may be easily contaminated and colonised by microorganisms	Properties strongly depend on temperature and humidity

Type	Pros	Cons	Additional remarks
Silicone-based	Slick and slippery texture Condom-safe Long-lasting Skin-safe (hypoallergenic) Waterproof (suitable for use in water)	Stain sheets Difficult to remove from the body Silicone toy-unfriendly More expensive Less commonly accessible	Have some warming up properties which may be preferred by some users
Mixed water-silicone	Easier to clean than silicone-based Longer-lasting than water-based Most sex toy-friendly	More expensive Less commonly accessible	

Sources: Niederwieser (2013); Queen & Rednour (2015); Bespoke Surgical (n.d.).

Clients should be educated about these essentials and practice relaxation in self-exploration. Use of anatomical educational boards, self-help guides, like aforementioned *Anal Pleasure and Health* (Morin, 2010), and digital or on-line resources, like *The Atlas of Erotic Anatomy and Arousal* by Cyndi Darnell (n.d.) should be encouraged.

Challenging misinformation and false beliefs

The best approach to challenging deeply rooted misinformation and false beliefs is the use of psychoeducational rather than the traditional educational (lecturing) approach. Psychoeducation, as defined by Roffman (2004, cited in Walsh, 2010, p. 3), "is a means of removing barriers to participants' understanding of complex, emotionally charged information and developing strategies for using the information in a constructive manner". It is not merely a process of passing distilled knowledge onto a client but a collaborative reconstruction of a client's cognitive representation of a problem. From a cognitive and health psychology perspective, the so-called "cognitive representation of the illness" is a way most individuals organise their thinking about any clinical problem or health threat. It comprises answers an individual gives themselves to five self-asked questions. These are:

1 What is it (identity)?
2 Why has it happened (cause)?
3 How long will it last, will it recur (timeline)?
4 What effects will it have (consequences)?
5 What can I do to make it go away (cure/control)?

This representation may be idiosyncratic and can be influenced by past experiences, social and cultural backgrounds, and views of other people (Leventhal et al., 1992; Tacchi & Scott, 2005). Clients may, for example, believe that the pain of anal intercourse is inevitable and is an integral part of this type of sexual contact (identity); is caused by the pathological, unnatural nature of the act itself (cause); will always be there (timeline); will have disastrous effects, like serious anal health problems (consequences); and there is little if anything one can do to eliminate or control the pain other than either take drugs or refrain from this form of sex (cure/control).

Getting to know this particular set of beliefs our clients hold on experiencing sexual anal pain is of paramount importance. It helps to guide the psycho-educational process in a more systematised way, addressing misconceptions, myths, false beliefs, or half-truths in a more subtle way, avoiding much cognitive dissonance, which could otherwise impede integration of new information and reconstruction of a pre-existing map of a problem. As some beliefs may be highly emotionally charged, this prolonged process of exploration of the understanding and experiencing of the problem will create a platform to address as many of the patient's concerns as possible.

Decreasing the influence of taboo and internalised homophobia

Challenging misinformation and providing factual knowledge should help to counter at least some of the taboo and homophobia associated with anal sexuality but may be insufficient in decreasing the influence of these deeply rooted, cultur-ally and socially fuelled factors.

Morin (2010) cites (p. 12) Sigmund Freud (2013), to describe the taboo pro-hibitions as lacking "all justification" and being "of unknown origin". "They are taken as a matter of course by those under their dominance". Morin further points to their all-encompassing quality and resistance to logical scientific inquiry or even first-hand experience and possible functions of anal taboo. These are: cul-tivating cleanliness as the key to spiritual purity, opposing sinful body against pure spirit, repression of homosexuality, and finally, guarding strict gender role division, where anal penetration is a symbol of feminisation and gender role trans-gression in men. It seems clinically reasonable to be mindful of these motives in clients' experiences and approach them psychoeducationally.

The term *internalised homophobia* was introduced by Sophie (1987, cited in Ellis et al., 2020, p. 205) to denote negative feelings towards oneself as a lesbian or gay man resulting from negative views of homosexuality prevalent in society. It was introduced as one of the key elements, i.e. one of the proximal stressors, into the minority stress framework (Meyer, 2003). Internalised homophobia has been sometimes cited as the most insidious and harmful factor, as it is constantly operational and exerts its influence from the inside of the personality (Grabski et al., 2019). It has been even described as "intra-psychically malignant" (Forstein, 1988, cited in Davies, 1996, p. 55). Internalised homophobia and other minority stress processes have been linked to various adverse health outcomes in gay people (Lick et al., 2013), including sexual function and satisfaction (Grabski et al., 2019) and, as presented, pain on anal intercourse (Grabski & Kasparek, 2020).

It is rather commonly accepted by gay affirmative therapists that it should be addressed in any gay person entering therapy. There are many recognised sources on the therapeutic management of internalised homophobia and minority stress (e.g., Davies & Neal, 1996; Kort, 2008; Pereza et al., 2014). As healing is rather a process than a zero-one event, it will require time, accumulating of positive experiences with anal sexuality and, even more broadly with other gay people, and direct and active support from the therapist using their authority and integrity against stigma and stereotype.

Increasing mind–anus connection and inclusion of anal area into holistic positive self

Dissociation of mind–body connection is much more common than not. In everyday clinical mental health practice, the problem seems even to have mounted up in an accelerating everyday life. People tend to "abandon" their aching bodies and lose both the awareness of what the body might need and also what it communicates in terms of its relation to the *psyche*. This lacking connection deprives people also of any adequate healing influence on the body. This dissociation is in many cases even much more pronounced as referred to the anus. Anal taboo and homophobia lead to some sort of elimination of this body region from the sympathetic attention scope and rarely raises questions of the sort: "How are you now?", "What do you feel?" but rather centres attention around the process of defecation. Clients will surely benefit from being educated on this phenomenon and encouraged to treat their anuses as valid parts of the human psychophysical unity which have much more to say and do then getting rid of impurities. Apart from psychoeducation, therapist support, and modelling, self-experience work will be helpful to build or rebuild this lacking link.

Promotion of anal health and elimination of anal health problems

Any client should be educated on the essentials of preserving anal health. These include, apart from the already mentioned, relaxation: (1) Promoting efficient bowel movements and avoiding constipation. This can be achieved by a diet rich in fibre, which stimulates the intestines; (2) Healthy toilet habits, i.e. avoiding forced defecation, prolonged "sessions" with some typical accompanying activities like newspaper reading or surfing mobile internet; (3) Appropriate hygiene by regular washing, use of delicate detergents, and gentle wiping; (4) Promotion of greater anal awareness and mind–anus connection, thus increasing conscious responsiveness to the anus when it feels sore and needs careful attention, for example, planned relaxation exercises.

As with any other organ, anus, rectum, and bowels can be affected by medical conditions. These include, but are not limited to, haemorrhoids, fissures, fistulas, abscesses, inflammatory bowel disease, cancers, or sexually transmitted infections. A detailed account of each condition is outside the scope of this chapter, but a well-informed therapist should be aware of such a possibility, of a common nature of some of the problems (e.g., haemorrhoids) and disastrous consequences of the other, if not early diagnosed and treated (e.g., cancers). It would be thus a reasonable approach to get into the habit of routinely consulting your clients with a trained physician, preferably a proctologist. Symptoms like acute and chronic bleedings (caution: blood coming from the upper parts of the gastro-intestinal tube may be mixed with faeces and rather rusty than intensively red in colour), discharge, acute or chronic pain (also outside sexual anal intercourse), excessive itching, or any visible changes to the skin surrounding the anus; any palpable tumours outside and inside the anus or the rectum should be especially alarming.

As the anal taboo and homophobia pertains not only into the population of MSM but also into the medical world, and the issue of healthy anal sexuality is practically absent in the training of specialists (Morin, 2010), it would be advisable to establish cooperation with an open-minded clinician who would be willing to gain experience and expand their knowledge in this field.

Promotion of mental health

Mental health is of high importance to healthy and satisfying sex. A wide range of psychiatric disorders tend to co-exist with sexual difficulties either as a cause, a consequence, or interrelated phenomena (Jonusiene & Griffioen, 2013). Although formal research on psychiatric disorders or more generally mental health status and anodyspareunia is lacking (apart from one study, in which anxiety disorders were associated with intensity of pain on anal penetration in a univariate analysis; Grabski & Kasparek, 2020), it would be clinically justified to expect that commonly occurring conditions like a range of anxiety, mood disorders, or obsessive-compulsive disorder may present risk for anal sexual pain and should be addressed in the assessment and treatment plans. Substance use disorders or use/abuse should also be included into working out the problem. Some moderate use of alcohol, cannabis, or amyl-nitrite ("poppers"), for example, may promote relaxation and facilitate anal sexuality, but other substances may impose serious risk, either by artificially eliminating the pain and/or severely impairing a user's criticism without producing relaxation (e.g., cocaine, MDMA, ketamine, GHB; Morin, 2010). These problems need to be addressed, and clients need to be educated that (1) pain is a natural defence mechanism and a valid piece of information on the status of the anus, meaning that it is either not adequately relaxed, lubricated, or there is some sort of other problem, like a wound or injury; (2) anal intercourse is, when a person is adequately prepared and ready (both physically and emotionally), pain-free and pleasurable; and (3) some substances impose risk because of anaesthetic or judgement-impairing properties.

When mental health problems are present, they should be approached according to the existing standards of care. As some approaches like progressive muscle relaxation or autogenic training are commonly included into the management of some clinical problems, like anxiety disorders, including the anus, the rectum, and the whole pelvic floor area would be a reasonable add-on.

Summary

Pain on anal intercourse, or *anodyspareunia*, at least mild and casual, is rather common. Moderate or severe and frequent pain may concern around 10–20% of MSM. A substantial proportion of these men, but not all, may experience distress and benefit from clinical help. Possibly only the minority will eventually reach clinicians' offices due to the effects of taboo, stigma, and internalised homophobia. The causes or contributing factors of/for *anodyspareunia* are varied, and sometimes the genesis is multifactorial. An organic or medical cause should always be ruled out before commencing behavioural treatment. To do so, a thorough assessment is required and the help of an affirmative and informed proctologist needed. Proper relaxation is the foundation for pain-free, pleasurable anal sex and should be promoted. Clinical management of *anodyspareunia* is in its nature cognitive-behavioural, so well-known components, like psychoeducation and cognitive restructuring, bibliotherapy, self-experiential work and homework assignments are central to the therapeutic change. As the context of anal taboo and internalised homophobia may play an important role, an active and supportive role of a therapist is of paramount importance. The therapist should be knowledgeable of GSRD psychology and of gay affirmative therapeutic approaches.

References

Althof, S.E., Abdo, C.H., Dean, J., Hackett, G., McCabe, M., McMahon, C.G., Rosen, R.C., Sadovsky, R., Waldinger, M., Becher, E., Broderick, G.A., Buvat, J., Goldstein, I., El-Meliegy, A.I., Guiliano, F., Hellstrom, W.J., Incrocci, L., Jannini, E.A., Park, K., Parish, S., Porst, H., Rowland, D., Segraves, R., Sharlip, I., Simonelli, C., Tan, H.M.; International Society for Sexual Medicine. (2010). International Society for Sexual Medicine's guidelines for the diagnosis and treatment of premature ejaculation. *Journal of Sexual Medicine*, 7(9), 2947–2969.

Annon, J. (1976). *Behavioral Treatment of Sexual Problems.* New York: Harper & Row.

APA. (2013). *Diagnostic and Statistical Manual of Mental Disorders* (5th ed.). Washington, DC: American Psychiatric Press.

Beck, S.J. (2011). *Cognitive Behavior Therapy: Basics and Beyond* (2nd ed.). New York: The Guilford Press.

Bespoke Surgical. (n.d.). Anal Lubrication. [online] https://bespokesurgical.com/education/anal-lubrication-practices-2/ (Accessed: 14 December 2022).

Birnbaum, E. (2017). Surgical anatomy of the colon, rectum, and anus. In C. Ratto, A. Parello, L. Donisi, & F. Litta (Eds.), *Colon, Rectum and Anus: Anatomic, Physiologic and Diagnostic Bases for Disease Management* (pp. 9–18). Cham: Springer.

Damon, W., & Rosser, B.R.S. (2005). Anodyspareunia in men who have sex with men: Prevalence, predictors, consequences and the development of DSM diagnostic criteria. *Journal of Sex and Marital Therapy*, 31(2), 129–141.

Darnell, C. (n.d.). *The Atlas of Erotic Anatomy and Arousal.* [online] https://cyndidarnell. com/atlas-of-erotic-anatomy-arousal/ (Accessed: 14 December 2022).

Davies, D., & Neal, C. (Eds.). (1996). *A Guide for Counsellors and Therapists Working with Lesbian, Gay and Bisexual Clients.* Maidenhead, Philadelphia: Open University Press.

Davis, M., Eshelman, E.R., & McKay, M. (2019). *The Relaxation & Stress Reduction Workbook* (7th ed.). Oakland: New Harbinger Publications, Inc.

Ellis, S.J., Riggs, D.W., & Peel, E. (2020). *Lesbian, Gay, Bisexual, Trans, Intersex, and Queer Psychology: An Introduction* (2nd ed.). Cambridge: Cambridge University Press.

Felt-Bersma, R.J.F. (2017). Physiology of the rectum and anus. In C. Ratto, A. Parello, L. Donisi, & F. Litta (Eds.), *Colon, Rectum and Anus: Anatomic, Physiologic and Diagnostic Bases for Disease Management* (pp. 55–67). Cham: Springer.

Forstein, M. (1988). Homophobia: An overview. *Psychiatric Annals*, 18, 33–36.

Freud, S. (1913). *Totem and Taboo.* Complete Works, Vol. 13.

Grabski, B., & Kasparek, K. (2017). Sexual problems in homo- and bisexual men – the context of the issue. *Psychiatria Polska*, 51(1), 75–83.

Grabski, B., & Kasparek, K. (2020). Sexual anal pain in gay and bisexual men: in search of explanatory factors. *Journal of Sexual Medicine*, 17(4), 716–730.

Grabski, B., Kasparek, K., Müldner-Nieckowski, Ł., & Iniewicz, G. (2019). Sexual quality of life in homosexual and bisexual men: The relative role of minority stress. *Journal of Sexual Medicine*, 16(6), 860–871.

Hawton, K. (2004). Sexual dysfunctions. In K. Hawton, P.M. Salkovskis, J. Kirk, & D.M. Clark (Eds.), *Cognitive Behavior Therapy for Psychiatric Problems: A Practical Guide* (pp. 370–405). Oxford: Oxford University Press.

Hollows, K. (2007). Anodyspareunia: A novel sexual dysfunction? An exploration into anal sexuality. *Sexual and Relationship Therapy*, 22(4), 429–443.

Imieliński, K. (1989). *Seksuologia. Mitologia, historia, kultura.* Warszawa: Państwowe Wydawnictwo Naukowe.

Jonusiene, G., & Griffioen, T. (2013). Psychiatric disorders and sexual dysfunction. In P.S. Kirana, F. Tripodi, Y. Reisman, & H. Porst (Eds.), *The EFS and ESSM Syllabus of Clinical Sexology* (1st ed., pp. 890–927). Amsterdam: Medix Publishers.

Kort, J. (2008). *Gay Affirmative Therapy for the Straight Clinician: The Essential Guide* (1st ed.). New York, London: W. W. Norton & Company, Inc.

Leventhal, H., Diefenbach, M., & Leventhal, E.A. (1992). Illness cognition: Using common sense to understand treatment adherence and affect cognition interactions. *Cognitive Therapy and Research*, 16(2), 143–163.

Lick, D.J., Durso, L.E., & Johnson, K.L. (2013). Minority stress and physical health among sexual minorities. *Perspectives on Psychological Science*, 8(5), 521–548.

McNally, I., & Adams, N. (2001). Psychosexual issues. In C. Neal & D. Davies (Eds.), *Issues in Therapy with Lesbian, Gay, Bisexual and Transgender Clients* (pp. 83–102). Buckingham: Open University Press.

Meyer, I.H. (2003). Prejudice, social stress, and mental health in lesbian, gay, and bisexual populations: Conceptual issues and research evidence. *Psychological Bulletin*, 129(5), 674–697.

Mijas, M., Grabski, B., Blukacz, M., & Davies, D. (2021). Sexual health studies in gay and lesbian people: A critical review of the literature. *Journal of Sexual Medicine*, 18(6), 1012–1023.

Morin, J. (2010). *Anal Pleasure and Health: A Guide for Men, Women, and Couples* (4th ed.). San Francisco: Down There Press.

Niederwieser, S. (2013). *Fist Me! The Complete Guide to Fisting* (1st ed.). Berlin: Bruno Gmunder Verlag GmbH.

Paff, B.A. (1985). Sexual dysfunctions in gay men requesting treatment. *Journal of Sex and Marital Therapy*, 11(1), 3–18.

Pereza, R.M., DeBorda, K.A., & Bieschke, K.J. (Eds.). (2014). *Podręcznik poradnictwa i psychoterapii osób homoseksualnych i biseksualnych*. Warszawa: Kampania Przeciw Homofobii.

Queen, C., & Rednour, S. (2015). *The Sex and Pleasure Book: Good Vibrations: Guide to Great Sex for Everyone*. Barnaby LTD, LLC.

Reicher, M., & Łasiński, W. (1992). Jelito Grube. In A. Bochenek & M. Reicher (Eds.), *Anatomia człowieka II* (pp. 239–267). Warszawa: Państwowy Zakład Wydawnictw Lekarskich.

Reisman, Y. (2012). Let's Talk about Sex: Taking a Sexual History. In H. Porst & Y. Reisman (Eds.), *The ESSM Syllabus of Sexual Medicine* (pp. 233–310). Amsterdam: Medix Publishers.

Roffman, R. (2004). Psychoeducational groups. In C.D. Gaarvin, L.M. Gutierrez, & M.J. Galinsky (Eds.), *Handbook of Social Work with Groups* (pp. 160–175). New York: Guilford.

Rosser, B.R.S., Metz, M.E., Bockting, W.O., & Buroker, T. (1997). Sexual difficulties, concerns, and satisfaction in homosexual men: an empirical study with implications for HIV prevention. *Journal of Sex and Marital Therapy*, 23(1), 61–73.

Rosser, B.R.S., Short, B.J., Thurmes, P.J., & Coleman, E. (1998). Anodyspareunia, the unacknowledged sexual dysfunction: A validation study of painful receptive anal intercourse and its psychosexual concomitants in homosexual men. *Journal of Sex and Marital Therapy*, 24(4), 281–292.

Sandfort, T.G.M., & de Keizer, M. (2001). Sexual problems in gay men: An overview of empirical research. *Annual Review of Sex Research*, 12, 93–120.

Sophie, J. (1987). Internalised homophobia and lesbian identity. *Journal of Homosexuality*, 14, 53–65.

Tacchi, M.J., & Scott, J. (2005). *Improving Adherence in Schizophrenia and Bipolar Disorders*. Chichester: Wiley & Sons, Ltd.

Tiefer, L. (2012). The new view campaign: A feminist critique of sex therapy and an alternative vision. In P. Kleinplatz (Ed.), *New Directions in Sex Therapy* (2nd ed., pp. 21–35). New York and London: Routledge.

Tripodi, F., Silvaggi, C., & Simonelli, C. (2012). Psychology of sexual response. In H. Porst & Y. Reisman (Eds.), *The ESSM Syllabus of Sexual Medicine* (pp. 86–139). Amsterdam: Medix Publishers.

Vansintejan, J., Vandevoorde, J., & Devroey, D. (2013). The gay men sex studies: Anodyspareunia among Belgian gay men. *Sexual Medicine*, 1(2), 87–94.

Walsh, J. (2010). *Psychoeducation in Mental Health*. Chicago, IL: Lyceum Books, Inc.

Weiner, L., & Avery-Clark, C. (2017). *Sensate Focus in Sex Therapy: The Illustrated Manual*. New York and London: Routledge.

WHO. (1992). *The ICD 10 Classification of Mental and Behavioural Disorders: Clinical Descriptions and Diagnostic Guidelines*. Geneva: WHO.

WHO. (2018). *International Classification of Diseases for Mortality and Morbidity Statistics*. [online] https://icd.who.int/browse11/l-m/en (Accessed: 7 October 2021).

Wincze, J.P., & Weisberg, R.B. (2015). *Sexual Dysfunction: A Guide for Assessment and Treatment* (3rd ed.). New York and London: The Guilford Press.

Chapter 11

MSM and compulsive sexual behaviours

Silva Neves

It is evident, when reading all the chapters of this book, that many therapists have blind spots in the areas of GSRD. Adding to this, the blind spots created by the confusing and dividing opinions on "sex addiction" increase the likelihood that therapists will make mistakes unintentionally and even harm clients. I am optimistic, and I believe that most therapists are well-meaning professionals. Still, we must explore our blind spots and keep learning as new research emerges that may contradict our previous knowledge or old-fashioned ways of doing things. It is ok to change our minds and do something different! In this chapter, I aim to do just that: criticise the ubiquitous and often unchallenged narrative of "sex addiction", and offer a more sex-positive, ethical and evidence-based method from contemporary sexology, psychotherapy and a Queer perspective for therapists who work with clients presenting with sexual compulsivity.

This chapter is focused on MSM (men who have sex with men). Most of this population will identify as gay, queer, bisexual men, bicurious, pansexual, and nonbinary people. As such, I use the term "men" to mean anyone who identifies as such, including people assigned male at birth (AMAB). I acknowledge some men identify as "straight" and have sex with men. Therefore, I will use the term MSM to be as inclusive as possible.

"Sex addiction" and fear-based pseudo-science

Compulsive sexual behaviour (CSB) is a subject that generates many debates and even stentorian misinformation, filled with fear-based stories and sensationalised media about the inappropriate sexual behaviours of celebrities. Most people will have heard of terms such as "sex addiction", "porn addiction" and "love addiction", which have not been endorsed by our international scientific communities because of a lack of evidence (DSM-5, 2013; WHO, 2019).

Since the '80s, when Carnes (1983, 2001) invented the term "sex addiction" as a clinical discourse, numerous attempts have been made to classify it formally. Still, even after all those years, evidence of addiction has not been found. Grubbs et al. (2020) noticed in a meta-analysis on "sex addiction" research that they have been poor in both their methodologies and theoretical base. Indeed, much of it is

Doi: 10.4324/9781003260608-12

pseudo-science, which has unfortunately infiltrated the psyche of many therapists and laypeople as "truth".

For decades, people, mostly men, have been (mis)diagnosed with "sex addiction" and "porn addiction" without scientifically endorsed diagnostic criteria. The absence of such guidelines on "sex addiction" means that diagnosis is made mainly through each clinician's moral compass, with personal beliefs influencing their clinical thinking on how sexual behaviours should be "healthy", "unhealthy" or worse, what they perceive as a disease. Unfortunately, in sex and relationship issues, clinicians notoriously have many unchecked biases, especially when working with LGBTQIA+ people, those with kink and fetishes and people in multiple relationships.

The literature on "sex addiction" tends to conflate sexual compulsivity with sexual offending (Carnes, 2001; Weiss, 2011; Hall, 2019). It is the most common fearmongering narrative of "sex addiction" and "porn addiction", which posits the addictive behaviours escalate to the levels of sexual offending. However, this assumption has been highly contested (Ley, 2012). Indeed, escalation, one of the hallmarks of addiction, has not been observed clinically in sexual behaviours (Prause et al., 2017). Most people who struggle with sexual compulsivity report repetitive sexual behaviours, with some variations in behaviours, and with consenting adults. Although those behaviours may be unwanted for a multitude of reasons, they are not offending behaviours as they firmly stay within the boundaries of legal and consensual sexual contacts. I argue that sexual offending is an entirely different clinical presentation from compulsive sexual behaviours, and they should not be formulated as part of the same problem (Neves, 2021a). Most clients report breaching their relationship agreement in practising non-consensual non-monogamy (cheating). Those behaviours may be offensive to their partner(s), but they are not offending behaviours in law. The same applies to problematic pornography use. Many people may report struggling with their porn use or wondering if they watch too much of it, but most do not escalate their behaviours to watching illegal materials. I think this is important to remember because one of the familiar homophobic narratives that LGBTQIA+ people still face, particularly gay men, is that they are sexual predators, offenders and even paedophiles.

"Sex addiction" and homophobia

The pseudo-science and the sensational anecdotes of "sex addiction" and "porn addiction" have an uncomfortable parallel with the ones of homophobia. It is not so surprising, given that the term "sex addiction" took off in the early '80s when the epidemic of HIV/AIDS was raging. Everybody became afraid of sex, and the values of abstinence and monogamy made a resurgence. It was also when homophobic people took the opportunity to reinforce their message that gay men were promiscuous, diseased and dangerous to society. They proclaimed the virus was God's response to gay sin. At the time of the

HIV/AIDS epidemic, having a lot of sex was frowned upon as going against public health. It was just the right time for an unscientific conceptualisation such as "sex addiction" to flourish: if people couldn't stop having sex to the point of risking their lives with AIDS, it must mean they are addicts and mentally ill. Now that the AIDS crisis is behind us, the "sex addiction" field continues its fearmongering stories with pornography, attempting to make it a public health crisis despite evidence that it is not (Ley, 2016; Nelson & Rothman, 2020). Unduly pathologising sexual desire, arousal and behaviours under the pseudo-diagnosis of "sex addiction" or "porn addiction" because of poor theories (and poor training) may cause significant harm to MSM because it may add to their homophobic trauma of oppression and discrimination.

"Sex addiction" and religiosity

The "sex addiction" textbooks in the USA and UK are covertly religious (Neves, 2021b). It is puzzling to see that the use of prayer is promoted in those textbooks as viable interventions (Birchard, 2015; Hall, 2019). Indeed, for the LGBTQIA+ populations, this can be re-traumatising as many have suffered psychological abuse from religious groups. "Sex addiction" therapists strongly recommend their clients to attend 12-step programmes such as Sex Addict Anonymous (SAA) and Sex and Love Addict Anonymous (SLAA). It is highly problematic for MSM because those groups' messages are sex-negative, religious and heteronormative. The Sex Addict Anonymous book is sprinkled with religious messages throughout and gaslights us in making us believe they are not oriented in religious preaching, which is simply not true. For example, Step 6: "We're entirely ready to have God remove all these defects of character" (SAA, 2005, p. 21) is impossible to read in a secular way. Recommending those programmes to MSM as part of their "sex addiction" therapy can cause harm (Neves, 2021b).

Alejandro reflected on the gaslighting he received in his 12-step SLAA fellowship programme. His sponsor told him to pray to his Higher Power. When Alejandro told him he didn't want to pray because he had some complicated feelings about religion, his sponsor raised his voice, saying that 12-step programmes were not religious; the Higher Power could be anything he wanted. At the time, Alejandro felt awkward to be asked to do something he explicitly expressed he didn't want to do, but his sponsor told him that he was "sick" with this disease, and if he weren't willing to pray, he'd get worse. Alejandro was afraid to get sicker, so he did as he was told. It was re-traumatising for Alejandro because prayers were used in his childhood to gaslight him too. His father forced him to pray with him to ask God to make him "a real boy" because he was "more sensitive than the other boys". His father beat up Alejandro and justified his violence as corrective, "for his own good", and if he prayed enough, God would put him right. Later, when Alejandro came out, his father cut all contacts with him, telling him he was an abomination to God. In the 12-step programme with his sponsor, Alejandro felt the same story was being played out: he was asked to pray to be put right. Neither his sponsor nor his therapist paid attention to the religious re-traumatisation. Alejandro told me:

> both my sponsor and my therapist told me it wasn't a religious programme and I should just stick to it, but they kept using the word "God" and prayer all the time. I was so confused. At one point, I thought I was going mad.

Needless to say that the first part of Alejandro's therapy with me was to help him heal from the trauma of his 12-step/therapy-induced gaslighting.

"Sex addiction", heteronormativity, mononormativity and shame

Most clinical texts on "sex addiction" demonstrate a poor understanding of the diversities of sexuality, sexual behaviours, eroticism and relationship styles. Disturbingly, many books ignore contemporary sexology, preferring to base their treatment on addiction theories (Carnes, 2001; Weiss, 2011; Hall, 2019), with an implicit message that the goal of "sex addiction" therapy is "sobriety", which means to make the "sex addict" monogamous, or, at least, a "healthy romantic". Many "sex addiction" narratives incorrectly assume that casual sex, or sex with strangers, is the opposite to intimacy. In his book dedicated to gay men, *Cruise Control*, Weiss (2011) asserts that one of the rules for the "recovery" of "sex addiction" is: "You have to get to know the man you are going to have sex with *before* you have sex with him" (2011, p. 202). He also advises his gay male readers to take their "fuck buddy" to a non-porn movie, have a meal with them or spend the night with them after sex (p. 203). However, in the sex lives of many MSM, the very point of a "fuck buddy" is that the relationship is sexual, not romantic.

More recently, Zachary Zane, a sex-positive author, made a request on Twitter to speak to experts about porn for the research of his book. Weiss responded to his tweet with: "Small suggestion Zach. If u want to deal w the porn and sex issue. It's best to wear a shirt on ur profile pic. From one sex addict out here" (Twitter, 18/11/2021). We could read this tweet as an example of a shame response. People who stumble across images or other materials that evoke sexual arousal may feel shame about those feelings because they cannot own them. As a result, they may attempt to shame the people they find attractive as a way to stop feeling uncomfortable with sexual arousal. This is a common reaction conceptualised by the theory of the compass of shame (Nathanson, 1992), discussed in Chapter 3. It is essential to be compassionate with people who shame others because they are struggling with their own shame. In my career, I have encountered some "sex addiction" therapists who shame other people's sexual behaviours because they don't understand, disagree with, or feel uncomfortably aroused by those behaviours. In most cases, it is not because the therapists are bad people. I think it is because their clinical training is poor, they do not check their biases, they are uncomfortable with some sexual content, they haven't explored their own erotic mind, and they lack knowledge in sexuality and relationship diversities.

"Sex addiction" and conversion practices

The congruent therapist will use an addiction treatment if they assign a behavioural disturbance as an addiction. The literature on "sex addiction" is strongly biased by addiction theories over sexology. For example, "sex addiction" texts are concerned with "the addictive cycle", the idea of "sobriety" and recommend 12-step programmes (Carnes, 2001; Weiss, 2011; Birchard, 2015; Hall, 2019). Weiss (2011) explains:

> People become addicted to a certain behavior because it induces chemical changes in the brain. These changes are just as powerful and intensely arousing to them as the high other addicts get from alcohol or drugs.
>
> (p. 7)

His claim has been refuted multiple times by sexologists, psychologists and neuroscientists (Ley, 2012; Prause et al., 2017). The brain chemicals Weiss refers to in his book (serotonin, endorphins, dopamine, etc.) are naturally released when there is sexual desire, arousal, orgasms and/or an intimate connection. In other words, the release of these chemicals indicates that the brain functions as it should, and it is not a sign of addiction nor any other disease. The idea that MSM people have an impaired brain because of their sexual behaviours uncomfortably echoes the idea that was used when "homosexuality" was considered a mental health disorder, which led to developing harmful methods such as conversion practices (the practice aiming to "correct" same-sex attraction and sexual behaviours into heterosexuality).

It is worth noting here that the UK Government's (2021) review on conversion "therapy" found evidence that some LGBTQ+ people were offered conversion "therapy" by therapists who told them their same-sex attraction and behaviours were a symptom of sexual addiction.

Some "sex addiction" therapists offer aversion techniques in an attempt to halt sexual desire and urges. Somehow, the addiction field ignores helpful methods from the psychotherapy profession, which has a wealth of emotional regulation tools that do not involve painful aversion techniques. When those aversion techniques are applied to MSM, they can be particularly harmful as they are akin to what I would consider conversion practices.

Mark reported that his previous therapy was harmful. Mark reached out to a "sex addiction" therapist because he was distressed that he couldn't stop cheating on his boyfriend by regularly attending sex clubs. After hardly any assessment, his therapist, who positioned themselves as "expert" in "sex addiction", agreed that he was suffering from the disorder. Their implicit goal was to make him monogamous to be a better partner. His therapist told Mark he had to put an ice cube on the roof of his mouth to give himself a brain freeze or to bite on a chilli each time he had sexual desires, urges or even thoughts about going to a sex club. Mark thought it was a "strange therapy" but complied with the "expert" advice. Reflecting on his past therapy, he now identified it as "conversion therapy". He said: "This technique did nothing for me, apart from hurting me and shaming me. It didn't stop my urges either". Mark reported post-trauma symptoms after his past therapy such as feeling acute distress in sexual situations, remembering the physical pain of his aversion treatment. This is common for survivors who endured conversion practices. If the "sex addiction" therapist had opted for psychotherapy rather than an addiction and aversion treatment, they would have avoided traumatising Mark.

Diagnosis: words matter because they can harm

Words matter when we discuss diagnoses because those words can harm when misused. The ICD-11 (WHO, 2019) endorsed a diagnostic framework called "Compulsive Sexual Behaviour Disorder" (CSBD), categorised under "impulse control" and not addiction. There has been much debate, but WHO clearly informs us that "sex addiction" and CSBD are not meant to be interchangeable. Kraus et al. (2018) state:

> Careful attention must be paid to the evaluation of individuals who self-identify as having the disorder (e.g., calling themselves "sex addicts" or "porn addicts"). Upon examination, such individuals may not exhibit the clinical characteristics of the disorder.
>
> (2018, p. 109)

Many therapists continue to use the two terms as though they were synonyms, which might indicate a poor understanding of the ICD-11 diagnostic criteria. Braun-Harvey and Vigorito (2016) caution on the "premature evaluation" of "sex addiction" when therapists typically do not do a thorough assessment and assume their clients suffer from "sex addiction":

> Prematurely framing a sexual problem as a clinical disorder pathologizes normative behavior, affects the individual's self-concept, and invites overly restrictive sexual interventions.
>
> (2016, p. 26)

My experience concurs with this. I have heard many clients tell me that their "sex addiction" assessment was quick, the term "sex addiction" was not questioned, and they were rapidly ushered into treatments, programmes and group therapies without much consideration. A great majority of them reported that they were strongly recommended attendance to 12-step programmes at the end of their initial consultation.

The public can choose any words they wish to describe themselves and their behaviours. In laypeople's language, the term "addiction" usually means something they enjoy very much and occasionally they might overdo it (i.e., I'm a chocolate addict). This is not the clinical definition of addiction. The word "addiction" is considered a serious disorder and a brain-altering disease.

Magnanti (2012) criticises one of Carnes' screening questions: "Have you been paid for sex?", making the point that the "sex addiction" field automatically pathologises sex workers as a sign of being diseased. Magnanti (2012) writes:

> That makes no sense. Since when does being paid for something equate to a pathological obsession with it? You wouldn't screen people with suspected eating disorders by asking 'Have you ever been a waitress?'
>
> (p. 39)

As a therapist, I have a clinical responsibility to properly understand the psychological weight that the word "addiction" may have on clients. It is not merely an academic discussion over nomenclature. Those words have a direct and profound impact on clients' well-being. Colluding with the language of disease can increase clients' distress. It is not therapeutic, and it is not ethical nor evidence-based.

Regarding the ICD-11 diagnostic criteria of CSBD (which I will explain later), Kraus et al. (2018) assert:

> we do not yet have definitive information on whether the processes involved in the development and maintenance of the disorder are equivalent to those observed in substance use disorders, gambling and gaming.
>
> (2018, p. 110)

The DSM-5 (2013)'s position is:

> groups of repetitive behaviors, which some term behavioral addiction, with such subcategories as "sex addiction", "exercise addiction", or "shopping addiction", are not included because at this time there is insufficient peer-reviewed evidence to establish the diagnostic criteria and course descriptions needed to identify these behaviors as mental disorders.
>
> (2013, p. 481)

This raises an uncomfortable question in our profession: why do we continue to use the terms "sex addiction" and "porn addiction" at a time when there is not enough evidence of their existence? I believe that it can be harmful to use a diagnosis when there is none, to make clients think they have an illness when they don't, or to collude with their self-perception of being a "sex addict" and their sense of defectiveness when it is not the case. Providing treatments based on the pseudo-diagnosis of "sex addiction" and "porn addiction" may be harmful. Clients may not be aware that having addiction-oriented therapy for a problem that is not an addiction can be problematic. In my career, I have seen numerous clients who told me that their "sex addiction" therapist did not explain the theories they were basing their treatment on; they made them believe that their diagnosis and treatment were evidence-based (when it wasn't). It was sold as the only and best treatment for their condition, disabling clients from making an informed choice and giving proper consent to their treatment. This is a breach of several points in the COSRT code of ethics (2022):

7 Not exploit anyone emotionally, financially or in any other way.
9 Not express your personal beliefs to Service Users or others in ways that could cause distress.
29 Only provide or advocate therapy with robust and scientifically verifiable evidence bases.

I believe it is the duty of psychotherapists, psychologists and sexologists to help change the terminology in line with the current scientific agreement, just as we have done with other old-fashioned terms such as "nymphomania", "impotence", "manic depressive" and "hysteria". MSM are sensitive to the disease language, rightly so, given they were pathologised until 1990 (WHO, 1994). It is essential for MSM that the psychiatric, psychological and psychotherapeutic professions stop repeating the grave mistakes of the past. I have heard some "sex addiction" therapists say, "I use this term because it is the term everyone uses", or "Compulsive sexual behaviour doesn't roll off the tongue". I am afraid that those excuses are feeble when the consequence of those words can harm clients.

Words matter for clients and laypeople too. The identity of "sex addict" is linked with the unhelpful message: "once an addict, always an addict". The typical "sex addiction" mindset encourages people to believe that they have a chronic illness and the best they can hope for is a life of constant vigilance not to stumble across sexual content as those would be a "trigger". This kind of avoidance strategy makes for a pretty joyless life:

> The simplest and most effective strategy is simply to look away (. . .) Other strategies include making sure you're facing the wall in public places, so you're less likely to notice people or scan on the off chance.
>
> (Hall, 2019, p. 146)

The idea that it is probably not a good idea for an alcoholic to linger in the alcohol aisle of their local supermarket may make sense. But, in our Western world, sexual, erotic and titillating content is everywhere. Also, people naturally feel spontaneous sexual desire and arousal, and they should not be afraid of it. The essential aspect of pleasure with our sexuality must be embraced, not feared. Many of my clients were distressed and exhausted by the constant monitoring of their sexuality as a result of their past "sex addiction" therapy. It eroded their mental health, and they described feeling worse than before their treatment. These clients reported that their "sex addiction" therapists believed the treatment they offered was successful based only on one outcome: their clients didn't "relapse". In my view, clients who only learn how not to relapse but who don't understand their erotic processes and end up fearing their sexuality is not a good outcome of therapy.

I find the analogy with food helpful. Why would we encourage our clients to avoid the immense pleasure of enjoying a chocolate cake if it's one of their favourite desserts? Indeed, that would only make that person want the chocolate cake more. When clients relapse on the forbidden chocolate cake, the therapist blames the client rather than thinking that the very prohibition of the cake contributed to the relapse. Perhaps the therapist's strategy wasn't good, and it wasn't the client's fault for "not doing therapy properly". Instead, I help my clients enjoy the chocolate cake, one slice at a time, in a conscious way, well-integrated with the rest of their food menu.

Sexology

The more one has a sense of deprivation of pleasure, the more one will want it. This is when the knowledge of sexology is crucial. The Erotic Equation proposed by sexologist Jack Morin (1995) offers a helpful and simple guide to understanding our clients' erotic and sexual processes:

Attraction + Obstacle = Excitement

An obstacle to something we enjoy makes it even more exciting. Meeting a handsome stranger may produce exciting fantasies to have sex with them if we know we can't do it (either because we're in a monogamous committed relationship, or maybe because they are).

A robust sexological assessment is crucial in understanding the client's unique erotic landscape. Before the therapist and client can figure out the problems, it is important to identify what is good, functional, pleasurable and joyous and to affirm it. It helps with reducing shame and therefore is therapeutic in itself. I borrow the work of Jack Morin (1995) to help my clients explore their erotic minds with the following simple questions:

1   What are your sexual memories that lead to a peak turn-on?
2   What are all the ingredients that make these memories a peak turn-on?
3   What are your sexual fantasies that lead to a peak turn-on?
4   What are all the ingredients that make these fantasies a peak turn-on?

Often therapists feel that it might be voyeuristic to encourage a client to go into such fine granular details about their erotic mind, but, in my experience, it is a relief for clients because they often never had any opportunities to do so in a safe and non-judgemental space. Some clients might be anxious to start with; if so, take your time, and pace the session. You don't need to dive into these lines of enquiries all at once. Getting to know our erotic mind is vital because it is the map of our eroticism and our sexual behaviours.

The four cornerstones of eroticism

Jack Morin (1995) identifies the four cornerstones of eroticism which help clients understand their erotic processes and normalise them:

1   **Longing and anticipation**. One of Peter's significant erotic experiences is planning a visit to a sex club on some Friday nights. He makes the plan a week in advance, and the anticipation of going, getting closer to Friday, imagining what it would be like, wondering who would be there, and planning what he would wear are all potent erotic feelings during the week.

2   **Violating prohibition**. His family always told Numaan that being gay was wrong and anal sex between men was the worst of all sins. For Numaan, there is nothing more powerfully arousing than being a bareback bottom to multiple sexual partners while looking after himself by taking pre-exposure prophylaxis (PrEP).

3   **Searching for power**. The best sexual moments for Hai is when he role-plays as a Dominant and takes charge with his partner who enjoys being submissive. The sense of feeling powerful consensually towards his partner is a place of erotic and psychological well-being for him.

4   **Overcoming ambivalence**. Alphonse and Quentin are in a monogamish relationship. They sometimes enjoy inviting a third sexual partner, usually a stranger, through an app. They can be anxious and ambivalent about it: "should we do it?", "would it damage our relationship?", "what if it doesn't go well?", "what if the third person prefers one of us and rejects the other?", "what if one of us falls in love with the third person?", and so on. When the couple overcomes their ambivalence by deciding: "let's do it" or "let's not do it", the eroticism is enhanced in their relationship.

Sexual compulsivity

If "sex addiction" and "porn addiction" are not real disorders, then what is sexual compulsivity?

The greatest difficulty CSB presents for therapists is that sexual behaviours manifest in many ways because they depend on the unique multi-faceted aspects of clients' lives. It is therefore not possible, as in most clinical presentations, to offer a one-size fits all treatment approach that addresses behaviours with the primary goal of stopping those behaviours. CSB serves to meet specific needs in a client's life, and even if those behaviours are unwanted, they need to be thoroughly understood first before behavioural change can occur. The main sex-positive framework of CSB is to think that, somehow, there is a function to the "dysfunction", and it is important to explore what that function is before beginning treatment.

The ICD-11 (WHO) diagnostic criteria for Compulsive Sexual Behaviour Disorder (CSBD) are as follows:

> Compulsive sexual behaviour disorder is characterized by a persistent pattern of failure to control intense, repetitive sexual impulses or urges resulting in repetitive sexual behaviour. Symptoms may include repetitive sexual activities becoming a central focus of the person's life to the point of neglecting

health and personal care or other interests, activities and responsibilities; numerous unsuccessful efforts to significantly reduce repetitive sexual behaviour; and continued repetitive sexual behaviour despite adverse consequences or deriving little or no satisfaction from it. The pattern of failure to control intense, sexual impulses or urges and resulting repetitive sexual behaviour is manifested over an extended period of time (e.g. 6 months or more), and causes marked distress or significant impairment in personal, family, social, educational, occupational, or other important areas of functioning. Distress that is entirely related to moral judgments and disapproval about sexual impulses, urges, or behaviours is not sufficient to meet this requirement.

Having these diagnostic criteria is helpful because it highlights that it is very difficult for a client to meet *all* the criteria for the disorder. These criteria can be used to "un-diagnose" clients who come with a self-diagnosis. Many clients will meet some requirements, in which case they should not be labelled with the word "disorder" but perhaps someone presenting with sexual behaviour problems or with some sexual compulsive traits. As mentioned earlier, words do matter, especially for MSM.

Here are some of the reasons why most clients won't meet the "disorder" diagnosis:

1   The problem has to be a failure to manage impulse control, it is not about the number of times someone has sex. Shinobu is often aroused and meets many people for casual sex. He manages his intense urges, and he is able to wait for a while until he organises a "hook-up" at lunchtime or after work. In that case, his behaviour is not considered a disorder, even if he does it daily.
2   Most people who struggle with compulsive sexual behaviours can still function perfectly well in their lives: attending to their work properly, meeting the needs of their partner(s) and friend(s), and maintaining their personal hygiene and overall health. This does not qualify for the disorder even if clients want to change their sexual behaviours. Some clients will report poor performance at work or prioritising a "hook-up" over meeting a friend because of CSB, and many will say that they keep lying to their partner(s). Those are negative consequences of CSB, but it differs from "significant impairment in personal, family, social, educational, occupational, or other important areas of functioning".
3   Many people say they shouldn't be doing their behaviours because they're cheating on their partner(s), but they do it anyway. This is not indicative of a disorder, it is most likely what Braun-Harvey and Vigorito (2016) call an "erotic conflict" and "competing needs".
4   Some clients will attempt to change their sexual behaviours by themselves without success, and others will not have tried to change their behaviours until they get caught by their partner(s). For the latter, the diagnosis of disorder does not apply.
5   If clients report their sexual behaviours have become "out of control" within six months, a disorder does not apply, as it can be a normal process. For

example, someone who has experienced a significant and painful bereavement may have a bout of compulsive sexual behaviours due to their enormous grief, which usually wanes by itself over time.

6   It is essential to properly investigate the source of distress that clients present with. Most of the time, and especially for MSM, the distress will be caused by shame induced by society, books, podcasts and websites promoting "sex addiction" and "porn addiction". The distress can be caused by their partners' disapproval or friends telling them they're probably a "sex addict" because they have more sex than them. Most often, the distress starts when their partner(s) discover their hidden sexual behaviours and become upset. These are distress from external judgements and do not qualify for the disorder.

7   The clients who come to therapy for genuine distress from within themselves (breaching their values rather than someone else's) most often describe feeling satisfaction (or pleasure) from those behaviours, which also rules out the disorder. It is rare for clients to experience no satisfaction or pleasure from sexual behaviours, even the ones they want to stop. The few that describe no satisfaction or pleasure at the time of sexual behaviours may be in dissociation, which indicates the possibility of post-trauma stress symptoms rather than the disorder category of CSBD.

Assessments

Many clients will come to therapy because their hidden sexual behaviours have been discovered by their partner(s), and their life is upside down. They will often present with a lot of shame, guilt and distress for hurting their partner(s) and for doing sexual behaviours they don't understand and feel compulsive or out-of-control. These clients will often want to have a "quick fix", stop feeling the unbearable shame and guilt, and they want their partner(s) to stop hurting too and "go back to normal". Therapists must learn not to collude with the rush. Even though clients are in emotional pain, there is usually no immediate risk to life, and repairing the damage of the betrayal with their partner(s) and understanding what is going on for the clients take time. I propose a four-pronged assessment.

Initial assessment: investigating the clients' level of distress, checking their behaviours with the ICD-11 diagnostic criteria (mostly to reassure clients they don't have a disorder), their current life situation: safe housing, stable job, no immediate physical health concerns, etc. Therapists will need to check if clients have suicidal ideations, if they need an urgent sexual health screening for STIs, and if they are at immediate risk of harm (some partners may become abusive after discovering CSB).

Sexological assessment: exploring clients' erotic minds, erotic orientations, turn-ons, sexual pleasure, the Erotic Equation, the four cornerstones of eroticism, identifying erotic conflicts and competing needs.

Psychological assessment: identifying the clients' minority stress and possible trauma symptoms due to homophobia, biphobia and/or transphobia. Assessing traumas that still cause a disturbance. Exploring attachment styles and their relationship with CSB. Identifying the underlying disturbance of the CSB: what is the source of the clients' chronic stress? For many clients, chronic stress is what maintains CSB. It may be anything from minority stress and internalised homophobia to having a difficult life, such as having a career they hate or serious financial stress.

RAW assessment: enquiring with clients if they are Ready, Able and Willing. Although most distressed clients want to change, not as many are ready for the change. Feeling desperate for change does not equate to a willingness to change. Doing a RAW assessment can help predict the blocks that might happen in therapy with clients and identify if they need extra time to prepare for therapy. For example, some clients might not be ready because they need to move out of their house, and they need to attend to that first. They may not be able if their CSB symptoms are explained otherwise, for example, a neurological disorder or processing important grief. Therapists need to be careful not to encourage clients to stop or change their sexual behaviours if those very behaviours are their only coping strategies to manage with post-trauma stress symptoms. If it is the case, it is very important to help clients have more coping strategies before working towards behavioural change. Otherwise, the therapy can make clients worse and harm them. Clients may not be willing to change behaviours because it is hard to change. If they want to stop a particular sexual behaviour because it is in conflict with their values or their agreement with their partner(s), they may need to be prepared to grieve the loss of the sexual pleasure the behaviour produced.

Effective, sex-positive and ethical treatment

The three-phase treatment (Neves, 2021a) is adapted from the trauma treatment proposed by Rothschild (2021). This trauma approach was designed to focus on avoiding harm in therapy. Given the high likelihood of harm in treating MSM who struggle with sexual behaviours, the CSB three-phase treatment is particularly effective for them. Of course, it is suitable for people of all sexual orientations and identities.

Phase 1: Regulation (helping clients with their impulse control and their emotional regulation)
Phase 2: Reprocessing (treating the chronic stress/disturbances underlying the sexual compulsivity)
Phase 3: Reconstruction (meaning-making of their lives, who they are and their connections)

These three phases are not meant to be strict linear steps; they are a guide for a good therapeutic flow. Each phase intertwine and overlap with each other depending on the clients' needs. Let's look at two case studies to illustrate how the three phases work.

Problematic pornography use: Patrick

Patrick came to therapy because he thought he was a "porn addict". He watched online porn from the age of 14 and never stopped since. He had a few short-term relationships with men but partnered sex was never satisfying for him, and he preferred engaging with porn rather than with other people. He frequently experienced unreliable erections with partnered sex but never with porn. He had a medical investigation, and there were no organic causes for his erection problems. He worried that his erection problems were caused by porn because that's what he read on some websites. He said: "I watched porn for so long, from a young age, I think I broke my brain". Nevertheless, he usually has pleasurable sexual experiences with porn. Sometimes he has a "quickie" if he doesn't have much time or for quick stress relief, and sometimes he enjoys edging in a long masturbation session. He has a few favourite scenes he tends to search on the porn engine: group sex, muscle men and public toilets. Watching group sex is highly arousing for him; this is the kind of scene that makes him ejaculate quickly because it is such a turn-on. He loves seeing multiple naked male bodies abandoning themselves in pure lust. The attraction to watch muscle men is mostly aesthetic. He doesn't consider himself a muscle man, but he loves to watch a sex scene between very attractive people that he probably wouldn't want to have sex with in real life. The public toilet scenes are a sweet reminder of what he used to do when he was younger. He loved the thrill of going to public toilets and having some quick, anonymous sexual encounters. He prefers not to do it in real life anymore, but he enjoys those memories by watching it on porn.

Patrick had never spoken about his porn use non-judgementally and in as much detail before. It became clear to him that his porn use had multiple functions: stress relief, sexual pleasure of edging and meeting different parts of his erotic mind: lust, aesthetic and fond memories, all of which I normalised as these were not indicative of any disorders. After a few sessions of exploring his erotic mind, Patrick already reported a reduction in his distress with his porn use because he now understood better what he was doing and for what purpose. He still felt something was "wrong" because of preferring porn so much more than partnered sex. I offered Patrick the option of thinking about digisexuality (people who prefer sex with a device) (McArthur & Twist, 2017). Patrick had never heard of it, but he found it interesting to research, and it further reduced his shame about porn use. Although there was a marked improvement in his distress, Patrick still felt that his behaviour was "too compulsive". We investigated the function of porn use apart from the ones we had already discovered. He quickly understood that porn watching was his only way to manage his emotional states: when he feels happy, sad, angry, anxious, and so on. Patrick grew up in a volatile household where both parents would scream at each other and hit each other. Sometimes those events would last a whole night. At a young age, both he and his brother quickly learned that one way to soothe themselves from their parents' domestic violence was to masturbate. They sometimes masturbated each other. Patrick described that it was the only "feel good" time in his childhood. By the time they were 15 and had a computer in their bedroom, they both learned that watching porn while masturbating was even a better soother because they could completely focus on the films and feel pleasure. For Patrick, those soothing moments were both relief and shame-inducing because it was when he became aware that he was very different from his brother who loved heterosexual porn. Patrick noticed that he focused on the male body and started to wonder if there was something "wrong" with him.

Later, when Patrick moved out of the family home, as soon as he could, he finally indulged in watching the porn he had always wanted to watch: gay porn. He remembers feeling a great sense of relief and pleasure then. However, homophobia wounded him. Not only were his parents overtly homophobic, but his brother also accused Patrick of being a "dirty poofta" who tried to turn him gay because of their mutual masturbation. This hurt Patrick, and it wasn't resolved for him until we discussed in sessions that his brother might have felt a lot of shame for his behaviours and attacking Patrick was one way of mitigating his shame.

Reflecting on his childhood, Patrick realised he had never learned other ways to soothe himself apart from watching porn. We spent several sessions adding new emotional regulation methods (Phase 1). His favourites became mindful breathing, butterfly hugs (crossing his arms and tapping on his collar bone in turns), jogging, and a simple and pleasurable distraction like peeling an orange and eating it. When Patrick felt confident that he had five other resources for emotional regulations, including masturbating to porn, he felt less compelled to turn to porn every time. He did not identify as a digisexual because he wanted a long-term relationship with another man. The problem was that he feared unreliable erections. First, I normalised that unreliable erections are more common with partnered sex even when there isn't a "dysfunction" (Rowland et al., 2021), which reduced his anxiety about his erections. We then worked on improving his erections with tried and tested psychosexual methods such as waxing and waning and the Kegel exercise (Campbell, 2020).

Part of this work addressed his internalised homophobia, identifying some of his homophobic parents' messages that he had learned to believe. We also worked on his beliefs about relationships. Patrick was surprised to identify that because of his childhood, he had constructed an idea that relationships were dangerous because someone could "kick off" at any time. Re-framing what relationships can be like, and not all of them will necessarily be like his parents', was a turning point for him (Phase 2).

Towards the end of his therapy, Patrick started to integrate all parts of himself: he had a better sense of himself by understanding the impact of his childhood and healing past trauma. He felt less shame about his porn use and turn-ons, and he continued to watch porn in a way that he felt in control of because he now understood his behaviours. He was able to look after himself better with new emotional regulation methods. Overall, Patrick reported that his therapy was not about his porn use, it was about feeling better about all the parts of himself (Phase 3). When we finished therapy, he was in a relationship with a man, and they had good sex.

Compulsive sexual behaviours: Hugo

Hugo has been in a monogamous relationship with his partner for ten years. He cheated throughout his relationship, going to sex clubs and saunas. Occasionally, he paid for a sex worker. His partner Allan found PrEP pills and confronted Hugo about them. He confessed his behaviours to Allan, which was a relief for him (no more secrets) but hurt Allan very much. Hugo came to therapy because he was aware he had cheated on all his past relationships, he didn't know why he kept doing those sexual behaviours, and he wanted to stop them. Hugo described feeling "intoxicated" by the thrill of going to sex clubs and saunas. Unpacking what he meant about that, he understood that the feeling of "intoxication" was extremely horny to the point of "not thinking straight". We investigated his erotic mind: what was so arousing for him? It did not take long for Hugo to identify that in those sexual spaces, he felt safe and free of shame (the shame only hit afterwards when he returned home to his partner). He felt enhanced sexual pleasure in those spaces because he could have sex without worrying about what others thought of him. Indeed, in sex clubs and saunas, there was no conversation, but there was a lot of lustful desire. Hugo knew that someone would find him attractive and desire him in those places. He described feeling a lot of love in his relationship but didn't feel wanted in the intensely lustful way he did in sex clubs. He preferred steam rooms and dark rooms in those spaces, mainly for mutual oral sex and occasionally anal sex. He was confused because he enjoyed his sex life with Allan, but it was not at the same intensity. Hugo described that there was "nowhere to hide" with Allan, and it often felt anxiety-provoking.

Hugo described his childhood as awful. He grew up in a small town, and his parents' mindset was to repress all feelings. Hugo was reprimanded for feeling sad, anxious or scared. He was only allowed to feel good. His parents also focused on his academic success and weren't interested in his mental health. His father was homophobic, saying "a dead son is better than a gay son". He fled his small town to come to London for his University studies. He thought he could finally feel safe in London, but he encountered rejection in the gay community. His self-esteem took another blow, and he experienced depression. He reflected on his pattern of choosing "safe" men, by that, he meant people who were not demanding in any way and often whom he perceived as less attractive than him. The issue for Hugo was that these kinds of "safe" men were also not demonstrative about their sexual desire and did not express their lustful desire to him, so, instead, he turned to sex clubs to find the erotic energy he was looking for.

When Hugo was clearer about his erotic conflicts, the function of his sexual behaviours and his erotic mind, his self-awareness increased, which decreased his sense of compulsivity. In his therapy, Hugo started to experiment with delaying his urges to go to a sex club when he wanted to feel desired by others, as well as managing his anxiety when expressing his sexual desire to his partner (Phase 1). We worked on his internalised homophobia inherited from his father's homophobic language, and he learned to be more resilient in navigating the heteronormative world. He disclosed later in therapy that his father frequently beat him up, leaving physical scars and emotional wounds. I offered trauma therapy to heal his post-trauma stress symptoms and also to be compassionate towards his physical scars. I love using the analogy of the moon: we can see it has been bashed often, and there are many craters on the surface of the moon, yet, it is still beautiful, it still shines brightly and it influences our tide. Using this metaphor is not about minimising the hurt but reframing thoughts in acknowledging the permanent reminders of trauma (Phase 2).

In Phase 3, Hugo was ready to have existential conversations with me about the pain of losing the illusion that there was a perfect world somewhere, and the constant efforts to reaching that elusive happiness. Instead, he started to have a very different world view: we live in an imperfect world full of homophobia, and therefore we need to be caring and loving towards ourselves. When we do that, we can feel moments of happiness, coming and going, just like all other emotions come and go, as a constant flow in our system, including sexual desire and arousal. By the end of his therapy, Allan had left the relationship, a significant loss that we had processed in the course of therapy. Hugo took the opportunity to reach out to friends, other gay men and built a "tribe" together. The next person he chose to be in a relationship with was quite different from all his previous partners. He was assertive with his expression of sexual desire towards Hugo, and they both made a "monogamish" agreement which allowed for the occasional visit to a sex club. In his last session, Hugo described his therapy as "learning to be human".

Conclusion

Working with clients who struggle with sexual compulsivity is complex and made more difficult by divided opinions. It is an area that has been plagued by poor research in the "sex addiction" field. There is now more robust and exciting developing research being done in compulsive sexual behaviours which, thus far, continue to confirm that sex and porn use are not addictive behaviours. Indeed, working with addiction-oriented methods when there is no evidence of it encourages sex-negative thinking and makes it more likely for practitioners working with this framework to unintentionally harm clients. The "sex addiction" narrative is largely embedded in heteronormativity, mononormativity and religiosity, which is highly problematic for MSM. Therefore we can better serve our Queer clients with a sex-positive treatment informed by contemporary sexology, with robust understanding of GSRD knowledge. An effective and ethical treatment is one that helps people thrive sexually and relationally, without fearing their eroticism or shame.

References

Birchard, T. (2015). *CBT for Compulsive Sexual Behaviour, a Guide for Professionals*. Hove, East Sussex: Routledge.

Braun-Harvey, D., & Vigorito, A.M. (2016). *Treating Out of Control Sexual Behavior*. New York: Springer Publishing Company, LLC.

Campbell, C. (2020). *Contemporary Sex Therapy: Skills in Managing Sexual Problems*. Abingdon: Routledge.

Carnes, P. (1983, 2001). *Out of the Shadows, Understanding Sexual Addiction* (3rd ed.). Center City, MN: Hazelden.

COSRT. (2022). *Good Therapy: COSRT Code of Ethics and Practice*. www.cosrt.org.uk/wp-content/uploads/2022/02/COSRT-Code-of-Ethics-and-Practice-2022.pdf

DSM-5. (2013). *Diagnostic and Statistical Manual of Mental Disorders* (5th ed.). Arlington, VA: American Psychiatric Association. American Psychiatric Publishing.

Grubbs, J.B., Hoagland, K.C., Lee, B.N., Grant, J.T., Davison, P., Reid, R.C., Kraus, S.W. (2020, December). Sexual addiction 25 years on: A systematic and methodological review of empirical literature and an agenda for future research. *Clinical Psychology Review*, 82, 101925. https://doi.org/10.1016/j.cpr.2020.101925

Hall, P. (2019). *Understanding and Treating Sex and Pornography Addiction*. Abingdon: Routledge.

Kraus, S.W., Krueger, R.B., Briken, P., First, M.B., Stein, D.J., Kaplan, M.S., Voon, V., Abdo, C.H.N., Grant, J.E., Atalla, E., & Reed, G.M. (2018, February). Compulsive sexual behaviour disorder in the ICD-11. *World Psychiatry*, 17(1), 109–110. doi:10.1002/wps.20499. PMID: 29352554; PMCID: PMC5775124.

Ley, D. (2012). *The Myth of Sex Addiction*. Lanham, MD: Rowman & Littlefield Publishers, Inc.

Ley, D. (2016). *Ethical Porn for Dicks: A Man's Guide to Responsible Viewing Pleasure*. ThreeL Media. Berkeley, CA: Stone Bridge Press.

Magnanti, B. (2012). *The Sex Myth: Why Everything We're Told Is Wrong*. London: Phoenix.

McArthur, N., & Twist, M.L.C. (2017). The rise of digisexuality: Therapeutic challenges and possibilities. *Sexual and Relationship Therapy*. doi:10.1080/14681994.2017.1397950

Morin, J. (1995). *The Erotic Mind*. New York: HarperCollins Publishers.

Nathanson, D.L. (1992). *Shame and Pride: Affect, Sex, and the Birth of the Self*. New York, NY: W.W. Norton & Company.

Nelson, K.M., & Rothman, E.F. (2020, February). Should public health professionals consider pornography a public health crisis? *American Journal of Public Health*, 110(2), 151–153. doi:10.2105/AJPH.2019.305498. PMID: 31913670; PMCID: PMC6951382.

Neves, S. (2021a). *Compulsive Sexual Behaviours: A Psycho-Sexual Treatment Guide for Clinicians*. Abingdon: Routledge.

Neves, S. (2021b). The religious disguise in "sex addiction" therapy. *Sexual and Relationship Therapy*. doi:10.1080/14681994.2021.2008344

Prause, et al. (2017, December). Data do not support sex as addictive. *The Lancet. Correspondence*, 4, 899. www.thelancet.com/psychiatry

Rothschild, B. (2021). *Revolutionizing Trauma Treatment: Stabilization, Safety & the Nervous System*. New York: WW Norton & Co.

Rowland, D.L., Hamilton, B.D., Bacys, K.R., et al. (2021). Sexual response differs during partnered sex and masturbation in men with and without sexual dysfunction: Implications for treatment. *The Journal of Sexual Medicine*, 18, 1835–1842.

Sex Addicts Anonymous. (2005). *International Service* (3rd ed.). Organization of SAA, Inc.

UK Government. (2021). *Conversion Therapy: An Evidence Assessment and Qualitative Study*. www.gov.uk/government/publications/conversion-therapy-an-evidence-assessment-and-qualitative-study/conversion-therapy-an-evidence-assessment-and-qualitative-study#what-forms-does-conversion-therapy-take-1

Weiss, R. (2011). *Cruise Control: Understanding Sex Addiction in Gay Men*. Carefree, Arizona: Gentle Path Press.

World Health Organization. (1994). *International Statistical Classification of Diseases and Related Health Problems* (10th ed.). https://icd.who.int/browse10/2019/en

World Health Organization. (2019). *International Statistical Classification of Diseases and Related Health Problems* (11th ed.). https://icd.who.int/

Mindfulness-based approaches to working with chemsex behaviours in psychotherapy

Dr Benedict Hoff

Introduction

Chemsex is possibly the biggest public health challenge currently facing men who have sex with men (MSM) (McCall et al., 2015).[1] It is a complex presentation and requires a flexible, nuanced approach in therapy.[2] Cognitive Behavioural Therapy–based relapse prevention and its more recent mindfulness-based iterations (Bowen et al., 2011) arose as evidenced-based responses to the limitations of aversion/abstinence-based recovery models such as 12 Step programmes. In turn, sexology-informed approaches to working with compulsive sexual behaviours (Braun-Harvey & Vigorito, 2016; Neves, 2021) offer alternatives to the now ubiquitous "sex addiction" model proposed by Patrick Carnes (2001) and brought to the UK by Thaddeus Birchard (2017) and Paula Hall (2019).[3]

This chapter speaks from the perspective of these "new wave" approaches and sets out how a mindfulness-based and sexology-informed approach to working with chemsex behaviours can address both aspects of this unique presentation (substance use and compulsive sexual behaviours) in a way that is inclusive, non-pathologising, trauma-aware and sex-positive. It is intended as a practical guide for therapists, illustrated with clinical examples.

This chapter begins in Part One by drawing out what we mean by chemsex and then outlines the principles and suitability of a mindfulness-based treatment approach. In Part Two it introduces the five stages of the *SOBER Breathing Space* – a key meditation taught on mindfulness-based relapse prevention (MBRP) courses – as a means, not only of structuring the rest of the chapter, but as a possible way in which to stage therapeutic work.

Part one: principles

What is chemsex?

Chemsex is a term coined by sexual health professional, advocate, researcher and activist David Stuart, who sadly passed away in 2022, that describes an intentional sexual behaviour amongst MSM under the influence of one or more of the

Doi: 10.4324/9781003260608-13

following psychoactive party drugs: methamphetamine (crystal meth, tina, crank), mephedrone (meph, meow meow, M-CAT) and GHB and GBL (gamma hydroxy-butyrate and gamma butyrolactone also known as G, gina or liquid ecstasy). The drugs facilitate and enhance sexual experiences, often at private sex parties ("chillouts") lasting hours or days. GHB and GBL have a strong psychological disinhibition effect and are also mild anaesthetics whilst mephedrone and crystal meth are physiological stimulants that trigger strong sexual arousal and feelings of euphoria. Combining these drugs creates an alluring fusion of increased sexual arousal with a decrease in sexual inhibition (Bourne et al., 2014).

Arguably the success in Stuart's model of key working (see Stuart et al., 2017) is how it validates gay men's experiences of chronic minority stress and under-stands intrinsically the function of chemsex behaviours in alleviating its negative effects: social exclusion, internalised homonegativity and shame, low self-esteem and poor body image (see also Neves, 2021, p. 135). Its approach also takes account of and mitigates against the inevitable loss people will feel if and when they decide to move away from chemsex behaviours. This usually occurs at the point at which the chemsex behaviours start bringing significantly more costs than benefits. Such costs have been associated with an increased risk of HIV infection due to the frequency of condomless sex, sex between multiple partners and needle-sharing with poor mental health reinforcing risk-taking. Pakianathan et al. (2018) showed that 16.5 percent of MSM engaged in chemsex are five times more likely to be newly diagnosed with HIV. Their study also showed a nine-fold increase in Hepatitis C risk, with diagnoses of all STIs elevated. Kall et al. (2015) reported 29 percent participation in chemsex amongst HIV+ MSM. Chemsex is also associated with antiretroviral therapy (ART) nonadherence in HIV+ MSM (Perera et al., 2017). Many who use chems also experience anxiety and depression and a significant percentage live with enduring mental health difficulties (Dearing & Flew, 2015). Erection problems, delayed ejaculation and anorgasmia are frequent presenting psychosexual issues (see Fawcett, 2015).[4]

What is mindfulness?

There are various definitions of mindfulness, but none of these probably mean much to anyone who is reading them! Mindfulness is perhaps best understood through direct experience. In this spirit I invite you now to practise this short *SOBER Breathing Space* to get a (literal) sense of what mindfulness practice is about. All the meditations and accompanying scripts referenced in this chapter are available at: https://benedicthoff.com/training – see Track 1 for this particular meditation.

First of all **STOP** and step off autopilot. Sit in stillness for a few moments. Now **OBSERVE** what is happening in your body, emotional landscape and mind. Take a moment to rest in this awareness. Now gather your attention around the breath and simply **BREATHE** focussing on the sensations of breathing. Try and be with whatever you're experiencing rather than pushing it away. Then **EXPAND** your lens of attention and hold your entire experience in this softer, more spacious awareness. And with this awareness, make an intention to **RESPOND** rather than react to whatever challenge arises in the rest of your day.

What did you notice? Maybe there was relief at stopping and taking some time out. You might have noticed tension or stress in the body, or a busy mind. Maybe noticing the rhythm of your breathing told you something about your emotional temperature right now. And after this pause, perhaps other things came into your awareness: bird song outside or the light shining in a particular way into your room.

Mindfulness is a specific kind of attention where we notice what is happening in the different levels of our experience with a kind, acceptant and non-judgemental attitude. We're not caught up in regrets about the past or worries about the future. Whether these experiences feel pleasant, unpleasant or neutral, we have some capacity to be with *all* of them without needing them to be otherwise. We cultivate this kind of attention through the practice of focussed attention in formal meditation, which we can then bring to other aspects of daily life off the meditation cushion (Hoff & Phillips, 2018, pp. 71–89).

Mindfulness, addiction and sex therapy

The Buddha told it how it is – being human is hard and life, as the Buddhist saying goes, comprises ten thousand joys and ten thousands sorrows. He suggested that a primary source of our suffering is how we habitually relate to these "joys" and "sorrows" – through craving and aversion. We can crave a sense pleasure, we might yearn to be someone or be someplace else, or we might be constantly reaching for what comes next. And this craving for what feels good can lead to aversion or struggle against what actually *is* in this moment, particularly if that's unpleasant. From this perspective, we are all addicts. We all experience the human instinct to push away negative experience, grasp after what feels good and make the mundane more interesting. And we all have our go-to ways of doing this – our crutches. Whether these develop into substance addiction or compulsive behaviours or just remain relatively benign coping responses, the underlying human tendency to need to "fix" our experience is the same.

Buddhist teachings spoke to the founders of MBRP as they searched for an alternative, "middle way" for people who were not making progress through aversion/abstinence-based approaches to addiction recovery or alternative CBT-based relapse prevention programmes. This middle way encourages non-judgmental observation and acceptance of experience and discourages identification with labels like "addict" or viewing addiction as an illness. It also foregrounds insight, understanding and choice over the "ideal" of abstinence, which may or may not be a treatment goal for participants.[5]

As Meg John Barker writes (2017), the Buddha's teachings on craving and aversion are as relevant to sex therapy as they are addiction recovery since they are at the heart of many sexual difficulties. We grasp after certain sexual experiences and outcomes and compel our bodies to respond accordingly. But anyone who has struggled to sustain an erection or achieve orgasm will know, the harder we try, the more elusive a reality they become (ibid., 440). And when things don't "go well", we may start to feel that avoiding sex, fantasy and desire altogether is preferable to feeling the intense shame and embarrassment that tends to accompany sexual problems (ibid.). Mindful awareness can help clients notice the ways in which this push and pull plays out during sex and obstructs sexual pleasure and helps them to feel rather than think their way through sex.[6]

Mindfulness is usually more effective if it is placed at the heart of the work and allowed to infuse the therapeutic relationship rather than being "deployed" sporadically. This is because the benefits of regular practice are subtle and build over time. But for all the hype around mindfulness in the therapy world, very little is said about how, as therapists, we really do this. Pollak et al. (2014) *Sitting Together: Essential Skills for Mindfulness-Based Psychotherapy* (see also Barker, 2013) is an excellent resource here and provides a robust framework and methodology that, combined with aspects of MBRP and sex therapy, informs the staged approach to working with chemsex behaviours I propose later. Unsurprisingly, the place where we need to begin is with ourselves. So if you haven't already established a regular meditation practice of your own and would like to, I invite you to try each of the practices I suggest for clients in the following section and build one as you read.

Part two: practices

Stopping (and pausing)

Automatic pilot: how did I get here?

Have you ever been on a trip and arrived at your destination with little recollection of the actual journey? We do a lot on autopilot. Humans have an extraordinary capacity to perform quite complex tasks without much conscious awareness, all the time thinking, planning, worrying, dreaming. This is functional because habitual behaviours use fewer brain resources. But life's beauty can pass us by, or we can end up in places we would rather not have gone. The "autopilot" analogy is key in mindfulness-based approaches to working with addiction and compulsive behaviours, and it tends to resonate with how clients understand their experience.

Clinical illustration: Hassan

"How did I get here?" Hassan asked at the initial assessment. Hassan was a bisexual Emirati aged 32 and had transferred to London with his job five years previous. Hassan had a long history of using stimulants – caffeine, nicotine and cocaine. A search for social connection and new sexual experiences drove his first forays into chemsex and experimentation with new drugs. Hassan described intense shame around his attraction to men which "evaporated" when he had sex on chems. He also noticed that if he was still a little high on a Monday, his focus and concentration at work actually improved. Gradually and "almost without noticing", his weekend usage bled into the working week during which he would use both crystal meth and G. He had received two formal warnings from his line manager for anger outbursts and "insubordination" and was worried about being sacked. Hassan spoke with desperation and in rapid-fire. Recently, he continued, some "very bad things" had happened to him at a chillout party.

I noticed his distress at this point and invited him to take a breather and practice a brief meditation with me called Touch Points. Hassan was sceptical about mindfulness. The year previous he had approached his GP for a referral for an ADHD assessment, but she hadn't felt this was relevant to his current issues. She simply referred him to a generic recovery group (where he was the only queer person and the only person of colour) and "prescribed" some mindfulness meditations to help him relax and manage intrusive thoughts. The few times he'd tried meditating he said he'd found it impossible to settle and "clear his mind". He also reported his intrusive thoughts often becoming more intense, and "taking over". But when I explained we could meditate standing up and that it would be about cultivating body awareness rather than working with the contents of the mind or trying to make it go blank, he opened to the idea. After we'd meditated together, Hassan said he couldn't remember the last time he had actually stopped and made some space around himself in this way, without reaching for distraction or another fix. He reported feeling more grounded and less keyed up. By the end of the assessment we agreed that some "pre-therapy" elsewhere might be helpful before starting work with me. This involved some key working around harm reduction, a managed detox from G and attendance at a support group and arranging an ADHD assessment through an alternative GP. Four months later when he was ready, Hassan contacted me and we began our weekly sessions together.

Taking stock

"Stopping" is not about sobriety or abstinence here. Some services/therapists insist on a period of complete abstinence before they will work with a client. Certainly clients need to have stabilised sufficiently to engage in therapy. But if they have not developed alternative coping strategies and protective factors or they require a managed detox, encouraging complete abstinence may be counterproductive, harmful or even dangerous. It may also deprive the client and therapist of valuable learning opportunities around the moment-by-moment unfolding of triggers, cravings and reactive behaviours.

Rather, "stopping" at this stage, is simply about stepping off autopilot, honestly taking stock and noticing what's here. This is crucial at assessment stage because as therapists we need to be sure we are providing the right type of support at the right time. Clients may be extremely keen to embrace sobriety, begin therapy and believe you are the perfect person to support them. But if contacting you has happened as an automatic reflex response to overwhelming distress without conscious awareness of *why*, therapy becomes another "fix" that will fail to deliver. As Neves (2021) writes, clients need to be ready, able and willing to engage in therapy, and desperation can easily be confused with motivation (2021, p. 115). In Hassan's case, confirming an ADHD diagnosis, accessing the support of an ADHD coach alongside therapy and eventually starting on appropriate medication were important pieces of his recovery jigsaw. Similarly, clients with signs and symptoms of serious enduring mental health conditions such as bipolar or personality disorders should also be referred to an appropriate specialist so that a dual diagnosis can be ruled in or out.[7]

(Safely) setting the tone

Stopping to pause in the assessment and taking stock can be accompanied by strong feelings of sadness, loss and regret. Inviting mindfulness meditation into the assessment can be helpful in grounding clients who experience such intense upwelling of affect. In *Touch Points* (see Audio Track 2) the client directs attention to places where the body is "touching" – the eyelids, hands, legs and feet. Body awareness is a good way to soothe the mind. However, focussing on peripheral points and not sensations around the throat, chest and belly associated with "sharp points" makes it a good beginning concentration practice for those presenting with trauma or who are emotionally dysregulated (Pollak et al., 2014, p. 70).[8]

"Stopping" during the assessment also presents the opportunity to touch into the client's felt sense of things (through, for example, meditation or somatic enquiry), particularly if they are "autopiloting" through their story with an absence of affect. Sharing in a brief mindfulness practice together can also foster psychological contact and interpersonal attunement. More generally it helps set the tone for a mindfulness-based approach to the work and ascertain whether this way of working is aligned to the client's preference and expectations. Modelling a flexible and inclusive approach to mindfulness practice can be really important here too in dispelling any myths that can make a mindfulness-based approach seem inaccessible.

Observing

Triggers and cravings

Clients may start therapy impatient to practise mindfulness to manage their most intense experiences, in particular urges and cravings, but in the initial phase, a mindfulness-based approach is careful not to collude with the compulsion to "fix" things. Reaching for meditation only to relax or manage difficult thoughts and feelings, as Hassan's GP had suggested, tends to make for more reactive behaviour, something we are trying to move away from. Furthermore, doing so without the basic foundations of practice is usually counterproductive and potentially unsafe for less well-integrated clients. Therefore in the opening stage of therapy, I suggest to clients when they experience triggers and cravings simply to record their experience in a daily Triggers Diary (see Bowen et al., 2011, p. 72) or through journaling, voice notes and even poetry or drawing, noticing, in particular, physical sensations; moods, feelings and emotions; thoughts and reactive behaviour. At this stage they do not need to *do* anything else other than notice their unfolding experience and let it be. That may mean engaging in chemsex behaviours, and that's okay.

Clinical illustration: Gary

Gary was 60, white, British, living with HIV and a widower. His husband Steve had died of cancer three years previous. Gary described their relationship as "loving" and "full of companionship" but sexless. Following Steve's death he found himself experimenting with chemsex as an antidote to grief and loneliness but also as a pathway to new sexual experiences. Eighteen months before seeing me, he would party and play most weekends but now more sporadically. He no longer used G or mephedrone but had found crystal meth much harder to quit and had been attending Crystal Meth Anonymous 12 Step meetings. He found the meetings helpful and the gap between lapses had been growing. When he experienced strong urges or cravings, he would instinctively log onto a meeting, or contact his sponsor. The cost of his sobriety was the virtual celibacy he had imposed on himself. Partnered sex, dating apps, solo sex and pornography had become so enmeshed with using that Gary avoided them and found the idea of sober sex terrifying. He experienced unreliable erections, delayed ejaculation and anorgasmia.

After an initial assessment, Gary began completing a daily triggers diary and practising a short breathing space three times a day when he wasn't feeling triggered to punctuate his daily routine. He started to notice the different qualities of cravings depending on context and his own emotional weather patterns. Fridays signalled the start of weekends alone and had historic associations with using which unfolded according to a familiar routine. Gary noticed that even just passing the supermarket or ordering from the same takeaway could induce cravings which he experienced as a "rush" and a tingling/shivering sensation running down the back of this head into his spine. He rarely felt sexually aroused until – if he acted on these impulses – he had actually logged onto Grindr and started chatting with other guys.

This contrasted with "cravings" he experienced during the working week. Here there was no identifiable trigger, the tingling/shivering sensation was absent and he noticed the presence of an erection from the beginning. On the few occasions he allowed himself to masturbate, the "craving" would dissipate, but he would experience self-loathing that registered as a heavy feeling in his body. Sometimes he would then find himself thinking about using G. When he resisted the urge to masturbate, "craving" would often persist, and he would struggle to concentrate and find himself reaching for cigarettes or numbing out on Facebook.

Not all urges are the same

Distinguishing between arousal relating to spontaneous ordinary libidinal urges and arousal associated with cue reactivity[9] can be tricky, particularly if the cues relate to the sights, smells, sounds, sensations of sex itself and/or their associated memories. Over time Gary was better able to discern between the two. As Gary began to feel less threatened by feelings of desire, I invited him, as an experiment, to act on these libidinal urges more frequently and to try masturbating if it was appropriate and writing down what he noticed. Gary observed that he experienced less self-loathing after ejaculation than he had before, which he wondered was because he had been given "permission" to masturbate. He also experienced a reduction in craving for G. We hypothesized together it wasn't masturbation itself which was the cause of Gary's cravings, but the feelings of shame which histori-cally he had soothed with G. In these specific situations, we began to reframe pan-icked calls to his sponsor or urgent attendance at 12 Step meetings as the reactive behaviours, rather than acting on the natural and healthy urge to masturbate. This opened up a space where Gary could start re-engaging with solo sex and, eventu-ally, a pathway back to sober partnered sex.

Starting concentration practice

Alongside the Triggers Diary, clients can begin practising a daily concentration practice, the foundation of meditation. The focus of attention can be on sounds, the body, the breath, a word or phrase, or an object of sight such as a candle flame. Most taught mindfulness programmes start with the *Body Scan* and *Mindfulness of Breathing* as foundational practices before moving to open monitoring prac-tice and then loving-kindness meditation. However, with this client group I find starting with outer objects of awareness away from the core of the body is a safer, more trauma-sensitive place to start. *Touch Points*, mentioned earlier, is useful here, as is *Mindfulness of Sounds* (Track 3). "A little often" is a good mantra for practice: perhaps starting at five minutes twice a day and building up gradually to ten minutes and eventually 20 and beyond.

Body and breath

Deepening concentration practice

Once clients are comfortable with these basic concentration practices, they can then move onto ones focusing explicitly on the body and breath. *Compassionate Body Breathing* (Track 4) can be a powerful way for clients to become acquainted with the anatomy of breathing whilst dissolving shame around body image and regrets about the physical toll chems may have taken on them. Following body-focused concentration practice, clients can then move on to working with the breath in *Mindfulness of Breathing* (Track 5), a core concentration practice. Here we learn to attend to the breath without trying to control it and return our attention to it each time it wanders. Over time, clients can begin to relate to their breath as an anchor that grounds them in the here and now.

Leaning in: urge surfing

Regular concentration practice increases stability of attention so that eventually clients can start working with more intense experiences. *Urge Surfing* (Track 6) is a core practice in MBRP where clients learn to shift their relationship to urges and cravings from being one of fear, resistance and aversion to "being with". Typically the need to medicate against experience is the fear that unless we "do" something, the experience will increase exponentially in intensity until it becomes unbearable. Clients will have learned in concentration practice, however, that everything – from sounds, to physical sensations and the breath itself – comes and goes, like waves breaking on the shore. Urge Surfing uses the metaphor of surfing these waves to invite clients into staying present with the intensity of cravings without behaving reactively.

Clinical illustration: Hassan

Hassan initially struggled with longer concentration practices but over time, with some adaptations, was able to increase from 5 minutes to 15 minutes twice a day. At this point we introduced Urge Surfing, practising this in session using visualisations of a previous instance where Hassan had felt triggered and engaged in chemsex. Hassan would imagine himself at the point where he felt triggered but then pause. Rather than acting on the craving, he would imagine it like an ocean wave which he was surfing, using his breath as a surfboard to stay steady. As we repeated the exercise over a few sessions, Hassan became more skilled at riding the wave from its beginning, riding the crest of its intensity and staying on top of it before watching it fall in intensity. He started to use it with real-life triggers and, over time, began to trust that often, without any action on his part, the waves of desire would arise, fall and eventually ebb away.

Clinical illustration: Gary

Gary had gotten creative with the Urge Surfing exercise and adapted it to work with sexual urges as well as chems-related craving. If appropriate, he would follow his urge and masturbate, imagining he was surfing the waves of pleasure as he did so. If not, he would just allow the waves of desire to wash over his body – noticing and enjoying the physical sensations and appreciating these moments of sexual "waking" after months of feeling like his libido had "abandoned" him. Together we ran with the wave metaphor, integrating a mindful masturbation practice called *Wax and Wane* (Track 7). In the exercise, Gary would stimulate his penis just until it began to harden, then stop until his penis became soft again. Then he would restart stimulating his penis until it was semi-hard, before allowing it to soften again. Then he would stimulate his penis until it was fully hard and then allow it to soften to semi-hard, before stimulating it to full hardness again. Over time, Gary began getting more comfortable with the idea that, like all aspects of experience, erections come and go and that if he lost his erection, another one would probably be on the way.

Making psychosexual practices accessible

Mindfulness practices dovetail nicely with sensate focus which underpins much psychosexual work (see Weiner & Avery-Clark, 2017). However, the design of sensate focus programmes can exclude clients who are not regularly having partnered sex or who don't have (a) stable partner(s). It is important to be creative here and adapt practices so they are as inclusive and accessible as possible. For example, fleshlights can be introduced to Wax and Wane so that once clients are used to working with sensations produced by manual stimulation, they can build confidence around penetration (if that interests them). The therapist can also support clients to be more mindful about the partners they choose to play with. The Six Principles of Sexual Health comprise a good metric by which clients can judge a potential encounter to be conducive to exploring learnings from solo sex in partnered sex. These comprise: Consent, Non-Exploitation, Honesty, Shared Values, protection from STI, HIV and Unwanted Pregnancy and Mutual Pleasure (Braun Harvey & Vigorito, 2016, p. 47).

Expanding

Open monitoring

As clients' mindfulness practice matures and they are able to work with the more intense experiences that arise during concentration practice, they can start to broaden their lens of awareness in what is known as "open monitoring" or mindfulness *per se*. This is a more spacious kind of attention that allows us to see the bigger picture and brings the different layers of our experience – physical, affective and cognitive – into a clearer view as they unfold in everyday life.

Michael Chaskalson's (2014) *Choiceless Awareness* meditation (Track 8) is a good bridge for clients through which they can practice this "on the cushion" before experimenting with it in daily life. In this meditation we allow our field of awareness to open, effortlessly apprehending whatever arises from moment to moment: breath, body sensations, sounds, images and thoughts, and not holding onto any of them. Clients tend to get better at managing thoughts here – relating to them more as "mental events" or "moments" in the mind rather than absolute truths. If moving towards sharp points in concentration practice helps clients tolerate intense emotions by experiencing them as bodily sensations, then open monitoring supports the re-integrating of these with their narrative contents such as thoughts, images and memories (Pollak et al., 2014, p. 15).

Clinical illustration: Hassan

Once Hassan was able to hold the intensity of experience we were working with in Urge Surfing, we began going "beneath" the craving. What did he really need in that moment? Was there a longing for something? What was it that he was truly craving? Near the surface of his awareness were memories of being bullied by his classmates for his perceived effeminacy, derided by his teachers for his poor academic performance and his lack of prowess in competitive sport. He was punished by his father for failing to meet these demands of compulsory masculinity. Hassan had developed a strong inner critic comprising the internalised voices of these male figures and a familiar script ran in his mind that he was pathetic, shameful and a failure. Gradually we made contact with "Little Hassan" who had coped by people-pleasing to avoid punishment, avoiding close relationships with other men, and demanding very little from people. Chems facilitated an experience for Hassan which transcended the limitations of these coping responses and provided an approximation of authenticity, unconditional acceptance, shared intimacy and sexual assertiveness. But when at a recent sex party the "very bad things" he referenced in the assessment occurred in the form of a sexual assault, the "safety blanket" that chems provided for him had been pulled away. At this point in the work, more repressed memories of sexual abuse that he had experienced around the age of six from his uncle began to surface. He was able to connect these memories with the intense anger he believed was always at the point of exploding in his daily life. Anger related to absent parents who provided for him materially but who neither recognised his support needs at school nor provided the safety and protection we all need from our primary care givers. The therapeutic relationship between us provided an important reparative experience in these respects that allowed Hassan to experiment with being vulnerable with another gay man without the "safety blanket" of chems.

Horizons of possibility

"Expanding" is also a more outward, approach-orientated way of relating to the world that clients can start experimenting with. They can begin to explore what, moving forwards, they want to include in their "pie of life": this may include making better lifestyle choices, taking up a hobby or doing some retraining or upskilling and/or creating new connections and social networks. They may also want to start re-engaging with dating and partnered sex if they have chosen to take a break from these during the initial phases of therapy. Vidyamala Burch's *Connection Meditation* (see Audio Track 9) is a good practice to cultivate this outwards orientation towards the world. Thus far, clients should have begun to experience the power of acceptance, kindness and compassion for themselves. The *Connection Meditation*, an adaptation of the Buddhist *metta bhavana* (loving kindness) meditation, invites them to extend this further outwards in ever-increasing circles, both to people they know and people they don't.

Clinical illustration: Gary

Solo practices such as Self-Focus and Wax and Wane helped Gary to reconnect with his body and embrace, rather than avoid, his own desires. Gradually he felt more relaxed about trying partnered sex and, when chatting with guys online, was better able to discern suitable sexual partners and was more confident in stating his needs and asserting his boundaries. During sex he felt more grounded in his body and enjoyed the experience of his own pleasure rather than "spectatoring" and agonising about what the person was thinking or whether they were having a good time. At the same time Gary began to notice the proliferation of thoughts that accompanied the arising and falling of his erections and how these would often pull his attention away from physical sensations. By gently acknowledging thoughts rather than getting caught up in the story around them, and then refocusing attention back to physical sensations, he found he was more able, in his words, "to go with the flow". When the thoughts became compelling, Gary brought to mind the words of the *Connection Meditation* and reminded himself that his partner was also a human being and, therefore, like him, also vulnerable to sexual shame and anxiety, despite Gary often feeling that he was the only person who experienced these things. This helped him soften into the experience and reduced sexual inhibition.

Responding

Bringing it all together: the SOBER Breathing Space

In the final stages of therapy clients usually have a well-established concentration practice and become more adept at using open monitoring to discern between different elements of their experience both inside and outside of formal meditation. In turn, their awareness of triggers and cravings is usually quite well-tuned with a greater ability to "lean in" and ride out challenging experiences rather than medicating against them. And their relationship with the world tends to be more approach orientated, with a greater capacity for exploration and discovery over safety and retreat. This is a good point to introduce the *SOBER Breathing Space* as an overarching practice that synthesises all the experiential learning up to this point. It can be framed as a mini-meditation that clients can carry in their back pocket.

Relapse is recovery

Relapse often lurks in the background for clients as the "boogie man under the bed" and something to be avoided at all costs. However, aversion to something which in all likelihood will happen at some point in their recovery tends to only increase the intense self-judgement associated with an initial lapse and therefore the likelihood of experiencing a full-blown relapse. Reframing relapse as an inevitable part of recovery and an important learning experience can help reduce clients' anxiety. Using the *SOBER Breathing Space* in challenging and high-risk situations can interrupt the relapse process and help them exit the "relapse highway" at an earlier junction than might otherwise have been the case. In particular, clients can be encouraged to really notice what thoughts are arising in the Observe stage of the meditation as they often play an important triggering role in relapse.

Clinical illustration: Gary

> Gary had become friends with Tim, whom he'd met online. They liked hang-
> ing out and having sex from time to time. Tim had moved away from chems,
> and Gary felt Tim understood him, in particular, his difficulties around sober
> sex. One weekend Tim invited Gary to a friends' birthday celebration at a
> local gay club. Gary knew the club well and didn't feel it was likely to pres-
> ent many triggers. Gary got hit on by another guy, and they spent the evening
> dancing together. Afterwards he asked Gary back to his place where they had
> a few drinks and made out. Eventually, to Gary's surprise, he produced some
> crystal meth and asked him if he'd like to smoke with him. Gary noticed
> familiar physical sensations around the anticipation the invitation triggered
> and a proliferation of thoughts that began with warnings about taking up the
> invitation but which then shifted into rationalisation about why it wouldn't
> do any harm. Gary then found himself "swept onto the train" and did indeed
> use. After the initial rush and a few hours of being high, he noticed he was
> starting to come down and the urge to maintain the high arose. He knew this
> was a point where the lapse would morph into a full-blown binge and took
> himself to the bathroom and led himself through the steps of the *SOBER
> Breathing Space*. When he reached the Breathe stage, he practised using his
> breath to surf the urge he was experiencing for long enough to create a space
> to pause and "peel" himself away from the situation, call a taxi and go home.

Compassionate acceptance

In their book *Mindfulness for Health*, Burch and Penman (2013) discuss the concept
of primary and secondary suffering in relation to the experience of chronic pain and
illness. There are the actual unpleasant physical sensations in the body – primary
suffering – but also the additional pain that arises when you resist and react against
this experience – secondary suffering. This analogy is also relevant to substance
use. During a comedown the body is usually in a deteriorated state – starved, dehy-
drated and exhausted – and the mind ridden with agitation and anxiety. A common
way to react to this is by piling self-judgement, self-loathing and shame on top of
what is already hurting. My adaptation of Burch and Penman's *Compassionate
Acceptance* meditation (Track 10) encourages a more skilful response to pain or
difficulty by bringing tenderness, kindness and compassion to our experience to
help dissolve this secondary suffering.

Clinical illustration: Hassan

> Hassan was engaging in chemsex behaviours less and less frequently and was
> more comfortable with sober sex. He noticed that since starting his ADHD

medication, his cravings for crystal meth had reduced. When he relapsed, Hassan described descending into a "pit of self-disgust and despair". He admitted feeling that he'd let me down and worried that I would "drop" him as a client. These were opportunities to model the compassionate acceptance that Hassan struggled to extend to himself. We talked about how compassion literally means "to suffer with" and that I was right there beside him and wasn't going anywhere. It was in these moments that the depth of his self-disgust revealed itself. And once it had, we were able to work with it through a combination of talking, chair work and meditative practice. Slowly Hassan began to experience greater self-acceptance, both in terms of his sexuality and the ways he managed his shame around this. In turn, he noticed that his need for G to facilitate sexual experience also diminished.

Afterthoughts

This chapter began by drawing out what we mean by chemsex and outlined philosophically and practically the suitability of a mindfulness-based treatment approach before exploring how the five stages of the *SOBER Breathing Space* can be used as a way to structure the work. Of course, the reality in the consulting room rarely unfolds as smoothly as it does through the written word! Clients' recovery is usually messy with periods of forward momentum followed by crises, lapses and setbacks. However, by foregrounding insight, understanding and choice over the "ideal" of abstinence, this approach supports a more granular, moment-by-moment awareness of the complex interplay between core wounds, unmet needs, triggers and cravings and their relationship to specific substances. It also resources clients with practical ways to respond, rather than react to the inevitable challenges that arise. In turn, awareness of the cornerstones of mindfulness practice on the part of the therapist supports better selection and staging of mindfulness-based interventions so the therapeutic process can flex to the ever-changing reality of clients. It goes without saying that therapy will usually be just one ingredient in clients' "recovery cake" and that those committed to moving away from chemsex behaviours will be supporting themselves in a variety of ways. The healing potential of group-based meditation cannot be underestimated here, complementing and reinforcing these mindfulness-based approaches to chemsex recovery in one-to-one therapy. In this respect, *Evolving Minds* offers a weekly low-cost meditation class in central London for gay, bi and trans men whilst sexual health charity *Spectra* offers a mindfulness-based chemsex recovery programme that can be accessed for free online or in-person.

Notes

1 For an "on the ground" perspective see Warton (2017).
2 "Therapy" is used in this chapter to refer to counselling and psychotherapy; "therapist" is used to refer to counsellor and psychotherapist.

3 The term "compulsive sexual behaviours" will be used in this chapter as this language is closest to the confirmed diagnostic criteria currently in place by ICD-11 (World Health Organization, 2019).

4 Evidence of these psychosexual issues is largely anecdotal, and formal studies are needed to establish their prevalence amongst MSM engaging in chemsex behaviours.

5 Various empirical studies have evidenced the efficacy of MBAs to addiction recovery – for a meta-analysis see Li et al. (2017). In relation to the efficacy of MBAs specifically targeting chemsex behaviours, there is little empirical research thus far, but see my co-authored research and evaluation report (Hoff et al., 2020) for outcomes of an ongoing group-based intervention based on the MBRP model funded by Public Health England's HIV Innovation Fund, which I co-developed with Bex Freeman and sexual health charity Spectra.

6 There is a growing (but still limited) body of empirical studies demonstrating the link between mindfulness and sexual/relationship wellbeing: see Leavitt, C.E., Lefkowitz, E.S. and Waterman E.A. (2019) for a useful literature review.

7 Studies suggest that people whose ADHD remains undiagnosed or diagnosed but untreated are more likely to self-medicate with recreational drugs. The reasons for this can vary but include: improving performance and concentration, calming the mind, managing low mood and self-esteem due to poor academic/professional performance and a tendency towards seeking thrill-seeking behaviours and novel experiences. See Bidaki (2017) and Franke et al. (2021) for studies specifically into the link between ADHD and crystal meth addiction.

8 "Sharp points" in the Tibetan Buddhist tradition relate to thoughts, feelings and memories that may be out of conscious awareness. Meditation practices that move our attention to the chest, belly and throat tend to move us towards these "sharp points", whilst those that focus on objects farther away (soles of the feet, sounds, taste) tend to be more stabilising (Pollak et al., 2014, p. 14).

9 "Cue reactivity" refers to conditioned reactions to stimuli (cues) associated with substance use and that which may increase the probability of relapse (Rohsenow et al., 1990).

References

Barker, M.J. (2013). *Mindful Counselling and Psychotherapy: Practising Mindfully across Approaches and Issues*. London: Sage.

Barker, M.J. (2017). Mindfulness in sex therapy. In Z.D. Peterson (Ed.), *The Wiley Handbook of Sex Therapy* (pp. 437–452). London: John Wiley.

Bidaki, R. (2017). Prevalence of attention deficit hyperactivity disorder (ADHD) over methamphetamine (glass) abusing adults. *Focus on Medical Sciences Journal*, 3(4), 59–64.

Birchard, T. (2017). *Overcoming Sex Addiction: A Self-Help Guide*. Oxford: Routledge.

Bourne, A., et al. (2014). *The Chemsex Study: Drug Use in Sexual Settings among Gay and Bisexual Men in Lambeth, Southwark and Lewisham (Technical Report)*. Sigma Research. London School of Hygiene and Tropical Medicine.

Bowen, S., Chawla, N., & Marlatt, G.A. (2011). *Mindfulness-Based Relapse Prevention for Addictive Behaviours: A Clinicians Guide*. New York: The Guildford Press.

Braun-Harvey, D., & Vigorito, M.A. (2016). *Treating Out of Control Sexual Behavior: Rethinking Sex Addiction*. New York: Springer Publishing Company.

Burch, V., & Penman, D. (2013). *Mindfulness for Health: A Practical Guide to Relieving Pain, Reducing Stress and Restoring Wellbeing*. London: Piatkus.

Carnes, P. (2001). *Out of the Shadows: Understanding Sexual Addiction*. Centre City: Hazelden.

Chaskalson, M. (2014). *Mindfulness in Eight Weeks*. London: Harper Thomas.

Dearing, N., & Flew, S. (2015). MSM: The cost of having a good time? A survey about sex, drugs and losing control. *Sexually Transmitted Infections*, 91, A86, 211.

Fawcett, D. (2015). *Lust, Men and Meth: A Gay Man's Guide to Sex and Recovery*. Wilton Manors: Healing Path Press.

Franke, A.G., et al. (2021). Psychopathology and attention performance in methamphetamine users with ADHD symptomology in childhood. *International Journal of Mental Health Addiction*. https://doi.org/10.1007/s11469-021-00682-0

Hall, P. (2019). *Understanding and Treating Sex and Pornography Addiction*. Abingdon: Routledge.

Hoff, B., & Phillips, R. (2018). Mindfulness and the city: Taking notice as therapeutic practice. In C. Rose (Ed.), *Psychogeography and Psychotherapy: Connecting Pathways* (pp. 71–89). Monmouth: PCCS Books.

Hoff, B., Wang, D., & Freeman, D. (2020). *Mindfulness-Based Chemsex Recovery: Research and Evaluation Report for Public Health England's HIV Innovation Fund*. London: Spectra.

Kall, M., et al. (2015, April 21–24). *"Positive Voices": A RCT Pilot Survey of the Behaviour and Healthcare Needs of People with HIV: Study Methods and Respondent Characteristics*. BHIVA Conference 2015, Brighton, UK.

Leavitt, C.E., Lefkowitz, E.S., & Waterman, E.A. (2019). The role of sexual mindfulness in sexual wellbeing, relational wellbeing, and self-esteem. *Journal of Sex & Marital Therapy*, 45(6), 497–509.

Li, W., et al. (2017). Mindfulness treatment for substance misuse: A systematic review and meta-analysis. *Journal of Substance Abuse Treatment*, 75, 62–96.

McCall, H., et al. (2015). What is chemsex and why does it matter? *British Medical Journal*, 351, h5790. doi:10.1136/bmj.h5790

Neves, S. (2021). *Compulsive Sexual Behaviours: A Psycho-Sexual Treatment Guide for Clinicians*. Abingdon: Routledge.

Pakianathan, M., et al. (2018). Chemsex and new HIV diagnosis in gay, bisexual and other men who have sex with men attending sexual health clinics. *HIV Medicine*. https://doi.org/10.1111/hiv.12629

Perera, S., Bourne, A.H. and Thomas, S. (2017). P198 Chemsex and antiretroviral therapy non-adherence in HIV-positive men who have sex with men: A systematic review. *Sexually Transmitted Infections*, 93(Suppl 1), A81–A81.

Pollak, S.M., Pedulla, T., & Siegel, R.D. (2014). *Sitting Together: Essential Skills for Mindfulness-Based Psychotherapy*. New York: Guilford Press.

Rohsenow, D.J., et al. (1990). Cue reactivity in addictive behaviors: Theoretical and treatment implications. *International Journal of Addictions*, 25(7A–8A), 957–993.

Stuart, D., et al. (2017, October 25–27). *Outcomes of Behavioural Interventions in Men Who Have Sex with Men (MSM) Engaging in Chemsex*. 16th European AIDS Conference 2017, Milan, Italy.

Warton, J. (2017). *Something for the Weekend: Life in the Chemsex Underground*. London: Biteback Publishing.

Weiner, L., & Avery-Clark, C. (2017). *Sensate Focus in Sex Therapy: The Illustrated Manual*. London: Taylor and Francis.

World Health Organization. (2019). *International Statistical Classification of Diseases and Related Health Problems* (11th ed.). https://icd.who.int/

Conclusion

Dominic Davies and Silva Neves

We hope this book has helped you think more expansively about all the aspects of our clients' sex and relational lives that are seldom discussed in the mainstream psychology and psychotherapy discourse. Clinical sexology and relationship therapy should not be reduced to a few techniques and methods. As this book demonstrates, being GSRD-informed means diving into our clients' unique erotic themes with an affirmative and sex-positive philosophy.

Effective and ethical sex therapy with lesbians, Queer menopause, sexual shame, the sex lives of asexuals, the diversity of heterosexuality that does not conform to heteronormativity, working with intersex people, having a candid dialogue about trans people's sex lives, de-medicalising trans people's sexuality and centring it in the pleasure context instead, examining our engrained bias about various kink practices, treating anodyspareunia, working ethically with sexual compulsivity away from the 'sex addiction' model, and the power of mindfulness-based approaches to working with chemsex are all specialist areas that are hardly taught in clinical training nor written about. Yet, all these subjects are relevant to a significant number of GSRD-identified clients. This book equips you with the contemporary and cutting-edge knowledge of better serving the Queer population and embracing the Erotic Queerness in us all.

Experienced practitioners wrote each chapter of this book with expertise in their subject and were generous with offering the wealth of their knowledge to us. Therapists are sometimes stuck in the binary conflict of wanting to be 'good enough' with their existing expertise or feeling 'not good enough' when they identify needing to know more about marginalised populations. Being a good therapist may mean resolving this conflict by acknowledging both: we are good enough and can always learn more. We are very grateful to all the authors who contributed to this book and feel privileged to keep learning from each other.

Doi: 10.4324/9781003260608-14

Index

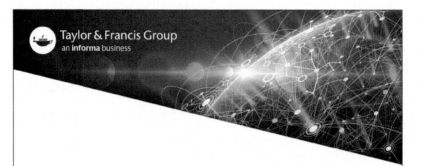